Reflections from the Wrong Side of the Tracks

Reflections from the Wrong Side of the Tracks

Class, Identity, and the Working Class Experience in Academe

Edited by
Stephen L. Muzzatti
and C. Vincent Samarco

ROWMAN & LITTLEFIELD PUBLISHERS, INC.
Lanham • Boulder • New York • Toronto • Oxford

ROWMAN & LITTLEFIELD PUBLISHERS, INC.

Published in the United States of America
by Rowman & Littlefield Publishers, Inc.
A wholly owned subsidary of The Rowman & Littlefield Publishing Group, Inc.
4501 Forbes Boulevard, Suite 200, Lanham, Maryland 20706
www.rowmanlittlefield.com

PO Box 317
Oxford
OX2 9RU, UK

British Library Cataloguing in Publication Information Available

Library of Congress Cataloging-in-Publication Data

Reflections from the wrong side of the tracks : class, identity, and the working
  class experience in academe / edited by Stephen L. Muzzatti and C. Vincent
  Samarco.
     p. cm.
  Includes bibliographical references and index.
  ISBN 0-7425-3511-8 (cloth : alk. paper) — ISBN 0-7425-3512-6 (pbk. : alk.
  paper)
  1. Working class—Education (Higher) —North America. 2. College
  teachers—North America—Social conditions. 3. Social classes—North America.
  I. Muzzatti, Stephen L., 1968– II. Samarco, C. Vincent, 1964–

  LC5055.N7R44 2005
  378.1'98623—dc22   2005006690

Printed in the United States of America

∞™ The paper used in this publication meets the minimum requirements of
American National Standard for Information Sciences—Permanence of Paper
for Printed Library Materials, ANSI/NISO Z39.48-1992.

This book is for Luciano and Mary who've put up with me the longest, and for Kirsten, who puts up with me the most.

—S. L. M

This book is for my father, Paul, and for my daughter, Hadley, both of whom continue to shape who I am

—C. V. S.

Contents

Preface: Serendipity My Ass; Some Preliminary Reflections from the Wrong Side of the Tracks

The tracks. A line of demarcation between increasingly polarized worlds. On one side, comfortable, if not outright idyllic, environs where individuals move about in clean, spacious surroundings largely free of socioeconomic encumbrances to rightly pursue the upward mobility promised by the American dream. On the other, a far less pristine community, ravaged by deindustrialization, corporate violence, and environmental racism where folks struggle with long hours of physically and emotionally grueling, soul-crushing, and dehumanizing work (if they're "lucky"), the ubiquitous threat of unemployment, and the psychic, not to mention physical, pain that comes with not knowing whether there will be "enough" to cover the rent, insurance, utilities, and food come month's end. Such a dichotomy has long existed in the United States. Stark and as allegedly pedestrian as such pictures are often said to be, they are nonetheless accurate reflections of the increasingly polarized worlds people in this country inhabit. Colleges and universities in the twenty-first century are disproportionately populated by those from the former world. Tacky blue vests with name tags bearing the euphemistic title "sales associate" below a stenciled-in name are disproportionately worn by those from the latter. With college and university tuition skyrocketing almost as quickly as government funding for education (at all levels) plummets, this, in and of itself, shouldn't surprise anyone. What is surprising, and hence worthy of exploration, is the fact that there are some people from the latter of these worlds in higher education at all, let alone staffing the ranks of the professoriate. Perhaps this collection is an exercise in folly. Perhaps, as some of the most vociferous social commentators from the right assert, we are glowing anomalies; living, breathing exemplars of the potential for upward mobility that exists at the core of the meritocracy we should all be grateful for being born into. Perhaps. Though as this collection attests, there is much more to the current position of the contributors than hard work and dedication. To be sure, hard work and dedication did play a part in the position we and our working-class colleagues find ourselves in. But did we work any harder than our parents, siblings, friends, and neighbors? Is languishing over obscure translations of some long-dead nineteenth-century European social theorist's polemic into the wee hours of the morning, painstakingly writing, then rewriting, then revising to the umpteenth degree a paper that synthesizes his insights with the autoerotic ruminations of a twenty-first-century postmodern pop-culture critic any more grueling than being a wage slave for America's largest private employer for just under forty hours a week, followed by an additional fifteen to twenty hours of equally mind-numbing work in some other service-sector ghetto to be able to pay for the inadequate health care plan "provided" by the aforementioned abusive corporate entity? The obvious answer to this question is at least part of the reason we're both somewhat ambivalent about being academics.

Though the stories of your two editors differ somewhat, they also have much in common with each other and, as the subsequent chapters will illustrate, at least some commonalities with the experiences of the other contributors to this volume.

We were born just a few years apart, in different cities and different countries. We grew up in the 1980s, just hours away from one another in Toronto and Detroit, both the sons of working-class Italian parents. We were from good solid working-class immigrant stock, children and grandchildren of blue- and pink-collar laborers who made their respective cities what they were; autoworkers and truck drivers, migrant workers and domestic workers, construction workers and house painters and typists and hairdressers. We grew up in the city, not in the suburbs, not in a bedroom community. Yes, in the city, one of us near 8 Mile, that area made famous by the 2002 film bearing its name, and the other in the south-central end of the Borough of North York, a name no doubt less well recognized by American readers but, relatively speaking, no less renowned for being a tough, working-class neighborhood. Yes, our neighborhoods were definitely on the wrong side of the tracks, but contrary to the sensationalistic and one-dimensional media portrayals, they were more than simply bastions of poverty, drugs, and crime. They were vibrant, exciting places, where neighbors knew each other and helped each other, where you weren't likely to see contractors' vans parked on the streets during the day but rather parked in driveways at night, because most people did their own roof repair and masonry and plumbing and drywall, and if they couldn't, they certainly had a cousin or in-law or *paisano* who could. It was a place where those who had lawns took great pride in them, and the garden was as much a vital source of fresh tomatoes, beans, scarolla, radicchio, and cucumbers as it was a place of recreation, kinship, and intergenerational cooperation. They were places where girls and boys played handball in apartment parking lots, road hockey on dead-end streets, tag and British bulldogs on vacant lots, and for those of us fortunate enough to have bikes, stunt riding on any surface and in any place available. They were neighborhoods where people of color and white folks lived side by side, shopped in the same stores, and sent their kids to the same schools. They were places where you were as likely to hear Italian and Portuguese and Somali and Spanish and Vietnamese as you were English. And they were places where working-class parents raised and nurtured working-class kids in modest homes with pride and love and hopes of a brighter future for them.

Like many kids from working-class immigrant backgrounds, we were in-doctrinated about the importance of education at an early age. School, we were told by our parents, was a means to a better (i.e., economically comfortable, if not outright prosperous) life. Herein lies one of the most funda-mental and earliest ironies we experienced as academics from the working class. Our parents were at once blindly deferential to our teachers and as-tutely suspicious of the education system. Though they didn't articulate it in quite this way, they realized that going to school, particularly the academic high school, let alone the university, was a Faustian pact. It was necessary for our "advancement," our "betterment"—which would come at great cost. Un-like the parents of middle-class kids, our parents held few delusions about the operational imperatives of social structural forces and society's power dynamics. Though our parents had far less formal education than the parents of middle-class kids, they had a far more sophisticated understanding of how hierarchies operate, no doubt because they spent their lives at, or near, the bottom of several. They knew that attending university was about social class and power—getting to go to one was a manifestation of class and power, and once you were there, class and power were bestowed and reproduced.

Suffice it to say, growing up in these environments, and as a result of a host of other structural and transformative interpersonal factors better left for elucidation in subsequent chapters, serendipity had little part to play in our lives. For a start, it's no surprise that we both found ourselves attending large public universities, chosen more for their geographic proximity to our re-spective homes than for their academic pedigree. To be sure, one of us ulti-mately decided to attend his university because the other nearby choice had a reputation as being the university for, to borrow a phrase from Laurel John-son Black (1995), "those stupid rich bastards."

So, too, it is not surprising that we found ourselves, after some initial con-fusion, studying English and sociology and drawn to particular subareas within those disciplines. While neither of these disciplines is free of the legacy of racism, sexism, homophobia, and classism, either in its scholarship, politics, or constitution, and we both cringed as some of the more conservative canons asserted that our working-class roots were "part of the problem" (no quality literature in the home and a criminogenic culture, respectively), they both answered questions we had about the world, and, perhaps more important, provided us with the requisite conceptual tools to ask questions that weren't being asked in many segments of society. Our respective disciplines, and particularly their more progressive and radical elements, gave voice to and authorized our fugitive knowledges. In short, it's not surprising that given a particular set of structural conditions and interpersonal factors, two working-class kids took undergraduate majors in, and then pursued advanced degrees in, disciplines that at least offered the possibility of revealing truths about the world and promoting social justice by debunking myths, challenging authority (not only its capricious exercise, but the very legitimacy of its existence), and demythologizing power.

Finally, it's not surprising that in 1999 we first met each other, two working-class academics in our first "real," full-time, tenure-track jobs, at a small, private, church-affiliated, liberal arts college in the Midwest. Nor, for that matter, should it surprise anyone that within a fairly short time we gravitated toward one another. Though we at first knew little about each other's personal histories, it quickly became evident that we shared certain working-class sensibilities: disdain for unwarranted and misplaced academic elitism, scorn for the unapologetic and arrogant behavior of many of our colleagues, contempt for the sense of entitlement and consumerist attitude toward education evidenced by some of the more economically privileged students, and finally, some fear and a great deal of mistrust of administrators. Almost a year to the day that we first met, we found ourselves in a working-class tavern, deliberately chosen not only for its constituency and atmosphere but also for its physical distance from the college, doing what working-class folks do to cope with the abuse, disabuse, alienation, pain, and confusion that result from wage slavery—self-medicating. Here we were, barely a year into our careers as professors, Veblen's working-class functionaries (or if you prefer, Marx's wage laborers for the entrepreneurs of the education factory), shaking our heads, face in hands, simultaneously proclaiming and asking ourselves, "Where the hell are we? And what the hell are we doing here?" It was here, in this time and at this place, under these conditions, and within particular intersections of biography and history, self and society, that the idea for this project was born.

ABOUT THIS VOLUME

As is often the case in matters scholarly, the volume before you is the result of several years of work, several false starts, delays, grinding halts, and restarts, and the efforts, assistance, and support of many people. Some of our earliest collaborative work on this topic—in fact, work that served as a rudimentary outline for this book—was undertaken in the fall of 2000 and presented later that year at a regional sociology conference. It received, shall we say, a less-than-stellar response. At the risk of belaboring the point, there was nothing noteworthy or surprising about that. The paper was delivered in a session scheduled at a less-than-ideal time by two unknown academics (one of whom wasn't even a sociologist!) from a small school outside the regional association's official geographic scope, on an unpopular topic, from an unpopular perspective, employing a devalued methodology. Our session was one of those awkward moments that many academics face at one point or another, in which, at least at first, it appeared that the assembled presenters would outnumber the audience members. While the balance eventually tipped in favor of the audience with the late arrival of a few stragglers, there were still far more empty seats than full ones. In and of itself the experience would have been wholly unremarkable and likely would have been lost to our collective memories were it not for the response of one audience member. During the question-and-answer portion toward the conclusion of the session, a tenured full professor from arguably the most prestigious and selective (and not incidentally, most expensive) university in the southern United States stood and began his "question" by pronouncing in a loud and confrontational masculinist tone, "You think you're special? You're not special!" Apparently it was his contention that economic (and by "logical" extension, racial and gender) inequality in higher education was a thing of the past. As "evidence" of this, he asserted that not only were many, perhaps most, of his colleagues people with working-class roots but that his campus was "full of working-class students." While this may very well have been the case, our cursory examination of his academic pedigree (Duke), those of his colleagues (Boston College, Brown, Chicago, Georgetown, Harvard, Princeton, a couple from Stanford, and, yes, Yale), and the approximately $23,000 annual price tag for undergraduate tuition, all gleaned from his university's website, led us to believe that he may have overstated the point with his modifiers "many," "most," and "full of."

Needless to say, the good professor had missed the point entirely. Our conference paper, and the work that has grown out of it, including that presented in this volume, is not about us or other working-class academics, whatever their number, being special—gifted mutants wholly unlike those who grew up around them. Rather, it's about opening up a space, a space where we and others like us can articulate what we've been feeling for some time: that class matters. Class is more than something to be reduced to the status of an independent variable in a quantitative analysis; it is something that shaped and continues to shape our lives and the lives of those around us. We are from the working class (men and women, queer, straight, and bi, old and young, white people and people of color, etc.), and it affects the way we interact with others both inside and outside the confines of higher education, as well as with and within other social institutions.

Following some initial setbacks, and after we both left the college where we met for jobs at the larger public universities where we currently work, we undertook this project once again. We put out a call for papers at the 2003 Midwest Sociological Association's conference and received a very encouraging response. Our session, the title of which now graces the cover of this volume, was quite successful by several measures. While it drew not quite a standing-room-only audience, it was nonetheless well attended. This was particularly encouraging because, as is standard, not only were we "competing" for the audience with numerous other sessions in the afternoon of the conference's first day, but there was also another, very class-specific, dynamic in the mix: a free wine-and-cheese reception hosted by one of the major sociology textbook publishers taking place at the same time.

Because of the positive response the session received, we broadened our call for papers while simultaneously more fully developing our project. It was at this point that we were offered assistance by and support from Henry Giroux. We had long been influenced by Giroux's work, but when he agreed to read the project, offer suggestions, and introduce us to the intricacies of publishing, we began to understand something else about the lives of working-class academics: that we have power in solidarity. We owe Giroux a great deal.

We provided authors with relatively few guidelines, aside from the specification that their papers should be reflexive and critical retrospective narratives/autoethnographies that contextualize within a broader structural and institutional analysis their experiences as people from working-class backgrounds in higher education. The end result is what you see before you. In addition to those that we authored, four of the chapters were contributed by the original session participants (Phyllis Baker, Julie Harms-Cannon, Dan Martin, and Janelle Wilson) and are based loosely on their presentations of April 2003, and one was contributed by an audience member (Lyn Huxford). The remaining chapters resulted from the second, broader call for papers and represent the work of a diverse group of scholars. The essays come from academics in a variety of geographic locales, both inside and outside the United States, and in various stages of their careers (for some academia was a second or third career). The authors were trained and work at schools or research institutions on the eastern seaboard and in the Midwest, the South, the Pacific Northwest, Canada, Australasia, and the United Kingdom. They are students in various stages of graduate work; assistant, associate, and full professors, tenured and untenured; administrators, associate deans, former deans, and institute directors. Both women and men, some relatively young, some older, are represented. They come from a variety of sexual orientations and family arrangements. This volume falls short, however, in representing one set of vital voices; there are no people of color among its contributors. The one woman of color who was originally involved in the project had to withdraw partway through. This is a reflection of several things, not the least being the pervasive racism and segregation in higher education. More specifically, and evidence of the multiple stigmas working-class women of color face in academia, she informed us that her decision to withdraw was based in part on the fact that she was informed, not so subtly, that participating in such a project wouldn't help her "politically" in her (almost all-male, all-white) department, and that her efforts would likely be better expended on a project that would count more favorably toward her evaluations; a project, perhaps not incidentally, that reduces race and class and gender to independent variables in the statistical alchemy known as multiple regression analysis and more thoroughly serves the hegemonic imperatives of government-funded research.

A FINAL WORD ON ORGANIZATION

The arrangement of chapters in this volume, as is always the case, was somewhat arbitrary. As will become evident throughout, a host of common themes emerge in this text. There are numerous similarities but also many intriguing differences from one chapter to the next. In most cases, having little more upon which to base our original organization than abstracts, brief outlines, and a few quick telephone conversations and harried e-mails, we decided to sort contributions into sections based upon three distinct tones: (1) narratives that critique the meritocracy, (2) narratives that trace the effects of middle-class cultural capital on relatively new academics from the working class, and (3) narratives that explore the effects of class on longtime academics from the working class. Arguably, there is room for debate on how well we accomplished this task of sorting and compartmentalizing. However, in the final analysis, in this collection of narrative-based, critically situated essays, contributors explored how class has affected their personal and academic lives, and we hope the effect of the collection is cumulative. By including contributors from multiple disciplines—both established and emerging voices—the text articulates the pervasiveness of class bias in this country and deconstructs the mechanisms that obfuscate how class and power work.

REFERENCES

Johnson Black, Laurel. 1995. "Stupid Rich Bastards." In *This Fine Place So Far from Home: Voices of Academics from the Working Class*, ed. C. L. Barney Dews and Carolyn Leste Law, 13–25. Philadelphia: Temple University Press.

Acknowledgments

The editors of this collection gratefully acknowledge the assistance of a number of folks who have helped make this book possible. First, our deepest appreciation goes out to our working class colleagues who consented to author chapters for the book. Suffice it to say, without them the project would have never materialized. Their accounts, at times heartrending, at other times humorous, and always inspirational, reflect the best traditions of the academic enterprise. Thank you. So too we owe a great deal to the colleagues, regardless of their social class, who have mentored, inspired, supported, and commiserated with us over the years. While we are indebted to many, among those to whom we owe the most are: Livy Visano of York University; Wynne Wright, Keith Crew, and Chris Mullins of the University of Northern Iowa; Chris Leland of Wayne State University; Catherine Orban of Marygrove College; Paul Leighton and Gregg Barak of Eastern Michigan University; Jeff Ferrell of Texas Christian University; Walter Dekeseredy, Barb Perry, and Shahid Alvi of the University of Ontario; Craig Bernier of the University of Pittsburgh; Keith Hayward of the University of Kent; Gary Newell of Northern Kentucky University; Dan Crocker and Adrienne Lewis of Kirtland College; Marty Schwartz of Ohio University; Henry Giroux of McMaster University; Richard Quinney, Emeritus of Northern Illinois University; Frederick Barthelme, Stephen Barthelme, and Rie Fortenberry of the University of Southern Mississippi; Anthony Neil Smith of Grand Valley State University. As well, our colleagues in the Department of Sociology at Ryerson University and the Department of English at Saginaw Valley State University are due our gratitude, as is the support staff, particularly Cindy Dy and Anice Gibbons. We are also appreciative of the work of Melissa McNitt, Alex Masulis, and Alan McClare of Rowman and Littlefield. Last but not least, we would like to thank the family members and friends who share our milieu and who enrich our lives, particularly Rob Caruso and John Stalletti from Keele and Lawrence, Joe and Ciela; Lisa; Melisa and Guy; Melinda and Hadley; Mike Makowski and Therese Makowski; Frances Cocagne and David Cocagne; Angela Samarco; Vito, Greta, Mason and Bandit.

Introduction

Social class has long been a matter of inquiry and contestation among social and cultural theorists. From squabbles over competing operational definitions, to questions of whether one's class is a result of individual achievement or social ascription, to assertions about the impact of social class on people's everyday/night lives, the debates continue to play themselves out, even in an allegedly "classless" society like the United States.

The starting point of our work here is that, contrary to public discourse and official pronouncements, a class system—complete with a highly stratified hierarchy—does exist in twenty-first-century America. The confluence of income, wealth, and occupational prestige, along with the less empirically verifiable, yet no less real, cultural and social capital that constitutes one's social class position, has a very real impact on the health and well-being of the populace. Social class not only continues to exist in twenty-first-century America, but it is still the best predictor of adult achievement and health (Duncan et al. 1998; Jones 2003; Short and Shea 1995).

We also start with the assertion that the class system is a system that works, often in subtle and unseen ways, to reproduce itself. While we in no way mean to suggest that this reproduction occurs solely in a structural-deterministic way somehow beyond the proactive assiduousness of human agents, we do want to draw readers' attention to the role of the education system—particularly higher education—in perpetuating inequality. The book also stresses, as will become evident throughout many of the essays in this collection, that students and academics are capable of resistance, subversion, and creative circumvention.

1

CLASS AND EDUCATION

A considerable incongruity exists between the Jeffersonian/Deweyite promise of universal education and vertical socioeconomic mobility. This is to say
that, contrary to the claim of equal opportunity and the role of universal access to education in facilitating upward mobility, strong and pronounced
barriers to higher education continue to exist.

For at least the last quarter of a century, some scholars in the field of education have been attentive to the relationship between social class and education. Many of their studies have employed an empirical approach and
sought to uncover the connections between class background, levels of academic achievement, and employment. Most paint a very similar and dis-
tressing picture: higher education is an arena that is still disproportionately
occupied by people from the middle and upper classes. This pattern is as old
as higher education itself, and despite rhetorical flourishes to the contrary,
statistics from recent history, at least, illustrate that this process is not abating
but rather increasing. In 1980, a student from the top income quartile was
four times more likely to earn a college degree than one from the bottom
quartile, and by the mid-1990s, almost twenty times as likely (Center for Popular Economics 1995; Jones 2003). While there are more people with a four-
year college degree today than at any time in U.S. history, college graduates
still constitute a statistical minority. According to the U.S. Census Bureau
(2004), just over a fifth (20.7 percent) of adults between the ages of twenty-
five and thirty-four hold a bachelor's degree, and considerably fewer (7.4
percent) hold advanced degrees. Successfully completing an undergraduate
degree, let alone earning a graduate degree, is intimately connected to one's
social class, not least of all the level of parental education. In her study, Jones
(2003) found that the attrition rate of first-generation college students ap-
proached 50 percent and that students whose parents had at least "some college" were twice as likely as others to enroll in doctoral programs.

Rarer than studies that examine the connections between social class and
university attendance are those that investigate the social class background
of university faculty. The few studies that do exist are quite instructive.
Among them we can point to the work of Lipset and Ladd (1979), who undertook such a study using national data and found that while there was a
marked expansion in college attendance after World War II (particularly as a
result of the GI Bill), the greatly expanding professoriate was drawn from
wealthier rather than less privileged family origins. So, too, in their study,
Oldfield and Conant (2001) found that the overwhelming number of faculty
they surveyed had parents in the top two tiers of the Nam-Powers-Terrie
(NPT) scale (the most widely used occupational status measure). Further,
they found that even in a university that had wide class diversity among its
undergraduate student populace, the faculty did not reflect this diversity, and

in fact the professors were three times more likely to come from privileged backgrounds than the students who filled their classrooms.

AUTOETHNOGRAPHY

The chapters you are about to read are personal accounts of the life experiences of working- and underclass academics. Each of the contributors explores how his or her educational experiences were affected by social class, and each contributor situates his or her experience within the broader system of macro circumstances that influence behaviors and attitudes. The use of personal narratives to qualitatively flesh out the intricacies of systemic order—the autoethnographic approach—is a valuable tool for exploring difference and for offering resistance to dominant paradigms. This is true for a variety of reasons. First, the autoethnography is, by its nature, an outsider's methodology. The outsider position is useful for critiquing rather than reproducing dominant systems of thought precisely because it does not rely upon hegemonic tools of order. Contributors are free to explore the bound aries of their experiences and the implications of their analyses without being obligated to conform those experiences to prevailing conventions. At its best, the autoethnography presents informed testimony from the heart of experience—tangible, authentic reports from the intersection of the global and the personal.

For the autoethnography to be valued, however, it is necessary to understand the difficult-to-define but nonetheless crucial visceral quality of personal narrative. At its heart, the autoethnography allows readers to hear a voice, a first-person subject identifying with and claiming subjectivity while at the same time recognizing the social-structural forces that inform the personal. The voice is critically important. Through it, readers can experience the language that makes up identity, the tone of struggle and confusion, the plea for resistance. You can also hear in these voices how deeply personal autoethnographies are. There is no way to read these accounts and not feel the contributors' investment in articulating their stories. Rather than see this quality as a hindrance to the method, we see conviction and adamancy as evidence of liberation. To the marginalized, silence and immobilization have long been outcomes of educational systems. The contributors' engagement with a narrative allows readers to feel the moment of truth opening up, the moment when, free from hegemonic academic boundaries, they are able to articulate their fugitive knowledges.

Finally, the autoethnography perhaps works best when it is presented as a collection of voices. A collection of autoethnographies allows patterns to emerge. If one academic experienced something, that experience is perhaps anecdotal. If another academic experienced the same thing, there's perhaps something suspicious afoot. If ten academics experience similar things, you have the makings of an important argument. That's what we have here.

Recently, however, the autoethnographic method has been criticized for being too self-indulgent and narcissistic to adequately represent what the empirical is intended to articulate (Sparkes 2000; Coffey 1999). While the use of the "I" voice and the engagement of subjectivity to advocate for a particular understanding of experience is, by definition, about the self, we agree with Tierney (1998) who asserts that "autoethnography confronts dominant forms of representation and power in an attempt to reclaim, through self-reflexive response, representational spaces that have marginalized those of us at the borders" (66). In fact, since we also believe that the boundaries of research and their maintenance are socially constructed, we also agree with Holt (2003), who argues that "a good autoethnography should not be dismissed. Autoethnography is not necessarily limited to the self because people do not accumulate their experiences in a social vacuum." Recent examinations of autoethnographies have argued that criticisms of the method are in fact means of reasserting orthodoxy and resisting change (Ellis and Bochner 2000). Such criticisms, in turn, function to preserve the dominant viewpoints that those using autoethnographic approaches may wish to question. This collection of essays wholeheartedly embraces the autoethnography as an authentic means of questioning systemic power.

REFERENCES

Blau, P., and O. D. Duncan. 1967. *The American Occupation Structure*. New York: Wiley.

Blumer, H. 1969. "Fashion: From Class Differentiation to Collective Selection." *Sociological Quarterly* 10: 275–91.

Center for Popular Economics. 1995. *The New Field Guide to the U.S. Economy: A Compact and Irreverent Guide to Economic Life in America*. New York: New York Press.

Coffey, P. 1999. *The Ethnographic Self*. London: Sage.

Duncan, G. J., W. J. Yeung, and J. Brooks-Gunn. 1998. "The Effects of Childhood Poverty on the Life Chances of Children." *American Sociological Review* 63: 406–23.

Ellis, C., and A. Bochner. 2000. "Autoethnography, Personal Narrative, Reflexivity: Researcher as Subject." In *Handbook of Qualitative Research,* 2nd ed., ed. N. K. Denzin and Y. S. Lincoln 733–38. Thousand Oaks, CA: Sage.

Granfield, R. 1991. "Making It by Faking It: Working-Class Students in an Elite Academic Environment." *Journal of Contemporary Ethnography* 20, no. 3: 331–51.

Holt, Nicholas L. 2003. "Representation, Legitimation, and Autoethnography: An Autoethnographic Writing Story." *International Journal of Qualitative Methods* 2, no. 1: article 2.

Jones, S. J. 2003. "Complex Subjectivities: Class, Ethnicity and Race in Women's Narratives of Upward Mobility." *Journal of Social Issues* 59: 803–21.

Lipset, S. M., and E. C. Ladd. 1979. "The Changing Social Origins of American Academics." In *Qualitative and Quantitative Research, Papers in Honor of Paul Lazarfeld,* ed. R. K. Merton, J. S. Coleman, and P. H. Rossi, 28–43. New York: Free Press.

MacLeod, J. 1987. *Ain't No Making It: Leveled Aspirations in a Low-Income Neighborhood.* Boulder, CO: Westview Press.

Oldfield, K., and R. E. Conant. 2001. "Exploring the Use of Socioeconomic Status as Part of an Affirmative Action Plan to Recruit and Hire University Professors." *Journal of Public Affairs Education* 7, no. 3: 171–85.

Sennett, R., and J. Cobb. 1973. *The Hidden Injuries of Class.* New York: Vintage Books.

Short, K., and M. Shea. 1995. "Beyond Poverty Extended Measures of Well-Being." *Current Population Reports* (November). Washington, DC: U.S. Department of Commerce.

Sparkes, A. C. 2000. "Autoethnography and Narratives of Self: Reflections on Criteria in Action." *Sociology of Sport Journal* 17: 21–41.

Tierney, W. G. 1998. *Tales of the Field: On Writing Ethnography.* Thousand Oaks, CA: Sage.

Treiman, D. J. 1977. *Occupational Prestige in Comparative Perspective.* New York: Academic Press.

U.S. Census Bureau. 2004. Earnings by Occupation and Education. www.ccnsus.gov/hhes/income/earnings/.

Willis, P. 1977. *Learning to Labor: How Working Class Kids Get Working Class Jobs.* New York: Columbia University Press.

I

SLIPPIN' THROUGH THE CRACKS:WORKING-CLASS ACADEMICS CHALLENGE THE MERITOCRACY

In this section, contributors explore the ways in which they learned about, and were affected by, the culture's belief in a meritocracy. The contributors' stories, while distinct, also articulate common experiences. In "Happy Accidents: The Unofficial Story of How I Became an Academic," Jennifer Beech argues that academics who come from the working class are not necessarily those people who have systematic plans for achievement. In fact, she argues that her lack of cultural literacy caused her to have only a hazy sense that a life in academe would be "better" than the lives of those around her. Without mentors, Beech survived attacks on her identity by adopting the coping strategy of "passing," a strategy that caused conflict with, and necessitated negotiation between, where she was going and where she had been.

In "Working It Out," Mike Presdee reveals how events from his experience as a working-class youth at secondary (high) school led to the development of a working-class intellectual understanding of the world. Presdee tells us that, like many young working-class folks, and like many of the book's contributors, he often imagined a "better life" wherein he's befriended by privileged schoolmates. However, the reality of the social structural forces and the interpersonal dynamics of his secondary school soon disabused him of fantasies he held about being taken into their homes, discussing cricket and Latin over tea, and holidaying abroad. Rather, he recounts how school events such as plays, concerts, and founders' days were celebrations of everything that he wasn't, and how he came to accept the "natural order of things," that he and others from his class were to be the ruled, not the rulers.

In his essay "Personal, Professional, and Political Paths to the Study of the Crimes of the Powerful," David Kauzlarich traces his movement from underachieving working-class high school student to tenured professor. He points to a variety of structural and interpersonal factors that began his journey and sustained him throughout. Of particular note is the emphasis Kauzlarich places on the role of his disciplinary niche—sociologically based critical criminology—in speaking to his experiences and engendering a unity of scholarship and political sensibilities. Academia, for Kauzlarich and some other scholars with working-class roots, is a requisite tool for challenging inequality and working for social justice.

In her piece "A Stranger to Paradise: Working-Class Graduate in the Culture of Academia," Dawn Rothe, a nontraditional graduate student, addresses the inner turmoil and intrapersonal conflicts that arise as a result of her transformation from waitress to undergraduate and graduate student. Her piece speaks to the question of what constitutes "hard work" and pays particular attention to her struggles to reconcile the relative values of physical and intellectual labor. More class-conscious than Marx's proletariat, Rothe struggles with the fact that the more "productive" she is, the more alienated she becomes. She also addresses the issues of academic cultural values and their contradictions.

In "Can a Working-Class Girl Have Roots and Wings? White Trash in the Ivory Tower," Donna Selman-Killingbeck reflexively addresses the construction of the working class as one engaged in excess—specifically, that she is too loud, too flashy, wears too much makeup, is too opinionated, and so on. Her narrative presents the way that she employs a variety of survival strategies to negotiate the terrain of a Ph.D. program and that of family life. Her story, perhaps not ironically, shares some striking similarities with those of other critical criminologists who have contributed to this volume. Like Berry and Kauzlarich, Selman-Killingbeck recalls the great surprise she experienced when she first was told, quite late in her undergraduate career, that she was indeed a "good" student. Perhaps even more poignantly, Selman-Killingbeck, like Rothe, reveals in her essay the survival strategy of overcompensation, a strategy that by no means goes unrewarded but also carries a great price.

In "Working Class Need Not Apply: Job Hunting, Job Interviews, and the Working-Class Experience in Academia," Stephen L. Muzzatti and C. Vincent Samarco chronicle how their parents' experiences disabused them early on of the belief in a meritocracy. Instead, for them as for Kauzlarich, academe became a place where they could learn about and insist upon class consciousness. Becoming an academic, then, and remaining an agent of change in academe, means negotiating forms of expression, the presentation of self, and a lack of cultural literacy.

1

Happy Accidents:
The Unofficial Story of
How I Became an Academic

Jennifer Beech

The phrase, "Don't get above your raising," may not be immediately clear to people who grew up outside the rural South. . . . It is not an injunction against wealth as such, even though riches carry the potential for corruption. Instead, it is a rebuke to pretense and snobbery, and a plea for respect for and loyalty to one's roots.

—Bill C. Malone, *Don't Get above Your Raisin':*
Country Music and the Southern Working Class

It is the second semester of my doctoral program, and after class my Shakespeare professor and I are walking to our cars in the overflow parking lot at the University of Southern Mississippi. Maybe for the purposes of chitchat, maybe out of genuine interest, he turns to me, "So, Jennifer, what brings you to USM for a Ph.D.?"

Okay, I'm ready. I've anticipated this question and prepared my response. Like Carolyn Leste Law and so many other academics from the working class, I'll attempt to fit in with a strategy of "silence and lies."[1] A moment of silence; brief, though, lest my hesitancy betray something. Then, the official story—the same one I tell on job interviews when asked how I chose my graduate programs: "Well, I knew I wanted to focus on *X*, and since *(insert school name)* had *(insert name of semi-well-known scholar)* on faculty, I applied." He buys it.

It's the short moments like these that are easiest to fake. A couple of well-prepared sound bites, the right hair and clothes, straining really hard to mask my southern accent, and I'm generally able to pass for a middle-class academic. Consequently, now with a Ph.D., I'm less able to pass as a member of my home community. My parents, a retired elementary school teacher and

9

a retired paper mill worker, are proud of me. Considering that I am the first Ph.D. from Woodly, folks there are proud of me, as well.[2] Proud of me, yes. Able to relate to me, well, that's another story. Quite often, I get the feeling that against the grain of this pride also run the emotions of resentment and fear: resentment that I somehow "made it" and fear that I now consider my- self better—that I've gotten "above my raisin'."

Have I gotten above my raisin'? Well, that's something that I have to ask myself from time to time, for the very rewards structure of the academy tells me that only a few achieve the Ph.D.—and certainly only a few from backgrounds like mine. I must be a particularly hard worker, maybe even a genius, a "scholarship girl" of sorts. That spin generally fits well with the *official story*. Indeed, even if it's bragging, that spin does what I need it to, particularly if it comes from those who recommend me. Lies? *Hmm*, not entirely. I mean: I don't want to sell myself short. Surely, I must be smart to have gotten where I am, right? I *did* work hard. Yet, to put that spin on, as I often feel I must, is to employ the strategy of omission: a blend of si- lence and lies, a half-story. Not the *unofficial story*, which I shall tell shortly.

In the autobiographical first half of his book *Lives on the Boundary*, Mike Rose[3] recounts his journey to academe, helping us understand how an aca- demically underprepared working-class Italian American kid from South L.A. finds his way to college, to graduate school, and eventually into a tenure-track professorship. Although Rose would eventually develop the habits of mind that lead to academic success, his story reveals that it was neither his genius nor his hard work that landed him in college or graduate school. That is, he did not simply pull himself up by the proverbial boot- straps. Instead, his story reveals that it was actually a series of well- connected mentors who pushed him into applying to various schools and who pulled strings to ensure his acceptance, along with scholarships and assistantships. Juxtaposing Rose's narrative with my journey from my own South L.A. (lower Alabama) into the hallowed halls of the academy, I am struck by how "lucky" Rose was, and I am grateful for the candor of his tale. As Michael Zweig, author of *The Working-Class Majority: America's Best Kept Secret*, reminds us, "A philosophy of individualism that ignores the place of luck and the shaping power of social relationships beyond the in- dividual accentuates the hubris of those who succeed and intensifies the sense of worthlessness of those who fail."[4] As my narrative will illustrate, I did not initially have a series of well-connected mentors who made the right calls and got me into the right schools; it was more a series of "happy acci- dents," rather than mere individual resourcefulness, that propelled me into good programs and that, in some ways unfortunately, helped me to get above my raisin'.

ACCIDENT ONE: "CHOOSING" AN UNDERGRADUATE INSTITUTION

The first accident, literally a car wreck, has served as a metaphor for my journey from beauty pageant winner decked out in fancy sequined or antebellum gowns to professor donning those three blue velvet stripes. As first runner-up to the Clarke–Washington County Fair Queen, I'd earned a half-tuition scholarship to what was then called Livingston University, and as an honors student, I'd earned an additional half-tuition academic scholarship to the same school. But, as that was the university where my mother had earned her teaching certificate for early childhood education, I rebelled by choosing the University of South Alabama, which offered me neither a scholarship for my brains nor my beauty. This meant that I'd have to work while in school, so one week after graduation, I moved to Mobile and took a job working forty hours a week at an eye, ear, nose, and throat clinic. The plan was that I'd work all summer, save money to help out with tuition and books, and cut back to twenty hours when classes began in the fall. This plan was thwarted when, two days before fall registration, a drunk driver going about sixty miles an hour rammed her Dodge pickup into my '69 Chevy Impala. Witnesses to the accident—two friends of the driver who were following her home from the liquor store because they "thought she might be drunk"— testified that the impact occurred when the other driver swerved into the left turn lane, where my vehicle rested.

While my parents were prepared to "take up the slack" from what my job didn't cover for college, they were not prepared to do this while also paying for ambulance, tow, medical, and car repair bills. And as anyone who has ever tried to get timely or fair compensation from a second-party insurance company knows, settlements are rarely either.

Family meeting. My father and mother (Nolan and Paulette) sitting stiffly on the brown plaid sofa, my brother (John) on the green Naugahyde chair, I with our schnauzer, Skipper, on the orange and brown shag carpet (this was the 1980s; we couldn't afford new furniture and carpet with each new decade):

> Nolan: Kids, your momma and I are proud of ya. You know we work hard and want ya both to go to college. And, Jennifer, your brother has decided he wants to go to college, too. You got those scholarships, and I'm not sure we're ever gonna get jack from that damned insurance company.
>
> Me: Daddy, I know where this is headed and . . .
>
> John: Jen, I wanta go too, and you got those scholarships!
>
> Nolan: And, yeah, your brother should'a worked hard, too, like you; (turning to John and shouting) then he'd have a scholarship, too!

Paulette: Besides, Livingston's a good school. I loved it there. You and John will, I'm sure. I bet some of my old professors are still there. Hey, you should look up Dr. Nawaz. He's in the school of ed. Maybe Dr. Nissan's still there. . . .

Me: Will they still give me those scholarships, even if I start winter quarter?

My question was as much defiant as it was genuine, for I knew nothing about the admissions process. In fact, I'd only intended to apply to South Alabama; I had only applied to Livingston when an application accompanied my scholarship information after the fair pageant. Soon enough, however, I'd learn that two halves do not always make a whole. According to Livingston's dean of admissions, a scholarship still awaited me, but I'd have to choose either the academic scholarship or the pageant scholarship. "Technically," he explained over the phone, "it does not matter which one you choose, as the tuition remission will be the same either way." Even then, I somehow felt that it *did* matter. During a brief pause, I peered around to see if I were still in the living room alone. Just Skipper.

"Miss Beech, are you still there? You want the beauty scholarship?"

"The academic," I mumbled more in the direction of the dog than the receiver.

"Pardon?"

"The academic scholarship!"

LIVINGSTON

At Livingston, I was a smashing success—particularly after one day, in a fit of frustration, I told John, "Look, you know I love you, but you're driving me crazy—always asking me where I'm going, telling me who to date, and I'm sick of it! Find your own friends. Tell ya what. Let's do this: You pretend that I'm at a different school, and I'll do the same with you. Then, we can meet up at home sometimes and see each other." I can still see my brother, his eyes cast off, not looking at me square—even though I coldly stared at him— his shoulders slumped, his hands dropped beside the pockets of his well-worn Levi's, a look of utter hurt, a posture of humiliation.

Two years before, John had returned after one semester at the University of Alabama—not because he couldn't make it academically, but because he couldn't bear the distance from things familiar. (This is not a flattering self-portrait, I realize. This is the part where I reveal the ugly decisions I made to fit in. This is where my story blurs with and diverges from my brother's.)

Ninety miles north of our parents' home was a safe distance for us. Livingston was a "suitcase college," one of those schools where the majority of students head home for the weekends. John and I both did this for about the first two months, and then I started to go home less and less. Beginning winter, rather than fall, quarter, my brother and I were the new kids on this campus of twenty-five hundred students, thus attracting the usual questions. When I would tell folks where I was from, I was often met with shocked responses: "No way! You don't sound or act like you're from the country," (read "hick," read "working class"), or, "Really! What do your parents do?" Although I didn't initially understand what motivated these questions, I quickly noticed that John was not getting shocked responses when he informed folks that he was from Woodly.

Livingston University was what John Alberti would likely deem a third-tier, working-class university—a small liberal arts school, originally a normal college, now catering to students who don't want to "be a number" or (more the case) who can't afford one of the larger state universities.[5] There, I joined the choir, began to take classical voice training, wrote for the school newspaper, acted in plays, and even became Miss Livingston University—this time to the tune of a full-tuition scholarship and an extra $500 for winning the talent competition with an Italian aria from the opera *Figaro*. I was a star. John and I took a few classes together, ran into each other occasionally at the only bar in town, and ate with each other from time to time in the cafeteria, but the more I became entrenched in school culture and the more he continued to go home every weekend, the less we connected.

My brother (in a rather dismissive manner, folks around campus would often refer to him as "Jennifer's brother," rather than as John) scored equal to or higher than me on most parts of our college entrance exams. He completed his B.S. in computer science the fall after I completed my M.A. in English. Today, he has replaced my father as a back tender on the same paper machine my father labored on for thirty-two years. When asked why he doesn't work with computers, John usually responds, "That stuff just wasn't for me. I mean, I like computers and all, but that wearing a tie and sitting in an office and acting all hoity-toity, that's not my style." In fact, it was the middle-class decorum of the academy that made John uncomfortable throughout college, so uncomfortable that twice he purposely failed the last business course required to complete his degree. In an effort to please our parents, he finally passed the class but now admits that he worried that completing the course would mean being stuck in the type of middle-class environment that had made him so uncomfortable for his six on-and-off years at Livingston.

It wasn't until I began to work on my doctorate in composition and rhetoric in 1996, when I began to read bell hooks, Victor Villanueva, Jr., Min-Zhan Lu, Henry Giroux, and others who forward border-crossing pedagogies, that I began to make sense of the psychological turmoil that not only my brother and I, but our whole family, had been going through since John and I started college back in 1986.[6] As hooks discusses in *Teaching to Transgress*, "Demands that individuals from class backgrounds deemed undesirable surrender all vestiges of their pasts create psychic turmoil."[7] Referencing the experiences of those like my brother, hooks points out that many students are unable to negotiate between the types of behavior expected in the academy and the types of behavior that make them feel comfortable in their home communities. While John had internalized his own "inferiority," I had made strong efforts to assimilate to a middle-class worldview, at the cost of what Victor Villanueva calls "fictive kinship" to my home community and literal kinship to my family.[8]

ACCIDENT TWO: CHOOSING
SOUTHERN ILLINOIS UNIVERSITY

My senior year, I was one of about four graduating English majors with aspirations toward graduate school. Looking back, I now see that while our professors genuinely cared about our welfare, they seemed quite unprepared to offer us the sorts of mentoring we might have received had we attended one of those top-tier universities. That is, while the letters of recommendation were forthcoming, little to no advice was offered with respect to how to choose a grad school. Despite an additional mathematics minor, my performance on the GRE was mediocre; I'd never heard that one should study how to take such tests. In winter quarter, those three peers and I applied to our "top choices"—which mainly meant the University of Alabama or Auburn. Did these schools offer fine programs in our preferred areas of study? Who knows! *They have great football teams; everyone in Alabama loves one of those schools; hence, they must be good,* we reasoned. The idea of researching a school, calling upon connections to get us in, and so forth, did not occur to us—did not, in fact, seem to have occurred to our professors.

There was a third school to which only I applied. On a bulletin board outside the main English office was an advertisement for graduate studies at Southern Illinois University. Since, according to the ad, there was no required application fee, on a whim, I applied for admission to the program and for a teaching assistantship. When in late spring I received the acceptance letter and an offer for an assistantship, I literally had forgotten that I'd applied. "Where is Carbondale?" I puzzled, standing next to the trash can in the post office. My next thought was that I'd been sent the letter by accident, that within a week, I'd receive another letter saying as much. As this was the only school to offer me an assistantship, I "chose" SIU.

THE MASTER'S

Shortly upon my arrival in Carbondale on a campus with twenty-five thousand students (ten times the enrollment of my undergraduate institution), I'd discover that what passed back at Livingston for middle-class decorum was here, at best, only a poor approximation.

Mid-fall semester. Bathroom stall in Faner Hall. Three of my fellow TAs enter: "Hey, listen to this. Earlier today, I saw Jennifer Beech walking down the hall, and all I saw was lips and hair!"

Strategy of silence. *Maybe, if I'm quiet enough, they'll exit without discovering I'm in here.* Fat chance! There are only three stalls in this bathroom, and these women all desire to use them. One knocks on mine. I open it, and laying on my southern accent with extra ferocity, I greet them, "Hello, feminists." (Back in Woodly, this would have been a huge insult to any woman.)

The first of my cohorts to defend my thesis, I graduated with As in everything except for a course in modern grammar. And I had made it thus far without having obtained a single student loan; just lots of credit card debt to pay for groceries and constant repairs on my '78 Monte Carlo. My parents had always warned me that student loans were a "surefire way to get in debt." When I'd informed them of the good news about grad school, my father's response had been, "You'll never make it on that stipend! I told ya you should have got that teaching certificate to fall back on." *Who was I to want to become a professor? Why wasn't it good enough for me to teach elementary or high school like my mom and the few other women from Woodly who went off to and always came back from college? A teaching job, after all, is a nice addition to the man's salary, and it allows the woman to be home the same time the kids are.* Common sentiment in Woodly is that a woman works only as a supplement to her husband's income. At home, then, my ambitions to a "career" as college professor appeared extravagant and disloyal.

CONVERGING AND DIVERGING WITH
JOHN, ONCE AGAIN, IN LIVINGSTON

At an odometer reading of 167,000 miles, that Monte Carlo blew up on me on the interstate in Eau Claire, Wisconsin—just as I was driving it home to "give" it to John for Christmas. *What was I thinking?*[9] He'd said he could use it for a work car to drive back and forth to the chemical waste disposal plant just outside of Livingston where he was then employed. An instructorship at a branch of the University of Minnesota had afforded me the funds to pay off my credit cards and to purchase a new Geo Metro. The plan was to drive the Monte Carlo to Alabama, hand it off to John, and then go car shopping with our Dad, who can, I'm still convinced, talk down any car salesman in Washington County.

Short on funds after purchasing a last-minute plane ticket at Christmas, I settled for giving John a Vikings sweatshirt and a beer mug bearing the Norwegian exclamation, "Ufdah!" Still, while home, John and I reconnected.

With only two years' difference between us in age, our fights have often been fierce, our resentments short-lived, and our bond strong. So, when my one-year appointment at the university turned out to be just that and I had tired of the bartending job I'd worked for eight months, John gladly flew up to Minnesota to accompany me on my move back to Alabama in January of the following year.

Till the next fall, I worked two to three odd retail jobs at a time down in Mobile. Then with a mid-August visit to John in Livingston and a stop in to see my undergraduate English professors, I succeeded in securing an adjunct teaching position at my old alma mater: teaching two first-year composition classes and two public speaking classes per quarter. John even invited me to share his one-bedroom apartment; I'd get the couch, of course. We planned to split expenses for a year, during which I'd save up enough money to go back to grad school. Considering John's low wage at the chem waste plant, this arrangement would help him, as well. Yet, just as I was set to move in, John received the phone call he'd been waiting for since completing his bachelor's. With a follow-up face-to-face interview and a subsequent job offer from the same paper mill our father worked for, John abdicated to me his apartment. Since this was all he ever really wanted—to work beside our father and to live in our home community—our parents and I were each genuinely happy for John's good fortune.

And I was happy to be teaching again, and especially happy to work with a student population whom I understood so well. Late fall quarter, with the sudden death of one of my most beloved undergraduate professors, the University of West Alabama (as Livingston University was newly called) offered me an instructorship at the prorated salary of $24,000 for the remaining academic year. In order to further my savings for grad school, in January I relinquished my brother's apartment and took a half-year lease at $140.00 a month on a fourteen-foot trailer—a place so small that, as my dad put it, "You'd have to go outside when you wanted to change your mind." Rather than change my mind, though, I now had to make up my mind about where to apply for doctoral programs.

ACCIDENT THREE: CHOOSING A PROGRAM FOR THE TERMINAL DEGREE

How ironic that six years after my initial application process for graduate school I'd come full circle back to Livingston. With the exception of one new tenure-track professor, the English faculty consisted of the same folks it had back in the fall of 1988, kindly professors who were as unprepared as ever to offer sound mentoring for how to choose a program. West Alabama's one new English professor did loan me her GRE study guide, something for which I am entirely grateful, and since she was finishing up her Ph.D. at the University of Southern Mississippi and spoke so highly of the program, I applied. *This time around did I research programs to match up my interests with their scholars and reputations or at least to make sure a program offered a decent stipend and health insurance.* Nope. Such academic ins and outs were still as much a mystery to me as they'd always been. Going on one person's recommendation and knowing little else about the program, I applied to USM. This was, perhaps, my happiest accident, for my second year in the program, I serendipitously discovered my academic direction, as well as my first effective mentor, when I signed up for a seminar called the Ethnography of Literacy.

USM

Backtrack to the overflow parking lot. This time around, I've made my best effort to approximate the look of a serious middle-class academic: short hair, subdued makeup, khakis, no nail polish. The Shakespeare professor, too, appears to favor khakis—*a good sign,* I think. My car's not as far back as his, and as I hang a right down my row, he remarks, "You said you're from Alabama, but I don't detect a southern accent."

"Oh, no," I retort with put-on Norwegian intonation, "That year as an instructor at the University of Minnesota Morris beat it out of me. That's for sure, yah!" Then, imagining I'm on the phone with my father, I dialect-shift, "Well, I'm fixin' to go. See y'all in class on Thursday." He smiles and waves good evening.

Speaking of Daddy (that's what we southerners call our fathers, whether we're two or fifty-two): he was very pleased to have me in Hattiesburg, an hour and a half away from Woodly, but not at all happy with my new look. First pointing toward my ears and then giving my new hairdo two thumbs down, he asked (as he also does every time I get made over for the job market), "What's with this uglied-up look?" To this day, he carries in his wallet a photo of me taken in the eighth grade the night that I won the Christmas Princess Pageant.

Mother had reprimanded him, "Nolan, now that she's getting her Ph.D., she can't go around looking like Miss America. Besides, I think she looks cute. We're proud of you, honey." They were. Now, with their house paid off and a bit of money saved, they were able and willing to help me with tuition and rent, and against their protests, I took my first student loan.

In the Ethnography of Literacy seminar, I learned that language is directly tied to culture and values, that to attack one's home dialect by deeming it "incorrect"—as the mainstream school systems do—is tantamount to attacking the identity of not only the speaker of the dialect but the identity and values of her home community. I began to read French sociologists Pierre Bourdieu and Jean Claude Passeron and to apply to my brother's and my experiences their theories of primary and secondary pedagogies.[10] Our differing successes and comfort levels with college made more sense as I began to understand that for those of us who are nonmainstream students, school enacts a secondary pedagogy that runs counter to our home world-views or our primary pedagogies, but for mainstream students, schooling is a continuation of their primary pedagogies. Reading David Halle's study of New Jersey chemical plant workers and Sherry Ortner's synthesis of several ethnographic studies of working-class neighborhoods, I grappled with the findings that working-class communities have a tendency for both male and female community members to associate women with middle-class habits and values and thus tend to ambivalently project class anxieties and resentments onto women at the same time they associate women with respectability and mobility.[11] Thinking from the perspective of Woodly residents, I saw that my desire to obtain a college education would have been tolerable had I simply gotten a B.A. and returned as a K–12 school teacher; they could have excused my "proper" speech as the necessary—even if unattractive—speech of a schoolmarm. In Woodly, John holds much more esteem because of the fact that he proved he could obtain the degree and then, instead, demonstrated his loyalties and showed himself "down-to-earth" by choosing the kind of manual, wage-labor job "real" men take; the very notion that he could have gotten a job related to his degree but chose his father's work pays a high compliment to our father and to other Woodly men.

The professor of that ethnography course, herself from a working-class background, sort of became my Jack MacFarland (the first teacher to mentor Mike Rose). She loaned me books, directed my dissertation, called in connections and wrote letters of recommendation when I went on the job market, and confessed to having difficulty herself in figuring out what exactly to wear to pull off the "proper" look for the job interview. Her balanced model of caring and honesty is what I follow today as I mentor students.[12]

REFLECTIONS FROM THE WRONG SIDE OF THE TRACKS

When I read the title of this collection, I hesitated to submit my piece, for Woodly does not even boast a traffic light, let alone a railroad track. But, as my brother recently reminded me (when I called to ask his permission to include him in this memoir), Woodly did at one time have a railroad. Settled in 1817 by farmers, Woodly experienced its boom when a major lumber company came to the community in 1902. According to our great-aunt Ina, "Most people either worked at turpentine or worked at logging." Today, the lumber company and the railroad that came with it are but distant memories for those of my paternal grandparents' generation. Still, with a population of about six hundred, this small community boasts two churches (one Baptist, the other Assembly of God), one catfish restaurant, and a volunteer fire department. Covering about sixteen square miles, Woodly rests on two perpendicular roads; these roads sit off the major state highway in a manner that almost prevents a stranger from happening into the community. One stop sign rests at the internal point at which the two county roads converge. In the twenty-first century, Woodly is simultaneously the rural South that William Faulkner and Flannery O'Connor write about and the globalized South connected to the world via the Internet. It is the South in which most of the students I teach grew up and still call home; the South that is, for many, the right side of the tracks, the side my students can't wait to get back to from college each weekend.

Such personal reflections as the ones I relate above are risky. Indeed, I wonder if disclosing these personal details will sabotage my career, given the very middle-class, individualistic values embraced by most in the academy. What I hope my narrative highlights are the struggles of those who do not have what has been recently identified as "affirmative action for the rich" or well connected. What I hope this piece further emphasizes is that my achievement of a Ph.D. and a tenure-track professorship are not so much evidence that the American dream is still alive but that individual hubris is itself part of the myth that works to blame those like my brother who "fail" to capitalize on the American education system—a system that promotes an accompanying literacy myth: the notion that the "good life" necessarily follows with the achievement of a certain type of (read, *middle-class*) literacy.

NOTES

1. Carolyn Leste Law, introduction to *This Fine Place So Far from Home: Voice of Academics from the Working Class*, ed. C. L. Barney Dews and Carolyn Leste Law, 3 (Philadelphia: Temple University Press, 1995).

2. I have chosen "Woodly" as the pseudonym for my home community because logging and paper industries provide the livelihood for many of the residents of Woodly and because the landscape of the community is, itself, comprised of acres of pine and oak forests.

3. Mike Rose, *Lives on the Boundary* (New York: Penguin, 1989).

4. Michael Zweig, *The Working Class Majority: America's Best Kept Secret* (New York: Cornell University Press, 2000), 102.

5. John Alberti, "Returning to Class: Creating Opportunities for Multicultural Reform at Majority Second-Tier Schools," *College English* 63, no. 5 (2001), 561–84.

6. bell hooks, *Teaching to Transgress: Education as the Practice of Freedom* (New York: Routledge, 1994); Victor Villanueva, Jr., *Bootstraps: From an American Academic*

of Color (Urbana, IL: National Council of Teachers of English, 1993). Min-Zhan Lu, "Conflict and Struggle: The Enemies and Preconditions of Basic Writing," *College English* 54, no. 8 (1992): 887–913. Henry A. Giroux, *Border Crossings: Cultural Workers and the Politics of Education* (New York: Routledge, 1992).

7. hooks, *Teaching to Transgress*, 182.

8. Villanueva, *Bootstraps*, 40.

9. Telling this reinforces for me that notion that writing is much more an act of discovery than simple transcription of events. Now, at the age of thirty-six, I am, frankly, amazed at how my twenty-five-year-old mind reasoned. Perhaps I imagined since I'd repaired or replaced just about every functioning part of my old car that surely it would make it fifteen hundred miles for me to bestow as a "glorious gift" upon my brother! I'm lucky John gets me gifts to this day.

10. Pierre Bourdieu and Jean Claude Passeron, *Reproduction in Education, Society, and Culture* (London: Sage, 1977).

11. David Halle, *America's Working Man: Work, Home, and Politics among Blue-Collar Property Owners* (Chicago: University of Chicago Press, 1984); Sherry B. Ortner, "Rereading America: Preliminary Notes on Class and Culture," in *Recapturing Anthropology: Working in the Present*, ed. Richard G. Fox, 163–89 (Santa Fe, NM: School of American Research Press, 1991).

12. This professor is so modest, she would be embarrassed were I to name her here. Suffice it to say that as one working-class academic to another, she has helped me to find "a place to stand" that is somewhere between the academy and my rural, southern, working-class roots.

REFERENCES

Alberti, John. "Returning to Class: Creating Opportunities for Multicultural Reform at Majority Second-Tier Schools." *College English* 63, no. 5 (2001): 561–84.

Bourdieu, Pierre, and Jean Claude Passeron. *Reproduction in Education, Society, and Culture*. London: Sage, 1977.

Giroux, Henry A. *Border Crossings: Cultural Workers and the Politics of Education*. New York: Routledge, 1992.

Halle, David. *America's Working Man: Work, Home, and Politics among Blue-Collar Property Owners*. Illinois: University of Chicago Press, 1984.

hooks, bell. *Teaching to Transgress: Education as the Practice of Freedom*. New York: Routledge, 1994.

Law, Carolyn Leste. Introduction. In *This Fine Place So Far From Home: Voices of Academics from the Working Class*, 1–10. Philadelphia: Temple University Press, 1995.

Lu, Min-Zhan. "Conflict and Struggle: The Enemies and Preconditions of Basic Writing." *College English* 54, no. 8 (1992): 887–913.

Malone, Bill C. *Don't Get Above Your Raisin': Country Music and the Southern Working Class*. Chicago: University of Illinois Press, 2002.

Ortner, Sherry B. "Rereading America: Preliminary Notes on Class and Culture." In *Recapturing Anthropology: Working in the Present*, ed. Richard G. Fox, 163–89. Santa Fe, NM: School of American Research Press, 1991.

Rose, Mike. *Lives on the Boundary*. New York: Penguin, 1989.

Villanueva, Victor, Jr. *Bootstraps: From an American Academic of Color*. Urbana, IL: National Council of Teachers of English, 1993.

Zweig, Michael. *The Working Class Majority: America's Best Kept Secret*. Ithaca, NY: Cornell University Press, 2000.

2

Working It Out

Michael Presdee

Reflection is a necessary yet often traumatic process involved in human change. Our collective personal histories come together to form the cultural milieu in which we live our lives, and only a close examination can show how the minutiae of everyday life take on important connotations.

It wasn't until I was in my late twenties that I began to think seriously about how my working-classness had affected the way I was, the way my friends were, what we did, who we related to, and how it both restricted us and created us. I had spent most of my life before sixteen in the working-class world of an English council estate, leaving school after sitting O-level exams and joining the Marines. Invalided out at twenty-two on a "war" pension, I reached my lowest ebb, unemployed and "lost" in Canada for eight months before, broken by hepatitis and exhaustion, I returned to England and a job as a government civil servant in the Inland Revenue. At twenty-four I was tucked up securely in the civil service and safely at home, back on the council estate.

It was not until after this that I went, by way of special entry and some fast talking, to teachers college and after several years of clinging to my "not knowing" began the long and painful process of "working it out." It has taken another twenty years to build the confidence to make that process public.

I have endeavored in my own way to work out how the layers of everyday life came together until I became, without knowing it, what sociologists call "working class." I have tried, from my own experiences, to unravel those taken-for-granted parts of our lives which make up what we call "our place." I always knew "my place," as did my parents, yet we never questioned how we came to know or why we accepted it all. We weren't a very "knowing" family, or a knowing neighborhood. We were not involved in politics and active struggle, and I felt no burning ambition to leave it all, do well at school, go to university, and join the "successful" middle classes. I wanted to travel and leave the estate, but not my group; I needed them. We and our neighbors simply tried and struggled and grew up. We were both restricted and creative, resistant and compliant, our own worst enemies and yet defiant.

In the writings that follow I try to trace the beginnings of my particular working-class intellectual understanding of the world that began in secondary (high) school, continued at college, and then simply hung over me throughout academic life like the "muck of ages, hanging like a nightmare over the brain of the living."

In the end collective consciousness will come from working it out together.

BIG SCHOOL

My previous primary school life was discarded as we were directed here and dumped there. Girls here, boys there. Some to grammar school, some to secondary moderns, and some to technical schools. My old familiar world disappeared, along with lemon sherbets and Biggles books. My early "love" Janice Kemp went too, erased from existence forever, and I didn't ask why, or where she was, or even if she was still alive. She was unimportant and no longer to be part of my world—that was now to be all male! Those years in primary school, which had made up so much of my life until now, would never be recognized by my new school; they would ask no questions about it, or care about what we learned, who our teachers had been, who our friends were, or what our lives had been like. It was all to be wiped from our memory, nonexistent and unimportant. Now we were entering the proper school, the real school, the big school, where generations of Gloucestershire young men had been taught since the sixteenth century.

Throughout that summer Mum and Dad prepared me for this new adventure, slowly piecing together, article by article, the costly uniform and baggage of grammar school life; some parts new, some handed down. There was a maroon worsted school blazer that they bought from the Golden Anchor clothes shop in town—"Gentlemen's outfitters and suppliers of school uniforms," it said in their advert—and inside the pockets of the coats and gray trousers was the traditional brand-new halfpenny for luck. Hanging outside the black and white timbered building was a huge golden sea anchor, and almost opposite was the ancient St. Mary de Crypt church where the original Crypt school had been founded in 1539. It was an old part of town, lined with long-established butchers' shops and "purveyors of fine wines" and the New County Hotel with its wooden revolving doors and hushed lobby. It was their part of town, and it seemed only right and proper that young "gentlemen" just off to grammar school should be "fitted" here rather than in the new-style stores like Bon Marché.

I needed several rugby shirts—one white and several in school colors—sports socks, gym shoes, gym vest, school tie, and cap. On the cap we were branded with gold rings so they could tell at a glance which of the four school "houses" we were in: Whitefield, Henley, Moore, or Brown. It was the first time that I had ever had clothes that hadn't been necessary for daily wear. During that summer the drawer under my bed gradually filled with neat piles of clothes that were to be used only on special occasions, once a week, winter or summer, rugby or gym. Clothes up to now had been functional rather than fashionable, and I had worn them continually until they were either too small or threadbare. Now I had clothes for different purposes, and I would no longer be allowed to play cricket and games in gray pants and black pumps, and I watched with satisfaction as the drawer filled and I became a person of substance for the first time.

The sacrifices made by Mum and Dad were huge as they bent the family budget to its limit until that passed-down and pieced-together uniform was complete. But those sacrifices were unseen, unthought about, untalked about, and unthanked; and my only recollections are of how, in spite of their efforts, I didn't measure up to the other boys with their brand-new everything, parading as they did, their complete sets of uniform right down to new school socks with the school colors at the top. Mine had been gathered together with cost in mind rather than the rigid demands of the school. I had ordinary gray socks from Woolworths, hand-knitted sweaters, handed-down bits and pieces; geometry sets, rulers, pens, and the first of many plastic and canvas satchels that frayed and fell to pieces with only average schoolboy use instead of the deep brown, shiny, stiff leather ones that were unaffordable and unthinkable. It had all been bought out of what was left after paying for food and rent, and how my parents even came close to getting it all together is still something I don't understand.

At primary school it hadn't really mattered, we were nearly all scrapped together, but now, for the first time, I would spend my days with children who came from a world whose way of life was unknown to me; a world that I had only peered into from the outside, or read about, or seen in films. These were the sons of the people who ran our world, my world, and they had money and lived on the other side of town in the big houses of Barnwood and Escourt Road. Their very appearance confused and confronted me. They looked different, talked different, and had an air of confidence in this, their rightful place, while I would always be an outsider, an intruder in someone else's world. For the remainder of my schooling I would try desperately to tunnel back to my world and the estate, as for five years I became a working-class mole, blindly undermining their attempts to capture

me until they would give up and release me, scarred and angry, back to my
family.

The school itself was built in a grand style and back to front, its main entrance, complete with mock classical pillars, facing the empty fields and hills
and used only by staff and visitors; while the boys used the back entrance
that faced the main road, our estate, and the action. The back we called the
front; and the front, their entrance, the back. The school stood there, a lump
of gray concrete, with its back to the people and its veneered front facing the
emptiness of the countryside.

The gymnasium was to most of us a hostile and uncompromising environment, containing cold concrete changing rooms and ancient showers
spitting out either scalding or freezing water, unable, with the rest of the
school, to find that necessary harmony and balance that would make any experience enjoyable. There were twelve spiteful nozzles attached to rusting
pipes that spat out their punishment over thirty or so naked bodies at a time
crammed into the short concrete box that made up the shower cubicle.
Overhead, cold air blasted down through the open skylight, putting the finishing touches on the whole stark process. Inside, the gym was the same
cold gray brick of the outside, lined with varnished wooden bars and decked
out with benches, boxes, and beams. It was here in the gym block that the
realities of home life were peeled off in layers for all to see. Shoes, shirt, underwear, and trousers hung up on pegs ready to be inspected by the rest of
the class and our teachers. I always tried to change in the darkness of a corner, quickly rolling my clothes in a ball and hiding them under my jacket so
nobody could see my grubby underwear with its frayed elastic waist, or my
worn-out shirt collars and cuffs, or my socks that had been continuously
darned with different shades of grey wool. There was no gay abandonment
of clothing here, only an embarrassed silent stripping in the half light of the
changing rooms that made me feel ashamed and vulnerable. Never before
had strangers to my world been allowed to penetrate so deep into my existence. They were not of me, and I knew that they didn't live like me. Their
eyes disapproved, taking in the evidence that would confirm for them that I
was different, behaved differently, lived differently. I had no secrets now
when I went back across the green to home; they had taken away my mystery, taken away my power: they had seen me naked.

Here at grammar school my life took on a solitary element, contrasting
with the "togetherness" of primary school, and I experienced, for the first
time, an intense loneliness as we were taught about individual competitiveness, and getting on, and how personal weaknesses could quickly become
other peoples' stepping stones. We never related very much, never talked to
each other about our problems or our feelings; whether we were coping,
whether we liked it all or not. We were thirty isolated individuals brought together for the express purpose of competing against each other for five

years, to beat down everyone around us, to come out on top, to stand out, to succeed. We were to become self-contained and confident, distant, untouchable by the emotions of the crowd. We were taught to become impartial, objective, unemotional, in control, intellectual; and it bred a deep loneliness in me that could only be dulled by my dreams.

In the first term we were separated alphabetically into three classes so they could watch closely how we responded to their new learning and new subjects. They started the process by calling me "Presdee." They spat it out in a sharp staccato manner: "Come here, Presdee. Shut up, Presdee! Yes, Presdee! No, Presdee. Be quiet, Presdee! Sit down, Presdee! Where's your homework, Presdee! Go away, Presdee!" I'd never been called Presdee before, only Mike, or Michael by my parents; but now I was reduced to a noun, an object, a thing—a Presdee! How could anyone warmly communicate with a Presdee? How could you commiserate, cajole, console? It was unemotive and meant to be so, the cold and detached voice of the superior over the inferior. These people had already learned, were already knowledgeable; they had what we didn't—knowledge and power: they were the masters! They were marked as such by the black academic gowns they taught in and the fancy dress they regaled themselves in at special assemblies when they paraded the colors and ermines of academic dress, complete with floppy hats and mortar boards, as they ascended the stage like academic mannequins, parading their plumage in front of the whole school. It reeked of superiority: they were superior to our primary schools, superior to our primary teachers, superior to our homes, superior to our parents, superior to us. It was the pomp and pageantry of privilege laid out for us, the chosen ones, to experience, to wonder at, to aspire to!

In that first term they laid the curriculum before us, a glittering treasure trove of "subjects," all with their own special teacher and special books. At the primary school we never really had subjects; we had English and arithmetic every morning and other things in the afternoons. We read exciting novels and poems and made papier-mâché Viking boats that took weeks to complete; we listened to the Glasgow Orpheus Choir and dug for carrots on Friday afternoons. Now we had "subjects"! Latin, Greek, French, biology, physics, chemistry, geography, history—even sport was a subject! No longer could twenty-two or more boys all play center forward at once; now we would mix science with bravery, develop "character," and play rugby.

Our first assignment was to cover with stiff brown paper the mountain of knowledge they had presented to us. It was almost an impossible task for an uncoordinated person like myself who became, quite simply, "dangerous" when armed with scissors and paste. I sat in the cold hall at home and found that nothing fit; the covers I made were either too big or too small. Dad, as always, took on the task for me, covering every book rapidly and skillfully, every corner magically fitting perfectly. He always had an ability to pack things: suitcases, parcels, sheds, barrows; and when he made up parcels for Mum's "club" he always seemed to know how much paper to use, and how much string, and he tied knots that slipped, moved, and tightened to order, with his short stubby fingers performing amazing acts of delicacy and precision.

Putting covers on my books was about as far as I got in a number of subjects; I was never really able to understand this new compartmentalized approach to knowledge. In the first few months the novelty of studying real "subjects" was motivation enough. Latin, the language of doctors, priests, and universities must be exciting, I thought. Dr. Rose used it when he wrote out prescriptions, and now I would be learning it and would carry it home with me in my satchel. But I never really got close to it, never mastered it, and simply carried it back and forth for four years without coming to terms with its strange sentence constructions and pronunciations. I never got much further than the simple conjugation of amo, amas, amat; the later complexities of the past indicative perfect and its ancient tongue twisters seemed to bear more resemblance to the Goons than to the Romans. For French we had a teacher who came complete with black beret and a full set of guttural sounds that were beautiful to listen to and impossible to make out, let alone repeat, and so I got no further in French than I did in Latin. My technique in both was remarkably simplistic, putting above each foreign word its literal meaning in English and then creating some semblance of meaning out of it all that often bore no serious connection to its real sense. In my translations Romulus did dreadful things to Remus, and my account of Horatio's exploits on the bridge remained in the realm of pure fantasy. By the time I had reached the fifth form, much of that mountain of knowledge that Dad had so expertly covered had been discarded, with my report for that year showing blanks by the side of French, Latin, woodwork, art, and music. Somewhere along the way, someone armed with hope and optimism inexplicably led me into ancient Greek, which, after another brief flirtation with the verb "to love," was added to the ever increasing pile of discarded subjects.

At the end of the first term they split us yet again into A, B, and C streams, and this time I lost my oldest friend, Bob Merrett, who had ridden faithfully over the fields with me for years and had kept me company during my long learning campaign. I would never be as close to Bob again, as we were slowly driven apart by the divergent worlds of the A stream and the C stream, but later we would meet and drink and talk, like old soldiers, about our play trips through the "Grand Canyon" and how we had escaped marauding Indians and how those lemon sherberts had saved us from starvation. Neither of us would ever understand grammar school, frozen as we were in the horseback world of primary school.

There were only three of us from my primary class left now, me, Chris Bullock, of conker and marble fame, and Roy Overthrow. All three of us were propelled into the rarefied atmosphere of the A stream, where we would be kept separate from the boys of the B and C classes. We were the chosen ones, with success just in front of us. By that first Christmas we had been equipped with a spectacular array of brown-covered books; had our first flirtation with foreign languages; knew all the rules and regulations; and, most important, had been taught the school anthem, "Carmen Cryptiensis."

"Vivat schola Cryptiensis, Vivat in perpetuum!"

It now finally dawned on us; this wasn't just for five years, this was to be forever!

I made few real friends in that first year, clinging to the old and feeling inferior to the new. The A stream was made up of a number of boys from that unfamiliar, other side of town, with its middle-class suburbs and professional people, and in the five years that we were together I never knew them, or talked to them much, as the class split and formed groups made up of kids from similar backgrounds. On one side of the class was a group of untidy and undisciplined misfits, failing in their work yet somehow bright enough to confuse the authorities and defy their assessments. On the other side was a sensible, successful group of students destined for the top, most of whom would go on to university life and success, no doubt ending up on the walls of our shrine to look down on other young boys forever.

My first friend was John Hudson. His father was one of the managers of the bakery on the edge of the estate, and he lived in a private house up on the Stroud Road. I had never had a friend from the outside world before, but we were both misfits of sorts and so somehow hung together. John was small and slightly hunched over, and I was fat with a pudding basin haircut. He played at being super middle class and I sat back and marveled at it all.

In all my schooling I never invited anyone back home. When I went across that green it was to be kept separate, untouched, unseen; mine. Yet I was proud to have John as a friend, especially when his father picked him up in their spectacular, pink and pointed Vauxhall Velox that made everyone sit up and notice. After a couple of years John's father was transferred. John disappeared over one long summer holiday, and my connection with that other world was gone; I went back to my split existence of "school" and "estate."

My only other friend was Roy Overthrow, who lived in one of the older red brick council houses not far from school. Roy had been with me in primary school and suffered badly from asthma and eczema, his rough hands turning blue for most of the winter, the cracked skin constantly being painted with brightly colored ointments. We spent a lot of time together, John, Roy, and I, John playing the posh superior and Roy laughing silently at my clownish antics. He could never get enough breath for a good hearty laugh—his asthma robbed him of that—so he bent over in silent convulsions of hysteria, his face turning deep red as his body fought for oxygen. Roy wheezed and spluttered at all my jokes as we clowned our way through our ordeal. He had lots of time off, spent at the hospital and doctors' offices, but he survived the five years, fingers taped up, better than most.

I had always hoped that Peter Latham would become my friend, but he never did. He was both very clean-cut and intelligent and a formidable fast bowler who had the peculiar action of turning both arms over at once before hurling the ball at the batsman. He also sang soprano in the choir, having a high-pitched voice that the music teacher raved over, and so he sang solos at special assemblies and played the lead female parts in our Shakespeare plays. He was everyone's favorite, and in the privacy of night I created a world where he and I were friends and he invited me to his home, where we would have tea together, play together, engage in deep conversations about Latin and cricket, and discuss going on holiday together. It was all there in my mind. What his home was like, what his parents were like, what his life was like. We were friends forever, and when I wandered around the green on my own, I talked to him and played with him, acting out our life together, oblivious to all outsiders. In the classroom he treated me with indifference, accepting my laughter and never reciprocating it. Try as I might, he was never interested; he simply took my jokes and ran.

I soon settled comfortably into the role of rebellious clown, perfecting, over time, the art of the quick quip and goonish behavior. It was something that I was good at, and I enjoyed being able to make the whole class laugh and sometimes even the teachers. It was as if I had control over them, just for that moment, making me the center of attention; in control, shaping what happened. I knew when I had them "with me," giggling along, trapped in the humor. I learned how, in times of tension or trouble, to escape through humor, wrecking people's defenses or their attacks. Teachers would try to fight back smiles, but when the edge of their mouths went up, I knew I had them, and their power, just for a split second, left them, until they regained their composure and carried on.

The prefects were the successes of the school. They wore gold braid around the edges of their blazers and gold tassels hung from their caps. They had special privileges, such as being allowed to cycle up the driveway and use the front door, and they had their own dining and common rooms. Their job was to keep the school in order and running smoothly, and so they were given the power to give out both detentions and lines. They regarded this power to punish, direct, and control us as part of their character building and education. These were the boys who had proved that they were going to succeed, that they would go on with their studies, go on to higher things: they were learning to be leaders. I was quite happy with it all and accepted it as normal. We all played the game, trying to fool them as much as we could and lie our way out of things that we shouldn't have been doing. We served our detentions when we were caught, and we wrote pages of lines that said, "I must not run in the corridor," "I must not talk on the stairs," "I must not laugh at prefects." They hated being laughed at and we knew it, and we resented them, disliked them, yet accepted them as part of the natural order of things: they were meant to rule, we were meant to be ruled. They were young chiefs, but chiefs nevertheless, and at lunchtimes we brought them their dinners and waited on them at their table, a sort of state school version of fagging (acting as servant to older students). Their only real chore was to read the lesson at assemblies, and we all took great delight when they nervously stumbled over the words and went red with embarrassment as we gloated over their discomfort, so that when they looked up from the lectern all they could see was six hundred grinning boys savoring every stutter. It was a process we were all part of. As they learned how to lead, we learned how to bait them, not to give in, how to appear unhurt, and how to survive. We presented our leaders with all the problems of control that they would have to face throughout their lives, and they learned that we could never be really beaten and would need to be contained and controlled to the end. It was here that I learned how they worked, what they wanted, what their weaknesses were, and how they were vulnerable. We tested them, poked them, prodded them; it was a training ground for all, and we all learned something.

The head stood totally remote at the top of the school, a short man, square jawed, with a severe hairstyle and a slight limp that was a result of his being at Dunkirk. He taught classics to senior students and various other groups throughout the school, and I managed to get through the whole five years without coming into close contact with him. He always wore a suit with waistcoat and tossed a big bunch of keys from hand to hand without looking down as he walked around the school. "Hard work and exactness" were central to his approach to education, which he thought would enable us all to follow our masters into the world of high tables and learning.

It all came together to form an air of eliteness that was overwhelming and oppressive. Now our terms were called Michaelmas and Lent rather than autumn and spring, and there, in the front of every boy's personal calendar was laid out the list of our masters for us all to admire and study—the academic livestock of the school:

Headmaster: Colin Ewan, M.A. Classical Scholar of Sidney Sussex Cambridge

Senior Master: A. L. C. Smith, M.A. Queens' Cambridge

A. C. Paget, B.A. Formerly Mathematical Scholar of Peterhouse Cambridge

A. W. Walton, M.A. Formerly Classical Exhibitioner of Selwyn Cambridge

J. Pryce-Jones, Keble, Oxford H. J. Skinner, M.A. Jesus, Cambridge

E. A. Strachan, M.A. Formerly Modern Languages. Exhibitioner of Oriel Oxford

D. A. Simonson, M.A. Formerly Classical Scholar of Christ's Cambridge

So the list of thoroughbreds went on, detailing their impeccable lineages and histories. Yet it was never explained to us what it all meant; you were supposed to just know, be impressed, be motivated. But I never knew, never understood how they came to go to such places, and I never asked, and I never cared. I knew they were different, better, superior, and I didn't want to know why; it was just so, and even now I don't know what an "exhibitioner" is! The whole edifice was propped up and rammed home by official and unofficial carnivals. Speech day, founders' day, open day, remembrance day, school plays, and concerts. On these occasions, out would come the orchestra and the school song, Oxford and Cambridge, black gowns and ermine; and we were always to be thankful, and if we were lucky, and if we worked hard, and if we committed ourselves to their ideals, and their ways, and their thoughts, and their beliefs, we might just be able to join them, their parades and their world.

On speech days we celebrated those who had finally made it, along with those who showed promise and ought to make it one day, and in 1961, Alan Bullock (Esq., M.A., Master of St. Catherine's College Oxford) gave out the prizes; the orchestra played "Incidental Music to Twelfth Night," "Give Ear unto Me" (from Psalm 17, Benedetto Marcello 1868–1739), and ended with "Jubilate Deo" (Orlando di Lasso 1532–1594), and I sat there, a voyeur, watching someone else's ceremony, listening to someone else's music, in someone else's world. They continued by reading out the list of those who had now joined the elite, who would be going on to Pembroke College Oxford, Selwyn College Cambridge, Queens College Cambridge, Leeds, Exeter, Lampeter, Liverpool, London, and Loughborogh. They went off to the Royal Naval College Dartmouth and the Civil Service Executive class; they got scholarships and prizes, advanced levels and ordinary levels. It was all there, listed in order of superiority, from Oxford to O levels; and when my turn came to join the lower ranks of the Marines, I didn't rate a mention!

Later in the ceremony they even called out the "distinctions gained by old Cryptians":

The Very Reverend R. A. Perry, Provost of Kuching Cathedral Sarawak

The Reverend J. E. Gethyn-Jones, Pembroke College Oxford, Honorary Chaplain to Her Majesty the Queen

Professor R. G. Austin. Formerly Domus Exhibitioner Balliol College Oxford, Professor of Latin University of Liverpool

F. S. Geldart, Former Scholar Queens' College Cambridge, Dept. Chairman British African Tobacco Company Ltd.

And right at the end:

H. S. Townsend, Chief Mechanical Engineer, Tasmanian Government Railways.

VIVAT IMPERPETUUM!

The headmaster told us all, "We must have men of first-class brains, first-class personalities, and first-class qualifications to teach first-class boys!" and said that the grammar school system was "the finest instrument of formal education this world has seen!" He reminded all the parents that they spent more on "tobacco and the pools" than on education and that this was simply not good enough. And finally the guest speaker assured us all that grammar schools bred "initiative, leadership, and moral courage," all of which would be looked for by employers and the country! We blessed it all with "Carmen Cryptiensis" and hoped it would all go on forever.

Mum and Dad never went; there was no point. I never won anything; I was never mentioned; Tony, my brother, was never mentioned; Mum smoked and Dad did the pools! These were events that celebrated what we weren't, and everything that they were. Mum and Dad left them to their singing and their dressing up, their strange songs and fine speeches, and got on with the business of surviving.

I progressed reluctantly through the academic syllabus they offered us, and Tony left with only an art O level to show for eleven years of schooling. Week after week, night after night, he talked for hours in bed about his dream of joining the navy. He would follow Granddad's footsteps and be an artificer and know about engines, keep the navy running. We created the details of his new life together in the bedroom under the cover of darkness until we had it perfect. We reveled in his future happiness and success, his dream life; but he failed his medical and instead became an apprentice at the local engineering factory. His dream of the navy would now be created on the water of the river Severn instead of the sea. When the news of his medical came through we cried together over the loss of his dream, the sadness locked in our bedroom, away from the rest of the home. I became engulfed in his unhappiness as he was left not knowing what he would do. He'd never thought about anything else. If there had been alternatives, there could have been no dream. It was the price he paid for the dream, and now there was nothing, only anxiety and a fear for the future, as he set about building a real life in a real world. It had been my first glimpse of what was to come after school, of what we would be like when they had finished with us, what we'd be ready for, prepared for, and how they wouldn't bother, how they wouldn't care.

I continued to frustrate my masters as they tried to guide me on the path of success. I had taken a glancing look and rejected it, not recognizing anything in it for me, and I spent my time aimlessly wandering through their maze of knowledge, oblivious to their pleas and confused by the deep sense of loss that I felt.

My courseload was reduced to just a handful of subjects as I entered my final year and the O-level exams. Art had become a thing of the past once it became clear early on that I was only good for putting things out, and cleaning up, and sweeping the floor. The woodwork teacher wisely refused to have me in his workshop, and music was at this level only for the select musical few. My final French report signed off with, "Some quite horrible work at times," and disappeared along with Latin. Viewed en masse, my reports showed the collective opinions of my masters as they struggled to provide an analysis of my abilities and potential. "Very slovenly." "Rather untidy." "His desire to be helpful often betrays him into speaking out of turn." "Poor—he has very little understanding of the fundamentals." "Does not seem interested." "Lazy and inattentive." "He is too boisterous and must learn to control himself for the benefit of others." "He does not really work." "Very weak." "Very poor, no care or effort." "When he begins to take greater care to speak his own language more accurately he may write it more accurately." "He must direct his energies into more useful channels." "His work is untidy and shows little effort." And when Tony drowned they showed little sympathy, noting only in their comments, "Missed two weeks, unavoidably I know, but make up for it!" "His recent absence must have been a handicap to him, but a considerable improvement is needed in most subjects. This can only come about by really hard and persistent work!"

In the last year they reached their conclusions: "Rather weak." "A little untidy." "His work is probably quite good but until I can read more of it, I can't be sure!" "His work continues to be slipshod and he continues to be quite cheerful about it." "Makes little serious effort." "A poor term." "No danger of over-exerting himself." Weak, lazy, disinterested and dirty, and unable even to speak properly!—they were giving up!

I did no preparation for the mock O-level general certificate exams, seeing no purpose to it all, especially as I would soon be leaving. There was no debate about it at home. I didn't protest, we didn't argue about staying on or not, it was never talked about. Dad had known all along that it would come to nothing, that there was little point to it, no good in it. Work was the only reality, our reality; not books, not learning, not Latin—only working life. There were no other options, no alternatives. I wanted to leave. If I stayed on, what would I do? What would become of me? What would I be? Teaching was for them, universities were for them, "leading" was for them. I knew already that I wanted to succeed where Tony had failed. I wanted to "join up," carry on the tradition, live out his dream and Granddad's stories. It was just a question of which force and when.

Throughout the mock exams I spent most of the time playing desktop cricket matches with a pencil, with scores one end and "way dismissed" the other. I managed a complete test series during the English literature exam, with England thrashing Australia as usual. When the results of the exams were carefully scrutinized they decided it would be safer for the school if I didn't do the proper exam in literature, protecting their record and saving me effort. I returned more of my books and my satchel grew increasingly lighter. It was almost becoming fun!

I was often punished. It was something we expected, invited, almost demanded. At school I was caned for writing out a betting slip during Latin, using a copy of the *Daily Mirror* racing page for the details. I'm not sure whether it was the betting slip or the *Daily Mirror* that incensed the teacher, but I remember the long walk to the deputy head's office and his speech about educating generations of Presdees, and how it was sad it had now come to this, and shouldn't I be ashamed; but I wasn't, and afterward, when I walked out, I smiled at the Latin teacher, who stood and witnessed it all. I went to the Jet and Whittle that lunchtime and passed the bet in the bathroom; they wouldn't stop me!

As I got older, my life became more like a battlefield with the battle lines rigidly drawn up, as if preordained. I had no answer to my feelings of injustice other than defiance and violence, which they in turn countered with more aggression in their attempts to control, contain, and make order. In time I created, with my friends, a veneer of violence that, like the spines of a porcupine, became part of us, an evolved defense mechanism that could be used, when all else failed, to attack and push back. Mainly, we lived with our spines just "there," bristling, and daring anyone to touch us or control us.

Yet it was all still confusing, because porcupines were useful in sport, especially in the front row of a rugby scrum or armed with a hockey stick. Gradually our very defiance and violence were appropriated by the controllers for their ends. They helped to make us, held us, controlled us, then unleashed us in their service. From the estate we joined the armed forces, became policemen and prison warders, security guards and bouncers. We were ripe for the unleashing: working-class watchdogs turned out to snarl and keep in order the mass of the working classes as we watched over the interests of the controllers. I was saved from delinquency by being delinquent for them, exercising my vice so they could be virtuous. I joined the Marines. Now I could be let loose on the enemy, their enemy, and be defiant, cunning, and violent—a legal delinquent—and instead of fighting authority I would fight for it. Or so they hoped. I became a state "minder."

That last summer became more mine than theirs as I idled my way through the few remaining lessons, going through the motions of revision and study. I had already been for interviews at the Navy recruitment center in Bristol and they knew I was determined to leave. My mind was already gone and they could do nothing about it. They gave up the struggle and officially wished me well in what they called my "chosen career." I had failed them and achieved no more than the boys of the C stream. I had wasted their time and betrayed them, and they would give me no more as they set me aside for the last few weeks until, before the end of the term, they released me and sent me back across the green, for the last time, and home.

They had tried to teach me that there was no life outside of theirs, nothing worthwhile outside of them. I was determined to defy them, to show them that we were real, that there were things we cared for, that there was a purpose to our lives. I hated them, their words, their way of life, their education: now it was finished!

EPILOGUE

I spent six years as a Marine commando, waiting on my masters, cleaning their clothes, bringing them their food, following their orders, fighting and firing on the "enemy" when directed. It was six years of practical subservience that laid down a sediment of servitude deep within my consciousness that would filter my experiences of everyday life forever, marking my thoughts and actions with indelible streaks and strands of working-classness.

When later I went to teachers college, I began the slow process of "crossing the great divide." At the age of twenty-five I talked for the first time to a middle-class person as an equal. Now I was surrounded by educated fellow students who came from that "other" side of town that I had always considered to be not for me. It was all confusing. Now I had to learn to argue without anger, reason and not hit, lose without seeking retaliation. I had to read poetry in old English and books with no story and write essays that weren't about my holidays. When I had completed my application form, they had asked for my second "subject," and when I rang to ask what a subject was, they sounded incredulous as I told them that on my estate we didn't have subjects, we didn't talk about subjects, we didn't "do" subjects.

Painfully and slowly I learned to be middle class, and I even became good at it, but that sediment was still there, still filtering in and contaminating my newfound middle-classness.

And it continues to do so now. In my career as a criminologist, it colors and controls how I respond to what I research, what I write, why I write. It has become organic to all that I do within an academic life where I am surrounded once more by the old enemy. I could never have imagined that I would one day be part of a subject so influenced, worldwide, by Cambridge University, or that I would continue my long struggle to be heard and fight to put forward "our" story, "our" view, "our" analysis against "their" view, "their" story, "their" analysis. As an "organic intellectual" in the Gramscian sense, I, along with others in this book, bear a responsibility to battle to bring meaning to the pain of poverty, to the pain of injustice, to the pain of the history of wasted lives. I do so for the sake of all who live on the other side of the great divide, my friends, my family, and the future.

3

Personal, Professional, and Political Paths to the Study of the Crimes of the Powerful

David Kauzlarich

My path from a disinterested and underachieving working-class high school student to my current position as a sociology and criminology professor may or may not be all that different from the avenue taken by other working-class academics. As sociologists like to say, albeit sometimes reluctantly, while distinctly unique individual experiences are part of the human condition, there is much that unites us. Be forewarned that generalization, the holy grail of positivism, is not my goal here, but perhaps there are parts of my story that may prove to be helpful in illuminating some of the challenges, frustrations, and, indeed, triumphs that are to a greater or lesser extent shared by those academicians from the working class. The first part of this chapter is a recounting of my journey from high school to the (dis)comforts of the ivory tower. The second part of the chapter explores elements of my somewhat paradoxical intergenerational mobility. Whether objectively, subjectively, or at times, both, academe can be at the very least uncomfortable, and at the most, hostile, to those from the working class. On the other hand, the security of tenure and promotion, the easy schedule, the incredible level of autonomy, and the chance to meet like-minded/similarly educated people make academe seem to be among the most satisfying and comforting of occupations. This paradox, like the notion of "strangers in Paradise" so well investigated by Ryan and Sackrey (1984) and their contributors, will be discussed here as it relates not only to educational background and experiences (e.g., proper language, growing up with books in the house, etc.), but also in terms of leisure and recreational activities, such as music, drink, travel, and partying.

I didn't even want to go to college after high school. Like many forthcoming high school graduates, however, I knew that I probably should advance my education in some way in order to increase my marketability as a job applicant. After all, in 1985, the glass factory where my dad worked as a laborer for about twenty years was not hiring. In fact, they were laying people off by the dozens. So, I found myself in the typical postindustrial conundrum: I certainly had enough of school, but there weren't any good jobs available that didn't require some academic work beyond high school. Had there been a full-time job opening at the glass plant, I would have no doubt taken it. The thought of landing a union job that would provide me with a bit more than a living wage, along with a decent pension plan and medical coverage, was about all that I was looking for. I also liked the idea of putting in a day's worth of physical effort. I liked the idea of coming home sore from a hard day's work, like my dad did. I wanted rough, thick, leathery hands like my dad as well. Hands like that just seemed to be a physical manifestation of honesty, the kind of appearance one only gets from pushing the body to do things that it ordinarily would rather not. I also would have liked to be rewarded for that hard day's work by hitting one of the many bars near the plant when the whistle blew at the end of the shift. My dad never did this, but I thought, nothing could be better than bellying up to the bar with good friends and coworkers, like in the beginning of the powerful film *The Deer-hunter*, shooting the breeze after slaving away in a hot, noisy factory. It would be liberating. It would even be cooler, I thought, if I worked on the night shift, so we could start partying at 6:00 a.m., not p.m.

Going to college wasn't exactly a popular activity in my family. My dad quit after a year, my mom didn't attend, and my brother and sister both had very short stints in higher education. The thought of me going to a four-year university right out of high school was out of the question. To begin with, I really didn't like school, and I wasn't a particularly good student, either. I cared a lot more about dating, singing, and playing guitar in heavy metal bands (the Anthrax, Megadeth, Judas Priest, and Iron Maiden genre), baseball, and partying than what I imagined to be dry and irrelevant material oozing from the stuffy confines of the classroom, where nerds and preppies listened to staid lectures. At the time, I thought that four-year colleges like the University of Illinois were for smart and rich kids—people with whom I would have difficulty relating. Even more arresting was the fact that, because of my indifference in high school to going off to college, I had failed to file appropriate financial aid and grant materials, which would be required for me to even get in the door of a baccalaureate institution. Mom and Dad, despite always being somewhat money savvy, just didn't have the several thousand dollars necessary to fork over to the state of Illinois for me to go off to a university. Going to a private college was an even more ridiculous proposition.

Finding no job waiting for me as I inched closer to graduating from high school, I decided to enroll in the area community college with a major in criminal justice. My parents indicated that they would be able to cough up the $13 per credit hour for my studies. I could live at home, so there would no increased expense in that manner. Plus, my mom and dad would let me use one of their older cars to drive the forty-five-mile round-trip journey to and from school. I felt really grateful to them for this, as I knew it was not without some sacrifice on their part. Finding virtually nothing else at the college interesting, I chose criminal justice as my major because I figured that being a cop wouldn't be that bad—it would certainly provide me with a decent income and benefits. I thought it might also provide me with all kinds of action and excitement. With all the naïveté of a seventeen-year-old, I thought that I might be able to party with fellow officers after shifts, as portrayed in way too many television cop shows and movies.

Community college provided me with a number of perks: Unlike in high school, I could smoke in the cafeteria, for example. I also picked up some interesting war stories from the criminal justice instructors. What surprised me the most was that I actually earned As and Bs in classes, without even trying. The stuff was real easy, a new life experience for me indeed. I remember one particularly crystallizing moment when it started to dawn on me that I might not be that bad a student after all. After an unusually challenging exam was handed back to me, I noticed a scribble to me from the criminal law instructor on the first page of the test: "Highest grade in the class. Good job." Wow, I thought to myself, this is incredible. I had *never* received a compliment like that in all my days at school. Mostly teachers talked to me when they gave me detentions or withheld certain privileges reserved for the well-behaved kids. I liked the feeling of validation that came along with the compliment from my college teacher. It came as a surprise to me that I actually started to like studying crime and law. I had never really had much interest in *any* school subject until this moment. Maybe this is why at my ten-year high school reunion everyone was shocked that I had earned a Ph.D. and was a college professor. At the get-together, they awarded me the somewhat dubious distinction of being "the Most Changed" person since high school. I actually had to walk up on a stage to receive that award. I didn't know whether to be happy or sad about it, but I was pretty sure that the award was given to the right person.

It was certainly not a given that I would continue my formal academic studies after I earned the Associate of Applied Science degree in criminal justice in 1987 (which, incidentally, I had been advised to keep off my vita when I was ABD since it could be more of a stigma than anything else). Drinking beer on the river with my brother-in-law on a lazy summer afternoon right before my community college graduation, it occurred to me that I needed to get the bachelor's degree to be even more competitive in the job market. At the time, I still wanted to be an agent of the state, preferably an Illinois State Trooper. Word on the street was that the Illinois State Police force was moving toward requiring more educational credentials. Right before I graduated with my AAS, I halfheartedly filled out the federal and state aid forms and an application to the cheapest school I could find, a small public university then known as Sangamon State University in Springfield, Illinois. That fall was to be the beginning of the end of my fascination with being a cop and an apolitical partier.

I remember thinking that the professor in my Law and Social Order class was really weird. First, I didn't understand why we were supposed to call him "Doctor." Was he a surgeon or something outside of class? Second, he always talked about how Native Americans, Asian Americans, and other racial minorities have been continually screwed by the criminal justice system in this country. As a white male growing up in a predominantly white working-class town, I was skeptical about his claims. After all, I pretty much bought the standard party line that the United States was indeed the land of opportunity and equality. This professor assigned several caustic books for the class, but one was particularly critical of the American system of justice: Jeff Reiman's (1984) *The Rich Get Richer and the Poor Get Prison,* widely regarded as a seminal Marxist critique of the U.S. criminal justice system. At the time I couldn't understand why Reiman would think that our system was "designed to fail," "protecting the rich," "picking on the poor," or "giving us a distorted view of what really threatens our health and safety." Although I was still unconvinced, I thought the professor gave me good food for thought. I ended up liking the class a lot and getting a B+, which was cool for me. Like many things in life, though, it really didn't sink in until sometime later that I actually agreed with most everything that the professor said, and especially with the type of perspective introduced to me by Reiman's book. Despite the book's encroaching influence on me, I did what I always did at the end of the semester: I turned in all my books where I bought them for a paltry percentage of what I had paid for them four months earlier. After all, ten bucks could buy a decent quantity of rice and beer. And who needed a bunch of books lying around anyway? Everyone I knew did just fine without all that.

Like many who choose to go on to graduate school, a combination of influences led me down the path to academe. In addition to the professor mentioned above, I was lucky enough to have a class with a professor who, for whatever reason, saw some potential in me. My next year and a half in undergrad was spent taking classes and independent studies with him and other lefties in subjects such as Marxist theory and critical criminology. I loved the stuff! This professor, who went on to fame for his studies of serial murder and serial murderers, made me read classic Marxist and critical criminology. It was at this time that I was first introduced to the writing of Richard Quinney, Jock Young, Bill Chambliss, and others. Quinney's (1977) *Class, State, and Crime* offered me a hammering critique of the classist nature of crime and criminal justice in capitalist societies. Young's work with Taylor and Walton (1988), *The New Criminology*, gave me a solid understanding of the purpose and potential of criminological theory. Chambliss's (1978) *On the Take* inspired me to want to study, understand, and *do something* about the crimes of those in positions of power. These books not only helped lay the foundation for my scholarly studies but also radicalized me politically by showing how in capitalist societies, structurally induced economic inequalities are reproduced in all social and political institutions, especially the criminal justice system. The metamorphosis had begun. I simultaneously became academic and political. I started thinking that perhaps being an academic meant being political as much as it meant being scholarly. I couldn't see any reason to disentangle the two, despite the admonitions from hardcore positivists I would occasionally come across in my otherwise highly radical, constructionist-oriented graduate training. I also couldn't imagine being an academic in any other area except sociological critical criminology, because what appealed to me most about academics was its emancipatory potential, its ability to freely question the status quo, and, to use a title from one of Marx's works, be "ruthlessly critical of everything existing." Unlike many of my colleagues, some of whom are working class, I would have not been interested in earning a graduate degree in any area of the natural sciences or many areas in the social sciences. They just weren't critical enough for me. They didn't have the edge that sociology and critical criminology seemed to possess.

Needless to say, I was no longer interested in being a cop. I asked myself: How could I be part of the problem? How could I reproduce the inequalities that I had now come to realize were embedded in the very fabric of our social and political institutions? I couldn't sell out to the system by getting a job, say as a probation officer, and endlessly question the legitimacy of my occupation. I also couldn't live with the futility of attempting to solve social problems by individualistic methods of treatment. So what *could* I do? Like so many other people who are not sure what they want to do or how to do it after getting the bachelor's degree, I made the logical choice.

Being awarded a graduate assistantship in the Department of Sociology at Western Michigan University was like winning the lottery. I couldn't believe that I would be given full tuition remission and a stipend for basically going to school and apprenticing under a professor. In a way I felt like I was stealing something, since the rewards of my studies seemed so disproportionately favorable compared to the work involved. Later I learned that by going to school at a regional university, I was in some ways limiting my options. No doubt reflecting my working-class, first-generation-college-graduate background, when applying to graduate schools I didn't think twice about the level of prestige associated with any particular university. It certainly didn't matter to me or anyone else I knew where I got my undergraduate degree, so why should it matter at the next level? To me, as to my folks and working-class friends, a degree was a degree, no matter where you got it. It was only later in my doctoral studies that I realized that, in the eyes of some fancy colleges and universities, I was basically an untouchable as far as being an employee. Notwithstanding the graduate assistantship, I chose to study at WMU because one of my undergraduate professors knew a guy there once. It was about as complicated as that.

As a graduate student, everything came together for me quickly—for free! I was surrounded by many smart working-class students who were also searching for something meaningful. I was also surrounded by a wonderful group of radical Marxist-feminist criminologists and sociologists who trained their students to question the legitimacy of positivistic science, to interrogate the claim that social science can be value-free, to use academics as a tool for challenging inequality, and to work for social justice. I also had classes with less radical but nonetheless competent and well-intentioned professors. These folks helped me become more intellectually and methodologically well rounded. I flourished in this near-perfect environment. I read endlessly, took copious notes on everything, and made an effort to engage almost every academic in the department in some form of intellectual discussion. Not only were these tasks things that I had learned to enjoy, but they were also activities that I felt compelled to do, given my less than stellar educational background. At the beginning of graduate school, I often felt disadvantaged in terms of vocabulary, so I would study dictionaries to improve my speaking skills and word choices. For most courses, I would read two or three times more material outside of class than in it. Aided tremendously by my mentor, I gained more confidence when I began writing and presenting papers in collaboration with other students and faculty members. I published my first refereed journal article toward the end of my master's training and had three articles in print by the time I was ABD. I had little doubt that I could be a university professor as long as I could continue to do progressive, social-justice-oriented scholarship and teaching. To this day, this is what sustains me in my profession. As long as progressive politics and sociology go together hand in glove (and research based on this nexus is rewarded, not punished, by my peers and evaluators), I will remain an academic.

When I was in elementary school, my dad lost three fingers to a pair of pinch rollers in a box-collating machine. He was trying to dislodge a piece of cardboard from this high-compression contraption when the "temp" guy he was working with unthinkingly turned the machine back on. A few days after the accident, my dad's purple and black fingers started to curl and wilt away. They were soon amputated. My dad didn't believe in suing people for things they didn't intend to do, so there would be no windfall lawsuit heading in my family's direction. The company, Owens-Illinois, gave him a few grand to tide him over while he collected disability and slowly recovered from the surgery. My dad, like so many working-class folks, went back to the same job a few months later. Fortunately, he worked accident-free for another twenty years. But while my dad was not technically victimized by another discrete factory accident, he did lose much of his hearing, and thus balance, because of the near-deafening cacophony that constantly emanated from the glass factory's machines. My dad, while functioning, is now semi-deaf and often falls and bumps into people because of his lack of balance.

To this day, I still wonder how his health might have been different had he become a lawyer, a doctor, a professor, or anything but a worker in a loud factory. Further, I wondered what such a factory would have done to me over time had a job been available after high school. Would I even be able to hear my buddies' jokes while bellied up to the bar after work? Would I drink *too* much, not for fun, but to escape from the industrial prison in which I worked? When I was in graduate school, Marxist sociology prompted me to question the whole capitalist system with its reliance on worker exploitation, worker alienation, and the extraction of surplus value. Critical criminology offered me a way to conceptualize and study the causes of corporate crime, including not only violations of worker safety laws but also environmental pollution and the sale and manufacture of unsafe products. My working-class roots all of a sudden met my academic interests in perfect harmony. I could *study*, not just be indignant about, crimes committed by people in positions of power against workers, consumers, and the natural environment. No wonder that I have never really been attracted to the natural sciences, business, or education. They would not allow me to undertake a critical, no-holds-barred approach to studying the crimes of the powerful and the victimology of the powerless.

As a professor, some of my successes and failures can be easily linked to my working-class background. For example, I have always felt more comfortable and competent teaching at a medium-sized regional public university than a small, private college. This is mostly because the students at a regional public university come from middle- to lower-class backgrounds. They tend to "get" my jokes; they are often familiar with the examples I give in class relating to music, sports, teenage indiscretions, and deviant behavior, and they tend to have friends or family members who work in factories or other manufacturing jobs and therefore understand the profound effect that unsafe working conditions can have on the quality of life. One of the ways I try to "do" critical criminology in the classroom is by spending considerable amounts of time discussing white-collar crime, especially crimes against workers, the natural environment, and consumers. Working-class students are less likely to have grown up in families that could afford water purifiers and thus seem to better understand how vulnerable the masses are to corporate pollution. These students also hail from backgrounds that often do not provide the opportunity to buy the best product but instead the cheapest one. The meteoric rise of Wal-Mart has been fueled by the working class. I find that many middle-class students say they wouldn't be caught dead buying clothes in Wal-Mart.

Having been a tenure-track professor at a small, expensive, east coast private college and now being a tenured associate professor at a regional, affordable, public university, I have noticed some differences in background between my colleagues and me. Certainly I have crossed paths with other working-class professors, but the majority of professors with whom I have worked come from at least middle-class families. Almost all of them went to more prestigious schools than I did at every level. Even as a published Ph.D., I have felt a bit inferior among my many colleagues from places such as Brown, Princeton, Pennsylvania, and Yale. Informal chats and other interactions around the office, dinner with colleagues, and various university functions have given me some sense of the profundity of difference between my upbringing and that of my non-working-class colleagues. As represented in table 3.1, I have found differences in, among others, the arenas of music, sport, tastes, and recreation. Again, the extent to which these differences are generalizable is an open question.

Music. Out of the several dozens of colleagues I have worked with both inside and outside the university milieu, I have met only a handful who like speed metal or punk. In my youth, these musical genres helped develop my opposition to authority, and to some extent they still reflect my suspicion of those occupying positions of power in bureaucracies. I

Table 3.1. Some Differences between Working Class and Non-Working-Class Academic Tastes and Backgrounds

	Working Class	*Non–Working Class*
Music	Metal, punk, rock	Classical, jazz
Art	Art? What's that?	Great familiarity
Drug use	Cheap beer, pot	Wine, scotch, imported beer
Recreation	Camping, fishing	Trips to Europe, Disney World
Books in house	A few, mostly Harlequin Romances	Many, no Harlequins
Swearing	Common	Uncommon
Clothes	Wal-Mart quality; JCPenney for wedding or funeral clothes	Saks, Lord & Taylor
Interest in sports	Baseball, football, hockey	Squash, tennis, golf
Foreign language	None, unless you count swearing	At least bilingual
Partying	Loud music, occasional fights; Too much alcohol and other drugs	Very soft music, relaxed chatting; Not enough alcohol and other drugs

study organizational crime and deviance, which are harmful acts motivated by profit and committed by people in positions of power. Like
punk, metal has anarchistic elements that are not captured by other musical styles. Such criticality in the face of the overwhelming pressure to
conform in modern society can also be appreciated by students in today's classrooms. Although I always risk dating myself and being
laughed at, I often reference works by Public Enemy, Rush, Megadeth,
and Rage Against the Machine in my lectures. While these references
may often pass over the heads of students who are Justin Timberlake
fans, I can tell that the students who do get the connection appreciate a
college professor who isn't so pompous as to deny the relevance of
popular culture—no matter how dated—to academic discussions.

Art. I had never heard of a single classical artist until I went to graduate
school, and even to this day I have little idea who the main artists are
and what drawings are considered seminal. Never being exposed to art
in high school or at home, I used music as my aesthetic release. I am as
lost as other working-class folks when a colleague makes an analogy to
an artist or corpus of work.

Drug use. Much of my youth was spent trying to score beer and then
drinking it. We drank what we could afford, mostly the cheapest, nasti-
est stuff around. Upon entering graduate school, I was introduced to
such delicacies as wine, scotch, imported beer, and good smokes. I
have yet to see a case of Milwaukee's Best or a four-foot gravity bong at
a university function.

Recreation. Along with art, Disney World and traveling abroad were perhaps the most foreign things to me as a youth and young student. The
former still is, but the latter is not, thanks to several lucky breaks I caught
when a couple of the universities I attended accelerated their funding of
study-abroad courses. Camping, fishing, and hiking are less foreign to
my colleagues than speed metal, but still a distant second to Europe.

Books in the house. Besides the occasional library book, not many classic
literary works lay around the house in working-class families. I don't
ever remember *being* in a house or apartment with bookcases until I
was in graduate school. That apartment was mine.

Swearing. Communication without some form of swearing is fairly un-
common among the working-class folks I hang out with. I have yet to
hear the "f" word more than once or twice in a faculty meeting, although
the choice of adjectives can be equally caustic.

Clothes. My male friends and family members wear suits and ties only at
weddings and funerals. Women wore dresses only for the same rituals.

Sports. Sunday football games, baseball seasons that seem to last forever,
and the punishing blows of hockey, all watched while inhaling bad
fried food and drinking cheap beer. Is squash ever televised?

Foreign languages. I may have known one or two people in high school who were bilingual. Now it seems everyone around me at work can speak at least two languages but me. This has been some source of embarrassment for me in various academic contexts.

Partying. University and departmental parties are usually laid-back affairs where people chat about important things against the backdrop of mellow music, oak bookcases, and fancy gourmet kitchens. Beer drinking games, loud/fast/rude metal in the background, and swearing are not common at such events.

This selective look at some of the differences between my background and current tastes and those of my colleagues is of course not exhaustive, nor may it be something that a lot of working-class academics find particularly unusual or uncomfortable in their work environments. For me, these differences explain why I sometimes feel considerably "out of the loop" in my occupation. For example, most of my colleagues seemed to do well in grade and high school. They even report liking the material. That is so different from my experience; in my group of friends it was very uncool to be so into the scholarly dimensions of school. In fact, I struggle with an interesting iteration of this in the present day, not because I find academics boring, but because most of my friends are not academics—they are working-class guys with whom I party (working-class style), watch hockey, fish, and ride motorcycles. These guys are home remodelers and mid-level contractors. They work in factories running drill presses. Most of them know just about everything there is to know about plumbing, electrical work, mechanics, and finish work. Now *that's* cool. It's not that I have to shed my academic skin to feel comfortable with them, but I do often feel uneasy when they introduce me to other people as "Dave, the professor," or "Cosmo, the doctor." I can almost see the eyes get wider, sensing that people all of a sudden have a different opinion of me now that they know my occupation. I wonder to what extent other working-class academics feel that being in their social loop does not often allow them to be fully in their academic loop, and vice versa.

I really can't complain about being both in *and* out of the academic loop. For all the differences noted above, they have almost no negative effect on my career aspirations. This is because I have been very lucky, not because I have necessarily beaten bad odds. First, I had an excellent working-class mentor in graduate school. He made me feel as though I could make academe my career because he did, despite coming from an even more rural and working-class background than mine. Second, both of the departments within which I have worked as a professor have many people who are open-minded, social-feminist progressives who mostly frown upon the bourgeois lifestyle. Many of these folks are not from working-class backgrounds, but their sociological criticality and their humanistically inclined beliefs have shielded me from what might otherwise be an uncomfortable work environment. I have been so fortunate to be surrounded by non-elitists that at one time I thought almost all sociologists were radical lefties, but after talking to several academic friends of mine who do not enjoy in their departments the kind of collegiality I do in mine, I realized that my situation is anomalous. My twenty or so publications would not necessarily be viewed as significant by less progressive scholars making decisions about my tenure and promotion. After all, I was trained in the tradition of radical sociology and critical criminology, both of which are heavily constructionist in nature and openly political. Such research is not appreciated in some sociological quarters; it cannot be easily done in the natural sciences, nor would the paradigmatic differences be tolerated in the majority of contexts in other disciplines. If it were not for radical sociology/criminology, I would be a cop or a drywaller instead of a tenured associate professor. My objective class status has indeed changed, but subjectively my class identity has not. The former has more to do with sticking it out in graduate school, politics, luck, and some hard work, while the latter reflects my roots in that small factory town and what that factory did—and could have done—to people under its employ. It is in this way that my academic discipline, certainly not my degree per se, is responsible for me feeling more in the loop than out.

REFERENCES

Chambliss, William J. 1978. *On the Take: From Petty Crooks to Presidents*. Bloomington: Indiana University Press.

Quinney, Richard. 1977. *Class, State, and Crime*. New York: Longman.

Reiman, Jeffrey. 1984. *The Rich Get Richer and the Poor Get Prison*. 2nd ed. New York: Wiley.

Ryan, Jake, and Charles Sackrey. 1984. *Strangers in Paradise*. Lanham, MD: University Press of America.

Taylor, Ian, Paul Walton, and Jock Young. 1988. *The New Criminology: For a Social Theory of Deviance*. London: Routledge.

4

A Stranger to Paradise: Working-Class Graduate in the Culture of Academia

Dawn Rothe

Higher education is typically the preserve of the white upper and middle classes. Beyond the palpable reasons for disparities and disadvantages that make it difficult for the working class to attend graduate school, the working class's educational disadvantage is embedded in the cultural limits of the working-class world: the expectations, social confidence, and cultural literacy. These disadvantages for the working class are endemic to the class system. They often lead to feeling marginal to the higher academic world and its ethos. The cultural ethos of academe entails more than learning the mechanical skills necessary to achieve within the profession; it includes the necessity to become socialized into a way of life that changes who one is. The virtues of this academic ethos are often in direct opposition to a lifetime spent forming self-defense mechanisms, survival strategies, and working-class values. Simply stated, one must take on a new and foreign identity that is not only challenging but leads to inner conflicts.

The ethos and virtues of academe remain an unchallenged force within the process of academic socialization, a force that constantly seeks to alienate the working-class academic's self from his/her identity. For instance, the virtue of recognizing one's ability and/or promoting oneself is a virtue that is highly necessary for survival within the academic profession. However, a working-class background establishes deep-rooted values of humility and a self-identity that recognizes one's place within the class structure: subordinate to the white middle- or upper-class individuals. This is one example of how the social skills that the working-class academic lacks are second nature to the white upper-class academic hegemony.

This treatise is a self-narrative that conceptualizes the trials and tribulations of my working-class self in a strange world. It is my intention to elucidate the barriers and constraints that exist within the academic culture vis-à-vis my personal account. Specifically, the focus will be on my experiences of alienation, lack of social confidence, lack of cultural literacy, and presentation of self in the academic world.

WHAT IS SOCIAL CONFIDENCE?

Universities not only espouse the dominant cultural perspective, they often fail to support or understand divergent working-class perceptions. This lack of understanding creates an atmosphere that is in conflict with a working-class person's level of social confidence. The process of academic socialization focuses on learning to "be the expert" in a given area or two. Universities promote sharing this intellectual "expertise" in classroom settings as well as social settings. As a working-class academic, however, I am constantly reminded of my place within the class structure. Thus, I feel like I have nothing of intellectual value to offer. After all, most of my life I have been reminded that there is no one outside of my close circle of family and friends that could possibly care about what I have to say. The dichotomy between the academic expectation of self-assuredness and the "inner-self" concept of inferiority hinders the necessary social confidence that aids in developing relationships and networks for professional success.

It is extremely hard to have social confidence in the academic world when one's work can no longer be measured as a success according to the working-class definition of hard work. Academe views the "process" of education as hard work. Yet when I was growing up, work was never about the process; it was about hard manual labor that concluded with a finished product. Coming from this tradition creates a lack of confidence in what one does within the university. For me, I must produce a finished product to believe I am performing hard work. Therefore, I have utilized a strategy of overproduction and course overload to attempt to compensate for my lack of finished product. The process of reading, researching, writing, or taking classes is never comparable to holding two or three jobs at the same time to feed my children or doing a backbreaking eighteen hours a day of hard labor regardless of the state of one's health. The schedule of academe appears as a utopia of freedom. Thus, any load I put on myself in order to feel that I "work hard and am successful" is never enough. I am still betraying my own body, my working-class ethic of hard work, and above all my father. I am left always feeling "less than," reinforcing the "I do not have what it takes" ideology. My own personal "survival strategy" that I have employed to try to achieve a sense of self-worth from this new form of "labor" has led to being further ostracized by fellow academics, particularly my graduate cohorts, and thus an increased lack of social confidence.

The processes of education are not the same as produced "fruits of one's labor." My lack of social confidence is only increased as my colleagues ridicule my survival strategy. My cohorts have labeled me as a reclusive person who has "no life," much less any personal troubles. The negative reaction to my overproduction is not restricted to my cohorts. My current department chair insinuates a similar understanding of "over"-ing with comments suggesting the strategy can only be done at the expense of a "social life." There is no understanding or sympathy for my working-class sense of accomplishment. My colleagues are not at all capable of seeing my strategy as a means to be a part of a social and cultural environment in which I do not belong and still be able to partially accept what I do for a "living."

The sense that one does not belong often results in feeling like an impostor. The impostor phenomenon is an internal belief held by many working-class individuals within the academic milieu that they do not deserve the success and recognition that they have earned. We are convinced we are less competent and less intelligent than the "typical" graduate student and are petrified that we will be discovered for who we really are. The impostor phenomenon has its origins in the working class's societal norms and values. When intellect is not nurtured or valued, a sense of one's intellectual ability is not integrated into the concept of self. Consequently, working-class academics often feel a need to overprepare (work harder than others), and this exacerbates the feeling of being an impostor.

It is hard to attain social confidence in the university setting when one believes that the white upper and middle classes are in academe because that is the way it has always been. The working-class individual sees being in the academic arena as pure luck. You not only do not belong, but you are there by a "sequence of accidents and lucky roulette spins."[1] Any "success" that I accomplish is thus a result of this luck. After all, how can it be due to my hard work when I cannot relate to academic standards of hard work? When I receive news that something I've worked on will be published, luck is responsible; when a book prospectus makes it past the editorial review stage, luck dictates that, as well. To believe it is anything else defies the working-class belief that whatever is going to happen will, and you have no meaningful role in that destiny.

The luck of winning "recognition" for a "job well done" is a near-death experience for the working-class graduate student. The traditional practice in academe and the way to confer value is to attempt to attain recognition for one's research. However, for a working-class individual, this is counterproductive. My working-class background emphasized humility and invisibility as positive characteristics. This is in direct conflict with the practices of the university environment, where self-assurance and visibility are positive character traits. I am left with an internal battle to confront. Perhaps worse than the battle is the public humiliation I experienced as I waged this struggle in front of the department's population. Ashamed of the attention, feeling un-worthy, and not understanding what I had done to deserve any recognition (as I still had not achieved what I saw as "good hard work"), I walked with my head held low. The rejoinder from others regarding my displayed shame was not from a working-class perspective; it was a response from the ethos of academia that assumes I must be too timid to teach or too shy to present my research at conferences. Both of these assumptions are far removed from the arduous task of accepting recognition for the working-class self. Instead, difficulty accepting recognition feeds the social insecurity that runs rampant within me daily.

Beyond the university setting, my lack of social confidence finds its way into "professional social settings." The "extra" social gatherings that are aimed at fostering social relationships are foreign and uncomfortable to me. I have the first dilemma when I enter the environment itself. It is the dilemma of "do I or don't I take off my shoes?" The working-class self says "take them off immediately," yet I look around and everyone else is comfortably walk-ing around with shoes. I choose the working-class value of no shoes in the hosting home and of course am noticed immediately. The next obstacle is the banal small talk. This small talk may serve a function within upper-middle-class social settings, but where I come from it is at best a waste of time and at worst pernicious gossip. Yet, sitting in a corner by oneself to avoid these discussions does not come without a price; there is always the painful reminder that to the middle-class gaze you have "no social skills." In short, the price of this critical and selective "aloofness" is the increased sense of being alienated, from within and without.

ALIENATED AND ALONE

Beyond confidence, there are underlying issues involved in the ethos, virtues, and practices of the academic socialization process that require a working-class individual to adopt survival strategies. As I became more and more aware of my social insecurity in the academic environment, I felt alien-ated and removed from that environment. The first process of socialization involves one's cohorts. The expectation that one develop academic and so-cial relationships with these strangers is both foreign and uncomfortable. In a largely homogenous middle-class environment, it may seem natural and fruitful for incoming graduate students to form these relationships. However, these relationships are far from desirable for the working-class student. I had little in common with my cohorts outside of a few shared courses during our first semester. This, coupled with my survival strategy of overworking, only served to further distance me from those with whom I was expected to have created a "lifetime and professional bond." Beyond the immediate problem of not fitting in, working-class folks often struggle to reconcile their definition of "relationships" with the institution's definition of relationships. For me, relationships take a long time; they involve learning to trust the other as well as being able to be yourself. The cohort environment is not conducive to this principle, nor, for that matter, is the overall academic environment.

The process of socialization into academe involves being "competitive." Again, this goes against the values of the working-class academic. If it is chance and luck that bring me to each day, why must I compete? After all, competition was a waste of energy when all that mattered in my background was my own hard labor, doing the absolute best I could at every job I undertook. "Success" did not involve competing with someone else, only against myself. Chances are I was not worthy of the "prize" anyway. I found out very quickly that competition was not just a straightforward attempt by one person to get something before everyone else, but involved chicanery and deception. This made the potential to bond with my cohorts even more difficult. The survival strategy from the streets resurfaced. I began to "look out for myself" in a bizarre and strange "political gamesmanship" that I had no knowledge of or experience with. Simply stated, I further retreated from any quasi-fostered relationships into a deeper recess of alienation.

"Using" someone in academe is not seen the same way in the working-class environment. Within the context of the university, people are resources that are at one's disposal to be used to "climb the academic ladder." Yet, this concept has been one that even my survival strategies cannot address. According to my working-class sensibilities, using someone else was not only a glaring indication of a general character flaw, but also one worthy of serious sanction. We were taught that giving led to attaining (externally and internally) but never by riding on someone else's ticket. After all, I was raised to believe that what goes around comes around. I still struggle with this academic value. The inability to adapt to this expectation leaves one in a lonely, low-ranking position within the political game: I am viewed as someone who does not have political savoir faire.

Once alienation within the academic environment invades one's consciousness it becomes an additional hindrance to adaptation. Adaptation, from a Weberian perspective, is vis-à-vis adjustments to conditions at each level, organizational, individual, and structural. The processes for these adjustments are believed to occur during socialization. However, as Berger and Luckmann's work suggests, socialization is the process of internalizing the objective reality of others as one's own reality. This objective reality, however, requires that it is the result of shared definitions that become taken for granted as real. This is antidialectic when examining the embedded contradictions of the working-class identity and that of the general academic environment. Adding the ongoing processes of alienation and decreasing social confidence, the hope for adaptation is slight. Hence, the working-class alienated identity is left to silently struggle with the unshared objective reality of academe.

I AM AND THERE AIN'T NO MORE

Growing up in a working-class environment quickly taught me to accept what I am because my position in life is not going to change: I will never be anything more than what I am. Thus, the "I am what I am" ideology is an acceptable personality trait to display. However, the overarching expectation that working-class individuals should abandon their background when they enter the world of academe contradicts the lifetime identity of the "I am" ideology. This is the most significant incongruity for working-class academics to overcome.

As an academic professional, you are expected to write personal statements that promote (and often embellish) your knowledge and research. This includes the processes of applying for a position, applying for funding resources, yearly reviews, and so on. For a working-class individual this task is laborious, treacherous, and hypocritical to your own identity. A strategy to survive this treason to one's self-identity can never fully appease the inner turmoil this task creates. I have sent (only in part, facetiously) personal statements to other working-class scholars that more resembled something in the "Personals" section of a newspaper than the expected "Notes on Contributors" standard. This was in part an attempt at humor, but it was also an attempt to postpone the inevitable, distasteful task of creating a personal statement of academic standards. After all, the standards I grew up with for discussing oneself included statements such as "am loyal, hard-working, and trainable." Humility was the key component to success in my world, recognizing one's place and admitting lack of knowledge about anything of value to the rest of society. This internal dilemma creates another basis for lack of confidence and alienation.

Humility is only a small part of the philosophy and practice behind the "I am" concept. Freely speaking your mind when asked for your opinion is also deeply embedded within the working-class consciousness. The subtleties of discretion or political correctness do not fit into the general conversational expectations of the working class. However, in the environment of academe, it is expected that you respond to questions or inquiries with reservation and civility, and in formalized language. The value of being forthright and "calling a spade a spade," something respected and expected in the working-class environment, suddenly becomes taboo. The double standards I find I must now try to live with (mine and those of academe) can have serious ramifications when I unconsciously or unknowingly intermingle these language expectations.

I am ostracized in my working-class environment if I forget which language to use among my family and friends. Within the academic environment, forgetting which text and tone are appropriate results in others coding me as politically unsophisticated or outright crude. Consequently, I am slowly learning that entering a scholar's office to ask about his or her political ideology is off-limits, openly admitting that some in my family have tried to "fight the law" and lost is not discreet, discussing relationships is reserved for the bar, and honestly responding to a question regarding one's teaching style is the academic equivalent of political suicide. I have also learned that those within my working-class environment think it rather snobby and standoffish to discuss attending a conference, ask for reimbursements, or complain about a small stipend. These examples may seem petty to some; however, they are further illustrations of the contradictions between openly being oneself and surviving in the university environment.

Along with language, what is considered acceptable attire is different in each world. At times language and attire are intermingled. When I was growing up, one of the first "survival strategies" I learned was thriftiness. This included the clothing I wore. It was not chic at the time to wear thrift-store seconds—it was essential. As I have entered this strange world of academe I have found that the virtue of thriftiness is not respected but is viewed as crude, cheap, and unstylish. The difference in language can further encourage the "downward" view of my thriftiness as I openly admit to (perhaps even brag about) a great buy by freely discussing the small amount of money I paid for a piece of clothing that received an "I love that outfit" compliment. Within the working-class environment, this bit of information would have been well received and positively reinforced. However, in the halls of academe, I have been told that this is not proper to say. It appears as if I am cut-rate. Cheap is not always a good thing.

Beyond the linguistic challenges to attire there are other consequences associated with these conflicting views of apparel. Growing up in my working-class household, there were two criteria for apparel: clothes had to be comfortable, and they had to be cheap. These criteria have practical reasons beyond social acceptability. To work hard one must be comfortable, and to have money for the essentials it is necessary to dress cheaply. The concepts of daywear, nightwear, and professional attire are missing from my working-class vocabulary and my working-class closet. The expectation for dress within the academic environment is very different. There is acceptable professional daywear, proper social clothing, and professional appearance attire. Attempting to intermingle these can not only be embarrassing but also can bring unwanted attention, enhancing the omnipresent awareness of my lack of social skills and social confidence.

My first encounter with this dichotomized concept of attire was at the first professional conference I attended. I did not have a suit, a dress, or any professional clothes, and I knew I would be walking and sitting all day. Thus, I dressed according to my working-class standards for comfort. Not a good choice. I felt even more out of place, which forced me to recognize again that I did not have the necessary social skills for my new environment. Before the second conference I attended, I was given some hand-me-downs that allowed me to fit into the professional environment. This gave me social comfort, but I felt I was walking in someone else's skin. I waited for the moment I could run back to the room and grab my old friends: oversized blue jeans and a big shirt. Although my closet has expanded now to include some professional attire (still secondhand), I find it most difficult and uncomfortable to be seen in these. My belief in being who I am must be suppressed so that I can transform myself into what I should be and what I should look like.

Attire is only a small part of appearance. Another component of appearance is the way one is able to carry oneself in professional and social settings. This can also be a telltale sign of a working-class background. How we carry ourselves in social settings is directly related to our level of comfort within a specific environment. It is linked with social confidence, alienation, and self-identity. For me, the embedded concept of being what I am and not appearing in any other way is natural and comforting. However, I find that as I am expected to portray a disguised version of me (a visual portrait of professionalism), I become further alienated from the strange environment I am in and from my own identity. This makes it all the more difficult to carry myself appropriately or to appear natural or comfortable. Instead of networking or mingling, I find myself retreating from social settings to avoid discomfort. When I do attend such events, I am drawn to the service staff to recover a sense of myself and to sneak a moment of safety from the unsure world I both love and dread. This is common practice for those of us who do not have the social skills of the upper middle class or the elite (hegemonic values). This is due to the practice of interpersonal homogeneity; "as individuals, we move in fairly homogeneous circles—living, working and interacting on an interpersonal level with others who are very much like us."[2] People seeking out commonality so that they can escape to a place of similar cultural expectations, language, and literacy.

Pierre Bourdieu emphasizes that social capital originates within class compositions. As social capital is attained vis-à-vis our own class structures, we fulfill the need for attaining acceptable social capital through alliances with other working-class academics; we seek out commonality with others of similar cultural expectations, language, and social capital. The consequences of seeking out those we are comfortable with can be as much of a hindrance to our professional career as it is positive for our personal sense of self. It can make it difficult to establish "foreknown knowledge" via social interactions and networks that are beneficial for success in the academic environment. This is in part due to the class structure within the academy as well as our failure to attain the "expected" cultural literacy necessary to be a part of the daily practices and expectations within academe.

WHOSE CULTURAL LITERACY?

Cultural literacy is an ambiguous term whose meaning fluctuates according to whose culture is being conferred. In general, cultural literacy refers to issues of social skills, knowledge of the "elite" cultural ethos, and common social experiences associated with the upper-middle-class lifestyle. All of these concepts of cultural literacy are generally unknown to the working-class individual. The working-class base of knowledge is not credited with having a cultural literacy and is not perceived as valid within the dominant hegemonic construct of cultural literacy. Instead, the working-class individual must wear an upper-class mask or face further mortification within the academic environment.

Perhaps the most significant indicator of lacking cultural literacy is centered on the knowledge of political gamesmanship: the foreknown knowledge of academic ethos, virtues, and practices. For many in the dominant middle to upper classes, the knowledge of how the university environment functions is handed down and/or taught within in college preparatory courses in high school. However, most working-class individuals within academe are first-generation academics and without the preparatory training for academe in high school. Thus they are left shortsighted and blinded to the expectations, practices, virtues, and values within the academic milieu.

My first costly lesson was centered on traveling to a national conference. I was told that the department had travel funds available for graduate students to attend a conference. What I was not told was that I was to keep receipts for all travel expenses if I expected to be reimbursed. Although this may seem quite logical to the upper-middle-class individual, tracking receipts was foreign to my working-class experience. Although my years of working as a waitress and bartender had taught me that the upper-crust businessman always requested receipts for lunch, dinner, and cocktails, I did not see myself as a "business professional." Thus, keeping receipts for my expenses at a conference was not part of my social knowledge. I applied within the department for these funds and waited for nearly two months to receive reimbursement (based on a flat rate of $300). As money got tighter and desperation grew, I went to the department assistant to ask when I might expect my check to arrive. It was only then that I learned I had to bring in all my receipts to be reimbursed. Hindsight was of no use. Information that had been taken as a given by others was unknown to me.

The working-class background also does not afford the opportunity to enhance necessary technological skills that higher academe assumes all students possess. The "leave no child behind" ideology was not a part of my reality. Neither my children nor I had any experience with a computer until my second year in college. It was then that I was confronted with the necessity of turning in "standard papers, 12-point font, double spaced." This sent a wave of panic through me. I did not even know how to turn on a computer. I was humiliated when we were directed to insert our floppy disks and begin our classroom assignment. Nearly in tears, I had to raise my hand and explain that I did not know where a floppy disk went or how to use a computer. Scrambling for enough cash to purchase a computer, I managed to teach myself how to type and become more familiar with what was once my enemy.

For the members of the working class, the process of furthering one's education is filled with paradoxes and dichotomies. Whether it is the expected nuance of language, the necessary technological skills, or the foreknown knowledge of the practices and politics of academe, these hindrances are supported by the dominant ideology and reiterated to the working-class student from the start. At the end of my first year at a community college I, along with my entire class, was told that only a small percentage of us would ever even make it to a four-year institution, so keep this in mind and don't expect too much; after all, the statistical research confirms that survival for those who attend a community college is extremely low. Essentially, the probability of a working-class person being successful within the academic environment is not statistically significant, so we were being spared the toil of trying. Again, we should know our place within the class structure and within the expectations of the academic system. In essence, we are often pushed out in a psychological sense. This further embeds social insecurity, alienation, and the need to disguise one's self-identity.

CONCLUSION

This narrative provides the reader a few glimpses into the trials and tribulations of my working-class self in a world of otherness. I hope that readers are able to identify with my attempts to reveal some of the barriers and constraints that exist within the academic culture. However, this must be stated with the caveat that we, as individuals, have different accounts of our personal history that make each of our stories unique.

Certainly these experiences are different according to our divergent ages and ethnicity, race, and gender. However, I believe that within the working class there exist many commonalities. It is these common experiences that we must address as a united group to strengthen us via shared experiences so that we can attempt to change the dominant hegemonic environment of academe.

NOTES

1. Naton, Leslie, "You Were Raised Better than That," in *This Fine Place So Far from Home*, ed. C. L. Barney Dews and Carolyn Leste Law, 74 (Philadelphia: Temple University Press, 1995)

2. Stephen Muzzatti and Vincent Samarco, "Working Class Need Not Apply: Job Hunting, Job Interviews, and the Working Class Experience in Academe." (paper presented at the Midwest Sociological Society meeting, Chicago, 2003), 14.

REFERENCES

Berger, Peter, and Thomas Luckmann. *The Social Construction of Reality: A Treatise in the Sociology of Knowledge*. Garden City, NY: Doubleday, 1967.

Bourdieu, Pierre. *Handbook of Theory and Research for the Sociology of Education*. Edited by J. Richardson. New York: Greenwood Press, 1986.

Clance, Pauline, et al. "Impostor Phenomenon in an Interpersonal/Social Context: Origins and Treatment." *Women & Therapy* 16 (1995): 79–95.

Dews, C. L. Barney, and Carolyn Law, eds. *This Fine Place So Far from Home: Academics from the Working Class*. Philadelphia: Temple University Press, 1995.

Leslie, Naton. "You Were Raised Better than That." In Dews and Law, *This Fine Place*, 66–74.

Muzzatti, Stephen, and Vincent Samarco. "Working Class Need Not Apply: Job Hunting, Job Interviews, and the Working Class Experience in Academe." Paper presented at the Midwest Sociological Society meeting, Chicago, 2003.

Putnam, Robert. "The Prosperous Community." *American Prospect*, Spring B (1993): 35–42.

Selke, Walker, Nicholas Corsaro, and Jennifer H. Selke. "A Working Class Critique of Criminological Theory." *Critical Criminology* 11, no. 2 (2003): 93–112.

5

Can a Working-Class Girl Have Roots and Wings? White Trash in the Ivory Tower

Donna Selman-Killingbeck

For most upper- and middle-class Americans, the epithet "white trash" is associated with images of women who have kids too young and too often with too many men. These women have a never-ending cigarette dangling between their fingers, wear too much makeup, drink beer out of the bottle, and have an attraction for unemployed men with big trucks. Usually, "white-trash" women are on "welfare" or work as waitresses, bartenders, or even strippers. One does not expect to find white-trash women in the hallowed halls of a university, let alone teaching the classes offered there. While many of us are doing exactly that, it is only rarely that we reveal our pasts and even more rarely that we discuss the road taken and the survival strategies that shaped our personal and professional lives. This personal narrative seeks to explore and expose the survival strategies that I have adopted as a working-class woman in higher education.

In *Cool Pose*, Majors and Billson (1992) demonstrate how black males, forced to mask their true emotions, utilize the strategy of a "cool pose" or tough-guy image in order to survive the societal remnants of a social history rife with discrimination and racism. This "pose" leaves black males distanced from their relationships and their own feelings. Similarly, working-class women wear different masks in different situations in order to survive a social context affected by a long history of sexism and classism. The "pose" I strike is shaped by the values, beliefs, and norms of my working-class roots, specifically the survival techniques of modeling, overcompensation, and resistance.

In *Crime as Structured Action: Gender, Race, Class, and Crime in the Making*, James Messerschmidt (1997) argues that "although gender, race and class are ubiquitous, the significance of each relation shifts with changing context" (8). In one situation, gender and class may be important in determining the strategy employed. In another situation, gender may trump class. In yet another situation, some combination of race, class, and gender may be relevant. The separation and intersection of professional and personal contexts have presented a multitude of unique barriers and conflicts to me as a working-class woman in academe. At times I find myself stifling what I think I know to be true intellectually (modeling behavior) to maintain the family peace, while at different times I find myself disrupting intellectual classroom discussions (resisting "the way things have always been"). Both strategies, dictated by class, gender, and situational context, allow me to survive.

I am Simmel's "stranger," "fixed within a certain spatial circle—or within a group whose boundaries are analogous to spatial boundaries—but his position within it is fundamentally affected by the fact that he does not belong in it initially and that he brings qualities into it that are not, and cannot be, indigenous to it" (Simmel 1908, 148). The narrative that follows explores and exposes the survival strategies employed by one working-class woman in academia. By discovering and uncovering the impact that my working-class roots have on my behavior in different contexts, I hope we academics will realize not only why some people behave as they do but also what we as members of a profession contribute to those behaviors and beliefs. Confronting our actions and beliefs as both insiders and outsiders can benefit all classes.

After several attempts at college, I finally managed to get it together and finish. I was quite content with a bachelor's degree and looked forward to beginning a career as a probation officer. That was the brass ring—a degree and a job that didn't require slinging drinks, shaking my stuff, or working midnights, all of which I did to get through my undergraduate program. Going to graduate school had never crossed my mind. First of all, I didn't know what graduate school was. After I found out what it was, I was certain that I didn't have what it took to (a) get in, (b) do the work, or (c) be successful at it. My grandfather's words kept sounding off in my head: "College? You won't even graduate high school. Just get married and quit wasting everyone's money." Several years later, he continued with, "Are you making a career out of school? It's time to get on with real life, have a kid and quit wasting time."

Three things happened that removed my doubts. Or I should say three people. I had written a paper on anarchist criminology for a capstone course. On the back the professor had written, "Please see me after class." Every thought imaginable ran through my head: *Did I plagiarize? Did I fail? Am I going to graduate? Guess I got too big for my own britches.* After having convinced myself that I was about to be dropped from the program and soundly berating myself for having the audacity to believe a degree was possible, I made my way to the teacher's office.

"Have you ever considered graduate school?" he asked.

I quickly responded, "Is that something I need to do to get my bachelor's? Because I'll do it. Just let me know when the class starts and I'll do the best I can to rewrite the paper so that I can pass."

After a chuckle he proceeded to explain to me what graduate school was and that he thought I was a good candidate. I thanked him for the grade and the discussion and walked out thinking the guy was nuts.

Several weeks later, my statistics instructor asked how I planned to spend the summer. I thought, "Why does he care? He must know where I work. Here it comes, some crack about dancers." He asked if I would be interested in tutoring a statistics course he was teaching over the summer. The school would pay for my hotel room and food and I would get a check! He did a great job of convincing me. His persuasion went something like this: "I am only asking because you are the top student in the class. I thought you would be good at it and I really need the help." Bingo! How could I possibly say no when someone needed my help, especially someone as smart as he was? While I was working for him, we spent a great deal of time discussing my future. He was adamant that graduate school was the way to go.

During that time I discovered that he was right. Teaching was fun and I was pretty good at it. Earlier that year, I had been assigned a research project on deviance. My teacher said, "For those of you that work full time, the best way to approach this may be to write about deviance in the work place." Later, he asked me for an electronic copy of my paper and permission to include it in a collection he was working on. Sure, I thought, this is about sex and crime. He'll probably share the paper with future classes as an example of what *not* to do for a project. Later, the instructor said he would like to include my paper in a book! My first thought was, "Please change my name." I had been working in a strip club and until then had been very successful at hiding this fact from *everyone*. I shared this situation with the office secretary and the statistics and criminology professors with whom I had become friendly. All of them were extremely excited about the publication. For me, the big deal was that my secret life was about to be revealed. The deviance professor and I discussed my confliction at length. He shared with me his own acts of deviance, the books and papers that grew out of those acts, and the work of other "respectable" people who wrote about deviance. His passion for the subject, the ease with which he shared his life story, and his respect for my writing and thinking provided by far the greatest encouragement I had ever received. He personally handed me an application to graduate school, offered a letter of recommendation, and made room in his office for an additional desk. So, on to a master's program I went.

My class background and condition also influenced how I experienced life as a graduate assistant in a master's program. When I found out that we were not allowed to have a job other than our assistantship, I nearly quit. I had been working since I was fourteen. Working was expected if you weren't married. To my family, school was a luxury; work was the real thing. So at first I lied and continued to work. Then I started thinking about what my father taught me—know the rules. Knowing the rules, working hard at a job and at school, and not drawing attention to yourself would lead to "success." At school I knew the exact expectations and I studied the code of conduct. In fact, I could oftentimes recite the syllabus for any given class. And I did work hard. I had to get As in everything, complete all assignments before the deadline, and never, ever admit that it was all just too much. This led to what I (not so) affectionately call my "grad school Barbie" period: Just pull the string and I'd say "Yes, I can do that, no problem. I'll even have it in early. Anything else you need done? Teach your class? Sure. Grade those papers? My pleasure. Edit that manuscript by tomorrow? No problem." In my world, complainers got fired, slackers were despised (it meant more work for the rest of us), and those who didn't know the rules usually got screwed. Over-compensation became an important survival strategy, and while it took its toll, it did not go unrewarded. I eventually found the policy statement about assistantships and work. It stated that as long as work didn't interfere with my obligations to the department, it was allowed. I kept that in the back of my head for a long time.

Knowing the rules has served me well as I continue through the choppy waters of graduate school, where I still find myself. Not long ago, for instance, I was assigned to work for two professors, ten hours per week for each. After a particularly long week, having dedicated in excess of twenty hours to reformatting one professor's survey materials, the professor called me at home. "I need you to go to the library right now and pick up my books." I responded that I had already spent twenty hours that week on his stuff and was an hour away from campus. His prompt response was "You no longer work for me." I knew the rules, though, and I kept a log of the time and work that I had done for him. CYA—cover your ass—was also a practice that I was very familiar with. Years of being viewed with suspicion, as all-around untrustworthy, had taught me to document everything. The graduate review committee, having viewed the documentation, responded in accordance with the rules and I was able to keep my job.

Having navigated the waters of a master's program successfully, I was hired as a lecturer. As I saw it, this was the ultimate honor. I was good enough to work with the people who had taught me. I felt like Sally Fields in her award acceptance speech: "You like me, you really like me." However, I knew that I had managed to trick these people. It wouldn't be long before they figured out that I had been faking it all along and that I really had no idea what I was doing. My fear was solidified when I overheard my aunt say, "Her teach? What could she possibly teach—Table Dancing 101?" So, I relied on strategies that had worked before. First, I tried to blend in. In an effort to appear professional, I got my hair cut short. After all, no woman teacher I had ever seen had long, bleached-blonde hair. I threw out my jeans and stilettos and went to the resale store, where I found business suits and conservative shoes. Second, I overcompensated. I signed up for every committee I could find. I volunteered to fill in when people were sick and spent long hours in my office. I spent the summer taking seminars on effective teaching. Basically, I modeled the behaviors of the people that I knew and respected in the department, albeit to the extreme. Finally, I avoided putting extra work on anyone else. I remember being told, "Donna, you don't have to make your own copies anymore. We have office help for that." To this day I am still very uncomfortable with that. I know how to run the machine. Why should they do my work? On one occasion, I was "caught" cleaning the sink in the coffee room. The student aide later admitted to thinking I was crazy. She said, "You *are* nuts. You wash the coffee cups and take out your own trash?" Overcompensation and blending in are often at odds with each other.

My working-class roots have affected my behaviors in the academic setting in many ways. For example, I still call my professors Dr. Such and such, no matter how much they insist that I use their first name. Something about giving respect where respect is due always rings in my head. I am much more comfortable with the office assistants and groundskeepers than I am with my cohorts. I rarely discuss my family life or my past. I have never figured out if I should take my shoes off when entering the department head's house for a party. Is it okay to sit on the floor? I think that grading papers with a red pen is a ridiculous display of power. My name is Donna, not Ms. Killingbeck or Mrs. Killingbeck, and yes, it is okay for you to call me at home.

My strategy of blending in and modeling the behaviors of those around me has been the source of many conflicts. In my world, women simply do not argue with men—not with your father, not with your husband, and definitely not with your father-in-law. Speaking up or challenging their opinions will earn you dirty looks, comments about being a know-it-all, and oftentimes the infamous, "Was I talking to you?" As women, we may know that what the men are saying is wrong and discuss it among ourselves, but as we have been told all of our lives by the senior women, "There is no point in arguing. It won't get you anywhere. Why do you have to keep on making trouble?" Needless to say, contributing to discussion in class or in a meeting is an unnerving situation. I can talk about an issue with a friend but freeze up as soon as it comes time to talk about the very same issue in class. The very idea of rewarding people for drawing attention to themselves by countering statements by the professor or debating with other students is foreign to me. This has been a challenge that has required some intensive work on my part. If at all possible, I will sit with a friend right before class and discuss what we think will be the topic of the day. We try to address any counterpoints that will be made in class before they happen. Usually this is not possible, so I

write out any comments I have before I say them, all the while trying to decide if they sound dumb.

At the first professional conference I attended I was lucky enough to present a paper I had spent months on. During the session, a renowned criminologist whom I had been quoting for years walked in. Afterward, a mutual
friend took the two of us out for a beer. My mind went blank; it was as if I
had forgotten everything I had learned in the past five years. Trying to save
myself, I asked when this criminologist's presentation was. He said, "It is
pronounced presentation, with an a, not with an e." Once again, it was confirmed. Not only was I stupid, but I didn't even speak correctly. The conflict
between being rewarded for drawing attention to myself in the academic environment and having been socialized to blend in at home is problematic.
Even when I examine the situational context that I am in, academic or home,
the messages are confusing, and the strategy I employ is usually the one with
which I am most familiar—to shut up and not draw attention to myself.

Since returning to graduate school, the pose I strike at school and the pose
I strike at home have collided. Last year I was asked to leave Thanksgiving
dinner at my family's home. Someone posed the question, "Who can tell us
exactly what we are celebrating here today?" My youngest cousin responded
in the typical manner, "We are showing our thanks to God for giving us this
great land and country." I laughed and mumbled, "Why doesn't someone tell
these kids the truth?" My uncle shot me a look and my cousin wanted to
know what I meant. So I gave him a quick overview of history as I saw it, the
one about pillaging, using trickery and theft and genocide to obtain posses-
sion of what was not ours, all the while using God to justify it. That was it. I
was told that "anyone who spreads that liberalist bullshit is not welcome in
my home." At the next family function, I kept my comments to myself, again
modeling the behavior of the senior women, in order to keep the peace.
Since that incident, word has gotten out around the family. Don't talk about
the death penalty around Donna. Don't talk about those lazy people on welfare. And absolutely do not talk about anything that has to do with race. I
was told that my family just does not trust me. I have sold out. I have become
an outsider.

In response to this, I have found a new survival strategy: I push buttons
with a touch of humor. The humor allows me to remain (somewhat) acceptable to them while at the same time allowing me to raise the questions and
issues I hope they will think about. For instance, a family member commented that since the quarterback of a big-ten school had been caught using
cocaine, he should never be allowed to play football again. The quarterback
was a poor role model for all of the younger kids. I responded by saying, "I
think you're right. Anyone who is a role model for kids should not be given
a second chance. I wonder how many senators, congressmen, business executives, middle managers, doctors, attorneys, bankers, electricians, carpen-

ters, real estate agents, and computer programmers have ever been in trouble? We should get them fired. Think of all the jobs that would open up." "She's got you there, Pops," one of the senior women said.

My use of humor is a form of resistance and has made its way into the classroom. For example, as I was outlining the paper guidelines for an introductory course I was teaching, I heard myself say, "Spelling, grammar, and syntax matter to the extent that they affect your ability to express your points clearly, powerfully, and articulately." I saw the eyes glass over and had to laugh at myself. I sounded just like, well, like a professor. I recovered by looking out the door and saying, "I think I'm losing my mind. For a moment I thought my old criminology professor was talking to you guys." Humor usually ends up being the self-deprecating type. For instance, when using the chalkboard, I always alert my students that I am a victim of spell-check: I have forgotten how to spell. When I attempt to use the overhead projector, I always let them know that I am technologically challenged.

By sharing this story I hope I have illuminated the effect my working-class background has had on how I adapt within the situational contexts of my personal and academic lives. Demonstrating the survival strategies that I have employed in both social contexts and the reactions to those strategies has required that I draw attention to myself in writing, creating a high level of discomfort. This particular narrative has taken over a year to complete and would not have been written if it had not been for encouragement from fellow working-class academics and frequent reminders regarding deadlines from the editors. Surviving, via modeling, overcompensation, and resistance, for me has been a process of interpretation, adjustment, reinterpretation, and readjustment of those strategies facilitated by the actions and reactions of others. Reflecting on where I come from and where I want to go has reminded me just how much my life has been touched by others. This is my personal story, but my hope is that by sharing these experiences we can gain insight into other people and ourselves. We are not traveling this path alone.

REFERENCES

Majors, Richard G., and Janet M. Billson. 1992. *Cool Pose: The Dilemmas of Black Manhood in America*. New York: Lexington Books.

Messerschmidt, James. 1997. *Crime as Structured Action: Gender, Race, Class, and Crime in the Making*. Thousand Oaks, CA: Sage.

Simmel, Georg. 1908 [1971]. "The Stranger." In *On Individuality and Social Forms*, ed. Donald N. Levine, 143–50. Chicago: University of Chicago Press.

6

Working Class Need Not Apply: Job Hunting, Job Interviews, and the Working-Class Experience in Academia

Stephen L. Muzzatti and C. Vincent Samarco

By all empirical measures, it is undeniable that the United States is a highly economically stratified society. However, most Americans underestimate just how stratified it is. This underestimation is attributable to several factors. Likely the most influential is interpersonal homogeneity—that is, as individuals, we move in fairly homogeneous circles—living, working, and interacting on an interpersonal level with others who are very much like us. Furthermore, aside from the periodic sanitized mediated images, most of us rarely see the depths of poverty and the zeniths of wealth that mark America's socioeconomic landscape.

Additionally, owing in large part to the pervasiveness of capitalist ideology, there is virtually no mention of, let alone elaborate public discourse about, social class (Wright 1997; Sennett 1998). Enlightenment-era ideals and the meritocratic lens of individual achievement result in an amorphous haze where all but a very few move about in an undefined and certainly unproblematized "middle-class" sensibility. However, closer inspection reveals this to be little more than a veneer, maintained and perpetuated by ideological state apparatuses. Statistically speaking, the United States has a greater disparity in income and wealth than any other industrialized nation in the world (Economic Policy Institute, 2004). This is a country where the top 1 percent of the population controls over 50 percent of the corporate stock, where the top 5 percent controls upwards of 75 percent of all the wealth; and where, even by conservative government statistics, between 38 million and 50 million people are poor (Economic Policy Institute, 2004).

Sociologists, economists, and other social scientists have long known that good income buys many things, among them nutritious food, health and wellness, comfortable surroundings, and a safe and healthy environment.

What many, however, until recent years have neglected is the way in which growing up in a middle-class home also buys respectability, confidence, cultural literacy, and all the additional privileges and opportunities that come with them.

This paper is about the lived experiences of two academics who spent much of our lives in various states of relative deprivation. The personal narrative elements are part of the sociology of lived experience and are offered up here as testimony to the fact that, while you may be able to take the boy out of the class, you may never be able to take the class out of the boy.

PERSONAL BACKGROUND

Vince's parents both came from working-class backgrounds. Both of Vince's grandfathers worked in automotive-industry factories and both stressed education in their households. As a result, after working a few years, Vince's parents attended junior college before meeting one another and marrying. After Vince's parents were married, they pursued undergraduate degrees. Through part-time jobs, grants, and loans, they were able to pay for school and afford an apartment, food, and clothes for their four children. When Vince's parents divorced, however, and his father moved from the area, those modest securities became luxuries. To make matters worse, Vince's mother was diagnosed as paranoid-schizophrenic and had to drop out of school. The family went on pubic assistance, moved into Section 8 housing, and, for a time, lived out of a van in a public park. Vince eventually earned scholarships to university and worked several nonacademic jobs after finishing his undergraduate degree before pursuing graduate work and a teaching career.

Stephen was born into a working-class immigrant family. His paternal grandfather was a farm laborer, and his maternal grandfather drove a cement truck for a living. His grandmothers held a variety of agricultural, domestic, and factory jobs over the course of their working lives. While Stephen's mother was a high school graduate, his father, partly owing to a language barrier, though largely because of economic pressures—specifically the need to find employment and contribute to his family's finances—did not complete high school. Stephen received small scholarships and also worked in the food-service industry, often thirty hours a week, to defray the cost of his attendance at a public university. Upon entering graduate school, Stephen received research and teaching assistantships, but economic pressures forced him to continue his food-service employment outside of the university.

SOCIAL CLASS AND ACADEME

Despite contemporary discourses about diversity, openness, and access, the gates of academe are still heavily fortified. For the most part, access to academe is still restricted to those who are able to reap the benefits of class privilege and cultural literacy. The presence of those from the working and underclasses within institutions of higher education is anomalous at best. The predominant perception is that those from the working and underclasses who have become professors have done so through conscientious diligence. The small number of professors from the working and underclasses is often constructed through the meritocratic lens of the American dream as being the hardest working, the most capable of manufacturing a systematic plan for achievement. Instead, achievement—conformity to the white hegemonic imperative—has depended more on masking and sanitizing fugitive knowledge. This retrospective narrative contextualizes the alienation and stigmatization of two university professors within a broader analysis of class, knowledge, and power.

This paper will focus on four manifestations where our own class experiences are often diametrically opposed from those of our colleagues. These areas are (1) the presentation of self, (2) forms of expression, (3) cultural literacy, and (4) class consciousness. While undeniably academically convenient, these areas are also meaningful interpersonal measures of class reality in twenty-first-century America.

JOB HUNTING AND JOB INTERVIEWS

Job hunting and job interviews are undeniably difficult, perhaps more so for members of one class than the others. Relative disadvantage may in fact exacerbate the problems of job hunting and job interviews for members of the working class. To begin with, the need, and subsequently the pressure, to "find work" is greater. This impacts the experience of working-class academics.

University costs are staggering. Scholarships, bursaries, grants, and teaching and research assistantships cover little, and hence the need to get out and get a "real job" is great. This often means working-class academics take on adjunct teaching or perhaps leave ABD, which further impedes the ability to complete the dissertation. Unlike some graduate school students who were able to effectively ensconce themselves in the graduate school program and when need be, fall back on their (or, more accurately, their parents') accumulated assets, this was not the case for us. As a result of relatively little experience and uncompleted doctorates, coupled with a tight academic job market, we felt that we had little choice but to take the first job to come along. In addition to these objective conditions is a subjective component of our working-class experience. Like many from our class, there was an internalized force that made us feel thankful for having a job. Seeing our parents, elder siblings, other relatives, neighbors, and friends struggle with chronic, sporadic, seasonal unemployment, how could we be expected to think any differently? To Stephen and Vince, as in the case of many working-class people, a "shit job" with low pay and poor to nonexistent benefits was better than no job at all. We felt our worth was determined by our jobs. This feeling is by no means restricted to members of our social class but is perhaps more pronounced among its members.

Hence, we embarked upon a job search. Unlike jobs for most members of the working class, jobs for sociology and English professors usually are not advertised in the *Detroit Free Press* or the *Toronto Star.* Nor can we draw upon contacts at the factory or the construction site. One of the first obstacles is simply finding out about jobs. Here again we face a barrier. Organizational membership is often vital for professional growth and development. This is probably no more acutely manifested than in access to the coveted *ASA Employment Bulletin,* the *Chronicle of Higher Education,* the MLA job list, and so on. Oftentimes, costs are prohibitive. Even now, with many organizations posting on the Internet for greater accessibility, a barrier remains, for this practice assumes that the individual has the appropriate hardware and software.

Most middle-class people are not only unfettered but often unaware of the financial constraints facing their working-class colleagues. Among the most notable of these financial constraints are the costs connected with application packets and travel to and from conferences and interviews.

Applications are costly to compile. In addition to basics, such as paper and envelopes, there are more substantial costs, such as college transcripts and mailing. A single application packet can cost upward of $15. When you multiply that by the fifty to one hundred packets applicants are forced to send, the costs can go well into the hundreds of dollars. An old adage says that it is easier to get a job when you have a job. While not the intended meaning, this is true for working-class academics. Like many of our brothers and sisters in the working-class occupational environment, our state of relative economic deprivation has often compelled us to steal from our employers. In our case, this employee pilferage has taken the form of inappropriate use of university photocopying, mail, and long-distance telephone services.

Travel to conferences, too, is a considerable financial strain that working-class academics disproportionately bear. While some costs are absorbed by employers, many incidentals at least are shouldered by working-class academics themselves. This often creates situations where the working-class academic is forced to operate and adapt under less-than-ideal circumstances.

For example, the inability to attend a conference prevents us from participating in the job fair and less directly in the networking essential to establishing contacts in our respective fields. Somewhat less burdensome are the instances in which we can attend but are forced to stay, not at the expensive conference hotel, but at a cheaper and more out-of-the-way alternative. Thus, we often miss out on the informal networking, such as dinner or drinks at the conclusion of the day's scheduled events. We are literally and figuratively on the margins.

Another, thankfully less common though potentially more disastrous phenomenon arises when the working-class academic is short-listed and invited to an on-campus interview. While it is the standard practice for the potential employer to pay for transportation and lodging, more dubious situations sometimes arise. Ideally for the working-class academic, the inviting institution arranges for travel and lodging and pays up front. Sometimes, however, the applicant is asked to pay up front to be reimbursed later. This may perhaps be negligible to a middle-class person with a significant or at least unencumbered line of credit, but the working-class academic who, like other working-class persons, is already overextended does not have the disposable income necessary and may well be removed from the running. Even more disastrous are scenarios in which the working-class academic is asked to bear the costs exclusively.

Coming from the working and underclasses, it is our experience that clothes were simply functional. With no, or limited, disposable income, neither of us paid particular attention to fashion. Rather, our focus was on clothes that were durable, functional, and, if possible, clean. Conversely, members of the middle classes and above were at liberty to concern themselves with the latest styles. Pressure resulting from colleagues' assumptions that we are middle class force us to attempt to adhere to sartorial norms with which we are both unfamiliar and uncomfortable.

During his first job search, Vince went to the Modern Language Association convention where most initial interviews in English are conducted. He spent most of his time before the interview learning from his graduate school professors what he might expect. He hadn't even thought about clothes. He brought with him the only jacket he owned—a blue blazer—along with a pair of khaki pants and a tie. He thought this is what English professors wore. On his first interview, he met with two members of a small college that thought of itself as a top-tier liberal arts college. When he knocked on the hotel room door, a polished male in his early fifties told Vince that the school had not yet finished with the previous interview. He said this through a yawn, without making eye contact. He asked Vince to wait in the hallway and abruptly closed the door. Vince fidgeted for ten minutes, going over what he would say. When the interviewer led the other candidate out and showed Vince in, he again did not make eye contact. Instead, he yawned

and waved Vince in. Vince met the other interviewer, and while he ex-
changed small talk with that person, he felt the first interviewer staring at
him. Instead of an initial question, the first interviewer said, "You didn't think
you had to wear a suit to this interview?" Trying to save the interview (and
thus the job) Vince replied, "Well, it's my lucky jacket." The first interviewer
did not smile. He said, "Not today."

When working-class academics secure university teaching positions, we
are again faced with a difficulty: the costs incurred in moving. Some universities refuse outright to pay for moving costs, while others concede to paying only a fixed amount ($1,000–1,500). Because of a lack of cultural literacy,
the working-class academic fails to realize, as is also often the case with
salary and other "payments," that this figure is often negotiable. Furthermore, as mentioned earlier, there's often a mind-set that afflicts working-
class academics that dictates that we should be grateful for just being offered
a job, and hence should not push the envelope with negotiations. This
proves to be a hardship in many ways. First, it violates the expectation of the
Mayflower move, making U-Haul the harsh reality. Furthermore, it often entails going into debt to get a job.

THE PRESENTATION OF SELF

Once a faculty position is secured, additional problems arise. As Goffman
long ago told us in his seminal work, *The Presentation of Self in Everyday
Life* (1959), while it is obviously affected by statuses and our concomitant
roles, much of the construction of social reality is a result of the proactive assiduousness of individual actors. As such, much of our daily experiences are
centered around an attempt to appear middle class. This includes, but by no
means is restricted to, the language we use, the clothes we wear, and other
personal effects.

As we come from the working and underclasses, as noted above in the
story of Vince's interview, it was our experience that clothes were simply
functional. Pressure resulting from our colleagues and students' assumptions
that we are middle class forces us to attempt to adhere to sartorial norms
with which we are both unfamiliar and uncomfortable. Vince, for example,
chooses to wear Polo shirts during the school week. He can afford only five
of them, so he wears the same shirts every week, but the fact that they are
Polo allows him this latitude. This name brand also allows him to mask class
position and make him appear to fit in. Colleagues have made remarks such
as "Didn't you just wear that?" and "Don't you have anything else to wear?"
Stephen, on the other hand, never having previously had the need to "dress
up," simply inherited a collection of dress shirts and ties from his father and
uncles. As a result, while technically dressed up to the middle-class gaze, he

often appears frumpy, mismatched, disheveled. Stephen has been aware of several occasions where his clothes have been a subject of derision among students. Our combined experiences in this area, perhaps more than in any other, constantly serve to remind us of our background and the differences in social class between us and others in our work environment.

Considering the cultural importance of the automobile in American life, it is not surprising that car ownership is yet another manifestation of the differences between us and those around us. As young adults, both of us realized that the costs involved in automobile ownership and maintenance were well beyond our means. Growing up in major metropolitan urban centers with extensive public transportation systems negated much of the need for automobile ownership. It did not, however, negate the desire for personal freedom inscribed in car ownership. The two cars Vince has owned in his lifetime have both been small, purely functional economy-model cars that were purchased more for reliability than dramatic looks. Each has lasted ten years. Recognizing the greater cost efficiency, Stephen opted to buy a motorcycle. It was only four years ago that he could afford a car, and even then it was a model that was more than ten years old with high mileage. Because our vehicles were clearly discernible among other faculty's late-model luxury sedans and coupes, we usually opted to forgo parking in the faculty lots and chose instead to park in the larger, more anonymous student lots. Because a car is possibly the single most universally recognized status symbol, it is little wonder that automobile ownership has proven to be yet another reminder of our class position.

Although somewhat less obvious to the casual observer, the home is perhaps a more significant status symbol than the automobile. As in the case of other similar-sized institutions, within the community of our small, private college setting with fewer than eighty full-time faculty, there existed a subtle pressure to entertain colleagues in one's home. Some examples from our experience include a theory-reading group, poker night, hosting job candidates, and so forth. This is very much outside the working-class experience, where the home was the place you brought only the closest family and friends. For college-related events, it is necessary to have inviting surroundings, ample space to host, the disposable income to purchase gourmet-like food and beverages, and the desire to politick. Vince has not participated in such events because he has found the disposable income required a significant and unnecessary barrier. As a result, he has been perceived as being aloof and disinterested in the social interactions of the college. Similarly, Stephen has also not hosted these social/professional events. In addition to his inability to furnish the expected quality of food and beverages, he feels a degree of embarrassment because he had a small apartment located in a very working-class neighborhood that cannot measure up to the opulent surroundings of his colleagues. In addition to these fiscal concerns, we also maintain a degree of deliberate distance. As is politicking, this subject is explored in a subsequent section.

FORMS OF EXPRESSION

As sociolinguists have long asserted, language is not neutral. And as is the case of many subordinate groups—such as people of color, women, and gays and lesbians—the working class is a group that is often seen but not heard. Even when audible, the language of the working class is often marginalized, dismissed, or outright ignored. Hence, as individuals from working- and underclass backgrounds, it is not surprising that we feel that we must be careful of what we say and how we say it. Growing up in working-class neighborhoods unfettered by the artificial Victorian notions of proper forms of speaking, we competed with others in our class to be heard. A sure-fire formula for success was volume, frequency, and ostentatiousness in speech. In the middle-class environment of the university, such tactics are frowned upon as wholly inappropriate. Consequently, we both daily struggle with conforming our voices to the dictates of appropriate speech while at the same time holding true to our backgrounds. Our classroom presentations and discussions are frequently laced with sentence fragments, non sequiturs, asides, profanity. Critical connections and critiques of power are embedded in our discourse. Power is distributed, narratives are broken, students work with their hands, and we get used to hearing the sound of our own voices. We do not adopt the same presentation with most of our colleagues. As in many interactions with people from working-class backgrounds and people from higher social classes, despite urges to engage in bell hooks's (1989) "back-talk," we muzzle ourselves and revert to conventional dynamics where we are talked at instead of talked to.

Representative both of past lived experience and a critical appreciation of society's power dynamics, neither of us feels particularly comfortable ensconcing ourselves in the trappings of authority and domination. Unlike many of our colleagues who demand to be called "Doctor" or "Professor" by students and in turn refer to them as "Mr." or "Ms.," we both are reticent to use the title "Doctor" or "Professor." We are also, as representative of the cacophonous exchanges of our youth, more comfortable simply using our last names. In addition to the two aforementioned reasons, encouraging students to refer to us by our last names speaks more directly to our experience, where we're more apt to use our last names among ourselves. At the outset of his courses, Vince makes a particular point of asking his students not to refer to him as "sir," clarifying by stating that he has "neither been knighted by Her Majesty the Queen, nor am I your commanding officer." Depending on how ornery he feels, he may also say, "Don't call me sir, I work for a living." Similarly, when asked by students what they should put on the cover page of their written submissions (Doctor/Professor), Stephen humorously deflects attention from his title by saying, "I know what my name is, put your name on the title page." In dealing with colleagues, we have not been as successful. When constructing the syllabus for a team-taught course, Stephen typed both his and his colleague's last names. His teaching partner, obviously taken somewhat aback, suggested, "Why don't we use our full names and titles?" Stephen, aware of what was going on, acquiesced without discussion.

CULTURAL LITERACY

Possibly the single biggest manifestation of class privilege is the amorphous "cultural literacy." This entails, but is not restricted to, such things as social versatility, social graces, knowledge of cultural forms, and travel experience.

One of the most noteworthy examples is travel experience. Unlike many of our middle-class colleagues, neither of us has traveled extensively outside the United States. Many of our colleagues were taken on family vacations as children or young adults, or traveled with their parents on business. By contrast, the only time Vince made trips of any kind was when he and his family traveled from Detroit to Scranton, Pennsylvania, once a year to visit his grandparents. Similarly, the extent of Stephen's travel experience was day trips to rural areas to participate in very working-class leisure pursuits such as fishing, or long-weekend car excursions from Toronto to Buffalo, New York. Vince's first extensive travel experience came as the result of a direct-marketing position he took following the completion of his undergraduate degree. Stephen first traveled by air when he attended a conference in Chicago as a graduate student. When our colleagues regale each other with tales of sightseeing in Europe and the Americas, we remain silent, reminded of the limitations placed on us as the result of our social class.

The decorum and deportment of the working class proves to be ample fodder for ridicule. Often incorrectly labeled as reticence, or conversely boorishness, the inability of the working classes to "carry themselves properly" in a variety of social settings is yet another liability of our class position that confronts us daily. This manifests itself both in mundane daily activities at the university and, perhaps even more acutely, during special events. Vince, for instance, has repeatedly been accused of being disengaged from discussions about campus affairs. In one meeting about potential changes to the college's general education requirements, he was the only member of his eight-person department who did not participate in the discussion. There were a host of reasons for his reticence: disdain for the proposal, an unwillingness to approve structural changes that, to him, advanced an elitist ethos.

He was certainly unwilling to voice any concerns in front of the chair of his department and an associate dean. The next day, he received an e-mail from the associate dean, chastising him for his "blank looks" and "lack of involvement" in something so important to the college. Similarly, in interactions with the same associate dean, Stephen was "good-naturedly" mocked in front of other colleagues for essentially being a nonentity in campus politics. Specifically, he was told that, for someone who looks so "radical," he was "awfully quiet and deferential."

The effects of our class background are even more acutely felt when the college hosts special events, such as commencement ceremonies, ribbon-cutting ceremonies, or other activities in which we, as faculty, are paraded about and expected to represent the college in mingling with community members, trustees, donors, and the like. At a faculty-board reception, we both experienced considerable discomfort in having to engage in what we viewed as "superficial cocktail party chitchat" with significant financial supporters of the college. Acutely aware both of our vastly different upbringings and our daily lived experiences, we felt we were part of an unmistakable employer-employee exchange. Unsure of how to proceed in these interactions, and concerned that a potential faux pas would reflect poorly on the college, both of us chose to withdraw from the mandatory jocularity and situated ourselves, both literally and figuratively, on the margins of the party.

CLASS CONSCIOUSNESS

As some writers (Feagin and Feagin 1997; Register 2001) have lamented, class consciousness is a virtually unknown concept in contemporary American society. This paper attempts to illustrate how, for us and for many like us, class is a liability. Perhaps even more of a liability is class consciousness. Unlike many from the working and underclasses, who, while certainly begrudgingly, nonetheless somewhat unconsciously accept our powerlessness and disenfranchisement, we find that our academic training negates such rueful ignorance. Because we are class-conscious, we often find ourselves at odds with our colleagues, students, and administrators in a variety of ways, on multiple levels. At the first level of approximation, there is some degree of discomfort with colleagues who we know have not only very different past and daily lived experiences but also a different worldview. Our inability or unwillingness to uncritically accept the hegemonic imperative as it pertains to everything from the recent debates on the war on terrorism to whether or not our former college should have built an aquatic center serves as a daily reminder of the difference that class makes in people's lives. This subjective alienation extends as well to our interactions with those whom some of our colleagues refer to "value neutrally" as the administration, yet we are unequivocally aware of as our bosses. While many would conceptualize this stance as cynical or antagonistic, we disagree. Conceding simplicity, we nonetheless contend that this view is a wholly accurate assessment of our relative position in the power relations at our college.

This healthy mistrust of those in positions of power is evidenced both in our displays of deference (referring to the college president not by his first name, as many faculty do, but by his formal title) and in the fact that we often find ourselves feeling more comfortable in interactions with staff members such as maintenance workers, groundskeepers, and food-service staff than with members of the administration. Furthermore, unwilling to perpetuate the hierarchical structure, we are reluctant to assign tasks to the faculty secretaries, a hesitancy not shared by other faculty members. Additionally, unlike many other faculty, who flaunt their position in dichotomously organized locales (locales such as taverns, organized along the dichotomous "college folk" versus "townie" lines), both of us feel compelled to remove ourselves from that dichotomous and hierarchical atmosphere to the anonymous working-class environment of estab lishments outside of town, and beyond our former college's immediate organizing imperatives.

CONCLUSION

Though the topic is not really addressed in this chapter, anyone with even a cursory knowledge of the way in which social stratification operates is well aware of the multitude of barriers facing those who reside in the bottom tiers of the social hierarchy. As such, it is not surprising that so few members of the working and underclasses have the opportunity to avail themselves of higher education. Most, in fact, are, to borrow from Feagin and Feagin (1997), "pushed out" of the educational system long before attending a university reveals itself as an option. Hence, it is even less surprising that very few of those from the working and underclasses rise to positions of professors within the hallowed halls of institutions of higher learning.

In the anomalous instances in which members of the working and underclasses become university professors, a plethora of daily experiences not only remind us of our relatively deprived upbringing but also disrupt and impede our lives in this environment.

The survival, perhaps even more so than the success, of professors from the working and underclasses is highly contingent upon our sanitization of fugitive knowledge, our obfuscation of class position, and our muzzling of class consciousness.

REFERENCES

Economic Policy Institute. 2004. www.epinet.org/content.cfm/books_swa2004.

Feagin, Joe R., and Clairece Booher Feagin. 1997. *Social Problems: A Critical Power-Conflict Perspective*. 5th ed. Englewood Cliffs, NJ: Prentice Hall.

hooks, bell. 1989. *Talking Back: Thinking Feminist, Thinking Black*. Boston, MA: South End Press.

Giddens, Anthony, and David Held, eds. 1982. *Classes, Power, and Conflict: Classical and Contemporary Debates*. Berkeley and Los Angeles: University of California Press.

Register, Cheri. 2001. *Packinghouse Daughter: A Memoir*. St. Paul: Minnesota Historical Society Press.

Sennett, Richard. 1998. *The Corrosion of Character: The Personal Consequences of Work in the New Capitalism*. New York: W. W. Norton.

Wright, Erik Olin. 1997. *Class Counts: Comparative Studies in Class Analysis*. Cambridge: Cambridge University Press.

II

ATTACKED FROM WITHIN AND WITHOUT: WORKING CLASS ACADEMICS AND INITIAL CONFRONTATIONS WITH ACADEME

The second section of this text describes the myriad effects social class imposes on working-class academics once they have become faculty. As is true in the first section, contributors articulate many similar experiences and concerns. The similarities in their experiences should be telling; they represent fundamental and predictable ways in which class and power are articulated in academe.

"Making Class Matter: My Life as a Semi-Earhole" by Donna LeCourt discusses the ways in which capitalist ideology and the workings of cultural capital prevent most working-class academics from reaching a place where they can see their identities as fluid constructs, tools for critical personal and cultural discovery. Reaching that place, a place of "hybridity," involves critical discoveries of one's own narrative and fundamental grounding in Marxist ideology.

In "White, Working Class, and Feminist: Working within the Master's House and Finding Home Again," Julie Ann Harms Cannon describes how academics who come from the working class do so by endlessly negotiating a double consciousness. Harms Cannon says that working-class academics, and particularly women working-class academics, never "arrive," will always be presented with the uneasy feelings of being outsider and insider, of feeling shame and pride, and of using and being abused by cultural capital.

William J. Macauley Jr.'s essay "'Gimme That!': The Working-Class Student Meets the Working-Class Subject" presents a compelling case for how negotiating a meritocratic system of higher education for working-class students leads inevitably to feelings of displacement. He argues that narratives, the sociology of lived experiences, can be a radical tool for lessening the feelings of displacement and for presenting the necessity of critical inquiry into how class and power work.

Daniel Martin's "Critique of Domination: The Pain, Praxis, and Polemics of Working-Class Consciousness in Academia" speaks truth to power, in the tradition of Alvin Gouldner and Dorothy Smith. He illuminates the reifying assumptions about class, and the way in which working-class identities in the academy are constructed, both by working-class academics and by others. In his analysis of the vicious departmental politics sadly so common in the academy, Martin critically addresses the ways in which privilege and disenfranchisement are taken for granted and normalized. His narrative illustrates the ways that preestablished political, theoretical/paradigmatic, and personal tensions in the department are embedded in wider class relations, and how, when challenged, those wielding middle-class power will only address such challenges within the walls of established institutional frameworks that privilege those existing power relations.

Tenured professor Janelle Wilson's "Working-Class Values and Life in Academe: Examining the Dissonance" speaks to the conflict between the values of her working-class roots and those of the academy, though she frames them differently than does Dawn Rothe's earlier chapter. Wilson's narrative provides examples of this clashing of values in four broad categories: communication, family, community, and work. She also discusses implications for working-class academics, their students, and the academic enterprise. Ultimately, she concludes that though painful and difficult, working through the dissonance brings a diverse and fresh perspective and promotes a broader, richer environment.

7

Making Class Matter: My Life as a Semi-Earhole

Donna LeCourt

"We need to keep open admissions policies; there are too many structural in-equities in education to ever do away with them." "But isn't merit what colleges should evaluate? Aren't you proof yourself that there is equal opportunity? That working-class kids can succeed if they're smart enough and work hard enough?"

This mock conversation is almost an exact replica of the ones I've had with colleagues and students over the years as I try to bring "class" into a conversation about higher education. It reveals, in situ, the contradictions I inhabit daily as a college professor with working-class roots attempting to teach in an institution whose very function is to erase class difference by offering class mobility via meritocracy. I both am and am not the representative the interlocutor above wants me to be. Along with the body that seemingly bespeaks success, I carry with me the traces of my history: a history that consistently reminds me of those other bodies—of those friends and family—who "merited" advancement more than I (they were smarter, worked harder) yet who continue to work with their bodies, subject to economic shifts that inevitably put them at risk while I remain ensconced in my comfortable tenured job. This is the contradiction of the working-class academic who can never forget the reality of class oppression because she remains allied with the working class through worldview, consciousness, and the material ways her body moves through space, consumes, and even socializes. In the academic realm, I am both self *and* Other simultaneously. I reside in Homi Bhabha "third space"—the space of the hybrid, of ambivalence and possibility—yet it is not a comfortable one nor one that most of us seek out.

In this chapter, I argue that this liminal space of the working-class academic can be an impetus to action, as postcolonial theory might tell us, yet I also seek to highlight how difficult it is to come to such a space—to be both insider and outsider simultaneously—given the way capital, class, and education align in U.S. society. Although hybridity is a laudable goal, much like Orwell's pigs, not all hybrids are equal in a postindustrial nation, particularly in the context of the cultural institution that claims to be classless because it provides class mobility.[1] To highlight why class identities seem so damnably difficult to claim, despite our current climate of identity politics, I provide a short history of my own journey from working-class student to professional academic by invoking the Hammertown lads' metaphor of "earhole" from Paul Willis's ethnography of British working-class boys in *Learning to Labor*.

Although dated, the insights Willis's work provides into how the working class "creates itself" through acts of self-identification and revolution provide an apt description for my own journey, where competing identifications vie for prominence in response to both capricious and structural material conditions. The movement of the narrative, in Hammertown terms, is seemingly from "lad" to "earhole"—from one whose affiliations lead to opposing the school's values in favor of working-class social being to the earhole's desire to conform to those same values in favor of material success via the middle-class habitus proffered in school.[2] The lads (or lasses as the case may be), that is, reflect an emphasis on collectivity within working-class groups that tacitly privilege "family and neighborhood inter-dependence over individual competition."[3] Within such a context, overt value is placed on the hard work of the individual yet not at the expense of these social relations; as a result, the individual who seeks success through hierarchical structures is admonished for failing to attend to his social obligations, for preferring structural advancement over social being. Individualism is highly valued, but only within the context of class solidarity.[4] School bespeaks hierarchical structure and further threatens such solidarity; as such, it is depicted by the Hammertown lads as that which is devoid of life, that which silences the everyday pleasure of being in the moment and with others. In contrast, the earhole is described as one who is "listening, never *doing*: never animated with [his or her] own internal life, but formless in rigid reception."[5] Identifying with school marks the earhole as one who exchanges "some loss of autonomy" for the "formal structure" of school and its ability to confer autonomy only through hierarchy.[6]

But there are also the "semi-earholes" that, in one lad's terms, are "a separate group from us and the ear'oles. . . . They all mess about with their own realm, but they're still fucking childish, the way they talk, the way they act like. They can't mek us laff, we can mek them laff."[7] The semi-earhole, the place in which I reside in most of this narrative, is marked by some opposition to school in favor of working-class social groups, but his actions are never as revolutionary and oppositional as the lads'. Semi-earholes are still childish in their inability to construct autonomy through alliance with their social group rather than school. Only the lads interanimate school experience with their own values, their own oppositional culture that allows school to become laughable. Semi-earholes take school too seriously; they do not seek to define themselves by behaviors that the school most would reject: sexual activity, disrespect for authority, the taking on of adult roles and activities. The lads' behaviors, however, do not denote the "values" of the working class, as the popular appellation "white trash" might have it; rather, these behaviors reflect a rejection of the structural imposition of power by institutions in favor of the working-class social networks that sustain their members in the face of oppressive material conditions. The habitus we might infer here is, then, one of pleasure in the everyday and mundane, of dedication to community that abhors privilege structurally conferred but not socially earned. In contrast, the earhole divests himself of autonomy in everyday life and thus earns the lads' derision by ceasing to live, by yielding the autonomy provided by rejecting school: "fun, independence, and excitement" in the everyday.[8] By looking to structure, the earhole already eschews class by focusing on the promises of deferred gratification (success *later*) that school might confer. The semi-earhole—me—vacillates continually between the two poles, neither an adult in taking control "back" from structure nor a child in seeking only to defer control to the formal structure of schooling.

The earhole is an apt metaphor here for two reasons. First, the metaphor invokes the reproductive power of schooling in a visceral way: "The ear is one of the least expressive organs of the human body: it responds to the expressivity of others. It is pasty and easy to render obscene" within the gaze of the lads.[9] But it also recognizes how class is not just a fact of upbringing or social situation. It is also an orientation to experience, to the practice of everyday life that is not simply encoded through the overt values of one's home nor the economic conditions that structurally impose class upon us. Rather, class is lived relationally, resting in a sense of shared interest as much as shared experience. In E. P. Thompson's terms, class is "always embodied in real people and in a real context,"[10] but class is also continually "defined by men [and women] as they live their own history, and, in the end, this is its only definition."[11] In short, class is *peopled and relational*. Such a definition recognizes culture not as an exterior imposition upon subjects but, in Paul Trembath's terms, a relationship where bodies serve "as the mediators of social events in place of the disembodied exteriority of culture,"[12] making bodies the central "presence of cultural influence."[13] Such social being, further, comes to be defined relationally, in opposition to some bodies and in connection with others. Institutions (school, media, economics) may set the parameters of such relations but never fully define how they are lived.

This understanding of class allows me to extend the concept of being a "semi-earhole" to one of class *consciousness* rather than class as a static attribute of experience. Class is neither a thing we hold like an identity placard which never changes its signification nor is it something we leave behind when we economically move to the middle class. It is a continual unfolding—filled with tension and loneliness for the semi-earhole—that brings one to an awareness of one's past, one's present, and the potential for change in the future. The semi-earhole, the hybrid, refuses to reside on this side or that, not through an act of will but by the necessity of the material conditions in which she finds herself.

FROM LASS TO SEMI-EARHOLE: THE PAIN OF TRANSITION

No one wakes up one day and decides to give her life over to an institutional structure like schooling, literally answering an Althusserian hail to "take me" as the subject of an Ideological State Apparatus. The movement is slower and harder to describe. It is pure caprice, in my experience, understood as an act of will only much later when I attempt to explain my life with a firm narrative line. But there is no logic, no linear focus to the narrative by which one moves from being happily ensconced in a warm, loving environment to being thrown in with those who will continually mark you as different, never allowing your seamless identification as a "lass" to be embodied unconsciously or comfortably again. That movement, as I usually tell it, begins for me in the literal move from a neighborhood elementary school to a large, urban junior high where I was the only student from Edgeworth Street School tracked into honors classes. Yet this version of the narrative allows me to assume such tracking was due to natural ability, to being "smarter" than my peers, indicating the acceptance of hierarchies brought on by schooling that previously had no meaning. Yet, if I probe this convenient narrative, I have to admit that I also knew/know that I wasn't actually smarter. So, why was I the only sixth-grader from my neighborhood of three-deckers, factories, and auto shops let into the sacred realm of "honors"? Quite simply, because my life as a semi-earhole began earlier than I like to imagine.

Those elementary school years are marked by much sameness: playing on the sidewalks of a busy city street; derisively shouting comments with my friends to the "rich folk" who brought their cars to the neighborhood auto body shop; trips downtown on the local bus where we laughed at the kids in school uniforms; my first crush on Timmy, who lived in the housing project a block away, or my enduring love for Juan next door; the normalcy of getting a prime listening spot outside for a "good fight" between my own parents or the neighbors. All these images come back to me as part of what it meant to be in my neighborhood in a large eastern city center where factory workers and welfare recipients mixed, where many races and religions came together in the harmonious sounds of living loud and living now. There is such joy in that sameness, in remembering how I loved to speak what we now call Ebonics, how truly obnoxious we all could be in calling attention to ourselves and our difference when cars passed, how we deliberately dressed to oppose current styles of TV (no Marcia Brady outfits for us, but army pants and work boots), how the noise of living—cars honking, couples fighting, TVs blaring, people yelling across the porches—was seamless and beautiful.

There was an underside to being a "lass," of course—the continual risk of violence for taking the wrong position, the lack of control felt when parents argued about money or news made it around that someone else had lost a job, the warnings from older siblings to avoid Nolan's bar down the street and not to take the shortcut to school through the alley where the "gang kids" were waiting to make a drug deal. But even such fears had an immediacy to them, a sense of living in the moment that may be the hallmark of youth generally but seems to me more pronounced in working-class contexts. Even now with my family and friends from those days, the rush of pure emotion in a reaction, the desire to win by being loudest—these actions *are* more present than are the endless discussions of abstract concepts that never reach a resolution in my current context. But the fear remains as well: throwing up when I signed my first mortgage, believing that even tenure does not equate with job security, having that nagging feeling that the firm ground beneath my feet can disappear at any moment. The mind cannot always erase what the body feels; economic security is as much affect as material.

My younger self, however, did not understand these contradictions; she was as much at home as Willis's lads, but I was a semi-earhole even then. I did very well in school and earned high grades and special approbation as a result: teachers trusted me to bring attendance to the principal's office; for three years I was a reading group of one, the only student given independent work to do during class time; I was the kid asked to tutor others. But I also transgressed: I began smoking in fifth grade, I got into fights as head cheerleader with other schools' girls, I intimidated the "richer" kids in catechism, earning a call home from the priest for threatening to "beat down" on someone. I was no angel—little different from my neighborhood friends in my almost violent opposition to structure—but my high grades made my teachers perceive me differently as they overlooked my transgressions in ways they wouldn't for the other kids. I sometimes wonder if my transgressions took on such an edge because of this very surety that I was not "like the others." Yet where did this marking of difference originate? Why did I desire to do well in school yet also resist it so strongly?

Far from thinking it is an innate quality, I attribute it to my older brother. Two years ahead of me in school, Bruce had made a name for himself with the teachers as the best student Edgeworth had seen in years, and accordingly, he earned the derision of his peers for his complete accommodation of school's values and rules. As a child who was struck ill at a young age, my brother was segregated from the neighborhood, continually bedridden or not allowed out of doors. As a result, he became a voracious reader, consuming all the Hardy Boys novels and about ten books a week from the local public library. His reading was not seen as aberrant because of his illness. While I was continually told to "go out and play" if I tried to hole up with a book, Bruce was allowed a different space than the other kids. Since it was determined that he would probably never work with his body, his mind had to be honed for a different kind of work. While literacy was not devalued or discouraged, as so many educators seem to assume, reading simply operated within a different value system in my working-class home. It was not for leisure or pure edification; it was pursued for a practical result. My father, for example, is a highly literate man who read a newspaper daily and subscribed to three national news magazines and two academic political science journals. Not the reading material one expects from a high school dropout, yet it served his needs in the service industry, first as a barber and then as a neighborhood bar owner. It provided fodder for the continual political and sports discussions that kept customers returning. Encouraging my brother's reading served a similar purpose: a preparation for work.

My brother's literacy, however, also provided the impetus to my own. I skated on the coattails of his reputation at Edgeworth, but I also was fiercely competitive with him. Winning in sports, in school, in neighborhood fights—to not "let the fuckers beat you down"—was a value and an interest I shared with the neighborhood. That my brother's illness changed the field of this battle was incidental; I was still in it to win. And along the way what I won was a literal separation from my friends in junior high school. Junior high stands out, that is, because it was the first time I was forced to understand "difference" as not what was conferred by my school performance but something marked by my neighborhood itself. In the neighborhood, we felt superior to those kids from the adjoining areas with single-family homes and two cars or to those who brought their foreign cars to the shop; thus, I did not yet understand that in the larger world, it would be my friends and I who were considered "lower" in the hierarchy. But this was driven home vociferously in that move to junior high. Assigned a group geography project in seventh grade, I invited Lucy, one of my group members, home to complete the project. Although I was able to dismiss the growing dismay on her face as we walked from school to my neighborhood as a personality quirk, Lucy's declarations to the rest of my group members that I lived in a "ghetto" were impossible to ignore. My confusion at her statement is telling: a ghetto, I assumed, was where Jimmy Walker lived on *Good Times*. Since we didn't live in a high rise in Chicago, how could we live in a ghetto? We didn't, but Lucy had no other way of characterizing a row of three-deckers on a major urban street, a stone's throw from a cemetery, the public transportation garage, a car wash, a body shop, and a glass factory. Lucy's reaction never made me ashamed, as it was obviously intended to, but it did force me to realize what class truly meant once I ventured beyond my neighborhood.

This dawning awareness of class hierarchies compelled many of my grammar school classmates to react oppositionally. They opted out of the educational imperative to be successful and defined themselves quickly as "troublemakers with no interest in school." By eighth grade, they could be clearly distinguished from others as a group called the "Edgies," a gang name coined from the name of our grammar school. (Not surprisingly, none of the Edgies whom I know of graduated from high school.) My reaction, prompted no doubt by now being surrounded every day by the middle class, was instead to hide my background from the derisive gaze of school and peers. Never again did I invite a classmate home unless I had been to her house first or had come to trust her. I threw myself into school, maintaining the "honors" status that ensured my teachers did not identify me as an Edgie. When Mr. Rodgers happened to ask one day if anyone in our class was an Edgie, I tentatively raised my hand only to hear his shock and surprise: I didn't, in his words, look or act like one. I never openly admitted it again. These years, then, begin what I call my life as a "semi-earhole" because they did not result in the complete accommodation to school's values my desire to "hide" my background seems to indicate. Rather, this period is marked by a separation of the social and the school. Rather than bonding by opposing school, I kept my lifelines to friends and other "lasses" in my social activities and out-of-school time. I lived, that is, a double life, but not one yet prompted by some abstract desire for success beyond school.

The gratification I sought was immediate. Immersed in finding my identity via social relations (a hallmark of the budding adolescent, but especially one reared in a culture where the social *is* where life happens), I did not have a social cohort in those honors classes. Constructing a safe place there, then, meant acting as the others did, while maintaining my "true" self at home, in cheerleading, and in home economics classes where tracking was irrelevant. In short, I performed in the academic classes, not for assessment purposes, but to maintain a sense of self that wouldn't disperse endlessly into loneliness. I performed the "good student," presuming she had little association with the girl who walked home to Grove Street. Rather than rejecting the tracking that made my family so proud (and which had also, not incidentally, been accorded to Bruce), I found a way to live elsewhere—to be a semi-earhole with an emerging, although latent, class consciousness. My only transgressions in school came in that form. When asked in art class to include on our "index information cards" our fathers' place of employment, I left it blank, taking the detention that went with my refusal to fill it in when directly asked rather than admit that my father was recently unemployed, the only six-month period in my life when I remember him not working. My entire life my father had worked two or more jobs, working ten- to fifteen-hour days. When he bought his own business—by risking everything we had in the ultimate "gamble"—the long hours got even longer. I knew well that the measure of a man lay in how hard he works; I would not and could not expose this hardworking man to the school's gaze just to satisfy some art teacher's demands.

By the time I reached high school, however, performing one self while being another became difficult to maintain. Having petitioned for special permission for me to attend the "rich" public high school rather than the one I was districted for, my parents assumed they were making a decision with my best future interests in mind. For me, the division between the classes in this new school was even more obvious: a clear line was drawn early on between those of us who lived on the "wrong side of the tracks," a metaphor only in that the separating line was not tracks but Park Avenue. Again tracked into honors classes, I was one of the few students not from the west side of Park Avenue, and I became more and more determined to demonstrate that I was as "good as" the other honors students. Although I had no conscious awareness of this as a decision at the time, it is obvious in retrospect as I changed my fashion—searching the stores with my mother endlessly for Izod clones (tigers instead of alligators) and yoke sweaters made of polyester blends rather than Northern Isle—and my extracurricular activities, joining the drama club, the newspaper, and Latin club rather than cheerleading. Between these three clubs, school, and my part-time job (I started working at fourteen), I had less free time than my classmates, but I was sure never to mention this fact in those honors classes. The work ethic so ingrained during my early years, I would recognize later, was one of my greatest strengths. Speaking the value of that ethic at this age, however, seemed impossible. At this point in my life, the joy I experienced through work—and the power it gave me to buy new clothes and save for college—only reminded me that I didn't think or act like those around me. My only token resistance in high school was in my choice of friends; I held on to those from junior high like lifelines. As resistance goes, however, it was an unconscious move; I simply couldn't "connect" with my honors cohort in the same way.

This beginning accommodation to school values and ways of being is nothing if not accidental, a happenstance of changing circumstances. It was not an easy transition, however. During those high school years I also managed to get suspended for drinking on school grounds, cut school constantly, and spent most of my weekends with working-class kids from other high schools. My substance abuse, I now realize, was a vehement attempt to retain some part of the lass I was slowly losing touch with, to allay the fear that I was losing myself. I continued the lesson I had learned early: how to remain "successful" yet still be social through acts of defiance. As long as my grades didn't suffer, my minirevolutions were tolerated.

My decision to apply to college was perhaps equally capricious. On the one hand, it was prompted by my honors cohort; everyone in every class I took was planning to go to college. It seemed, naturally, the next step. But it was not a natural step at home, especially not for a girl. After many arguments, it was decided that I could apply, but only because I "didn't have a boyfriend." It seemed to my family like a good way to spend time if marriage was not immediately on the horizon. To be fair, I doubt I would have opted to go away to school had there been a man in the picture either. My continual fight to attend the state college forty miles away rather than the one in our city was prompted simply by the desire to gain some autonomy from my parents. That autonomy would have been granted had I been dating—been seen as a "woman" within the only terms that defined one's worth, the ability to attract a man. Even today, when my mother asks me if I'm happy, I reply within this currency (but now oppositionally): "At least I'm not married with four kids to support." Her reply, "Maybe you'd be happy if you were," still resonates; maybe I would be. The life of lonely exploration I was about to begin could have been forestalled; I could have remained within the confines of living in the present. Instead, my life would become a constant deferral of gratification, an accommodation to a foreign system, a way of thinking and valuing that can still seem odd.

BECOMING AN EARHOLE: THE BONDS THAT SLIP

Although much has been written about the difficult transition that working-class students experience in undergraduate education—and I must admit, my chief concern in presenting this narrative is to help configure that experience differently—I did not experience much alienation myself. Again, I attribute this to context and history. Contextually, I attended a local state college that primarily enrolled students exactly like me: first-generation students mainly from the working class. As a result, student life—if not the academic program—was familiar, populated with many other "semi-earholes" for whom working-class identifications were still strong despite our pursuit of a college degree. While many of my peers at Fitchburg State experienced more ambivalence (and many chose to leave before graduating), my immersion in a large city school system where classes were already so divided meant, simply, that I had already begun to position myself in a way that allowed this conflict to be negotiated. Like many other students, I went home most weekends to the life that felt most comfortable. I saw college primarily as a credential: a route to a certain kind of job rather than the education in the "life of the mind" my professors obviously thought it to be.

By making school into a pure structure that one must negotiate to receive a particular reward, I treated college much like a job. It became a place to do work as assigned by the supervisor (professor) rather than an engagement with the worldview embodied in the academy. I crammed for the exam only to forget the material immediately thereafter. As an English major, I read all the assigned work (but never went beyond what was assigned) and wrote personal reactions or objective analyses of a symbol or character that seemed rather pointless but got the job done. I actively participated in discussion, but with the assertion always that my position was right; discussion never seemed an opportunity to explore, only to take a position. This kind of argument, honed on my neighborhood streets, was seen as overly aggressive by many of my professors, but it also had (ironically) enough in common with agonistic forms of academic argument that it helped me "get by." The only oddities I remember from this time were primarily my professors, especially Dr. Barker, who consistently lambasted social science majors and Tupperware parties in his neighborhood. His acerbic wit was continually directed at the vocational, yet I dismissed his views as the quirks of an eccentric man rather than as a position more aligned with the academy than my own.

In this context, then, my decision to attend graduate school strikes me as odd. No one else from my graduating class of English majors even considered it a possibility. Nor did I until it was suggested by the most unlikely source: my father. Impressed with my high grades in college, he thought graduate school might provide the credentials I needed to get a better-paying job. Although he discouraged me from pursuing English any further—it was accepted initially as a major only because I was planning to teach high school, a good job for a potential mother—it was primarily his prompting that made me consider the possibility. My choice of schools (I applied to only one) was again an accident of circumstance; I had no knowledge of the usual research that went into selecting a graduate school. I found a poster advertising a program in the teaching of writing at Washington State. Because I was student teaching and struggled mostly with teaching writing, this program appealed for its practical value, but it appealed even more because it was on the West Coast. I thought traveling might be fun. That I might be asking for trouble should have been indicated early as I read over Dr. Barker's recommendation letter, which made clear that I was a good student but, in a loose paraphrase, "good for Fitchburg State, which you must realize does not have much competition," and that my thinking had potential, but it was also "very regionalized and mired in received ideas." Or perhaps the fact that I was admitted under probation even with a 3.9 should have told me that this would be no Fitchburg State experience; I had yet to understand that grades meant little when they came from certain kinds of colleges. I departed for graduate school with little expectation, then, that I would again be making a move like the one to junior high from which I would never return. With graduate school came the return not only of the double life I thought I had put behind me but also a renewed desire for sameness—to be a student and thinker like the others surrounding me in school. I was finally taught that the working-class identity I had sought to retain had no place in academia and shamefully began to make moves to erase it entirely. I took on, that is, the desire for a particular kind of success—to be part of the professional class, to be an academic in control of her work life—that had once seemed anathema to me, the eccentricities of Dr. Barker. I began, instead, to become even more a Dr. Barker than he probably was himself.

I am haunted, in particular, by a scene from the first year of my master's program where I had to do an oral presentation on a project. Throughout the presentation on Marlowe's use of techniques similar to those of absurdist dramatists, I referred to the ambivalence created within his plays toward characters, scenes, and reality itself. Yet rather than pronouncing the word "ambivalence" with a short "i" and "a," I pronounced it ambee-vaylence, with a long "a" and "c." The teacher's correction of my pronunciation did not stick, but only made me more and more nervous as my pale, redhead skin heated up to what I am sure was a deep apple blush. Leaving the classroom, I overheard two students talking, wondering "how she ever got into grad school." How indeed! How could I cover up—and I did try desperately—that the ways of speaking, writing, and even thinking that seemed to come so naturally to others seemed almost beyond my grasp? The people I conversed with did not say words like "ambivalent." How does one avoid being caught when one's reading vocabulary so exceeds her speaking vocabulary?

By deliberately refashioning herself.

To this day, I check pronunciation of a "difficult" word with a colleague before even thinking of saying it aloud in a conference paper. In my master's program, I enlisted a friend to help me out at the library, having had no experience with any of the bibliographies and indexes with which all my classmates were familiar. I asked friends to edit my written work so it would sound more "academic." I deliberately sought out students who seemed successful, made alliances with them, and found myself copying their writing styles in an attempt not to let anyone in authority know how inadequate I was to this task I had set myself. With such attempts at mimicry, I successfully rewrote myself and my thinking. I know now, of course, that these ways of writing did not come naturally to any of my classmates, but it seems as if my mimicry took on a force much stronger than my peers' because it extended beyond schooling to trying to revise eating habits, conversational patterns, the way I dressed, even how I decorated my apartment. Remarks like a friend's casual comment that he had never met another Ph.D. student who had "so few books" in her house were taken to heart as I immediately began buying books at used-book stores to make up for my inadequacies. I later took it so far as to display my professional journals in my living room. I also learned how to "mask" working-class markers well—a skill I still employ when I believe the context demands that my appropriately professional and middle-class face appear: the cocktail party at the job interview; the seemingly innocuous dinner where I know to leave sports, television, and heated political debate at home; the reminder that admitting where I received my undergraduate education will immediately diminish me in the eyes of my interlocutor. My body learned in these years how to move in professional-class ways: how to dress, speak, and socialize differently; what to say and what to silence. Although I no longer seek a complete masking, I learned much in these years about what I risked when the mask slipped and how to consciously choose when that slippage might occur.

There are, of course, disruptive moments in this narrative of completely accommodating middle-class habitus through schooling, the most obvious of which was my return to the inner city and high school teaching after earning my M.A. I longed for a familiar space—with people I understood—that might fit with this new professional self I had created. But I hadn't counted on my new desire for complete autonomy, my inability to be subservient to structure and authority in a school system where one was told what to teach. I knew this curriculum was inadequate to the needs of these students—kids like I was once, from the working-class and poor neighborhoods of Boston and Chicago—yet my attempts to reconfigure the system fell on deaf ears. Since I did not have the authority to do so, I once again sought the credential that might allow me such power: the Ph.D. With the intent to return to inner-city teaching, I moved on, but again I never returned. Instead, I learned this time around to fully invest in the materiality of thought, giving up what little sense I had of the importance of the everyday reality of oppression and the need for direct action. Working-class pragmatics finally lost to the appeal of the abstract.

But such a rewriting of self was not easily accomplished. It came with a loss of connection, of a felt surety about self and being that would be stripped away. As my body became the cultural signification of meritocracy in the university, I was continually reminded that that same body signified differently at home. While I was at school, my friends invoked my experience as proof of schooling's liberatory function as in the conversation with which I began this essay; at home the discussion proceeded differently. A summer visit during my Ph.D. program to my godmother's house is a case in point. As we sat at her Formica table drinking coffee brewed from her stove-top percolator (she refused to use the drip coffeemaker I had bought her the previous year), she excused herself briefly to go speak with a neighbor. Through the open windows I was privy to their conversation as she explained that she couldn't come over for their shared snack time that night because her goddaughter was visiting. "Is that the one that's *still* in school?" her neighbor asked. "How long has it been anyway?" My godmother's reply of "Eight years" was met with quite a lot of laughter, but her closing remark was most telling: "We think she's a little slow." The inability to explain what one did in college after four years, how one was earning degrees along the way, went directly to the heart of how much I had changed. The B.A. was one thing (it meant I had done "college"), more than that was inexplicable, unnecessary, and even an indication that perhaps I did not possess the right currency to succeed. Continual questions at family weddings about when I was "going to get a real job" or "finally get married" only brought this message home even more poignantly. I was rewriting myself so dramatically that friends and family no longer knew how to read me; I signified too differently, I did not fit into any frame of reference they had. Attempts to explain my priorities fell on deaf ears; that I would defer living—making money, having a family, even going on vacation—in favor of some hope down the road seemed ludicrous.

While much of graduate school is peppered with stories like this as I became almost a stranger to myself, I thankfully recognize now that the story is not simply assimilationist. What I once saw as "slips" to be corrected I now recognize as attempts to speak a difference I had not yet learned to devalue. Once I gained more confidence and got over the reaction that my working-class accent was "cute" or "quaint," I tried to speak the difference that kept making itself apparent, yet these attempts were wrought with tension and risk. I remember clearly how the students and professor reacted in a composition seminar when I attempted to present another cultural perspective on the connections between literacy and schooling. In response to many articles bemoaning the low literacy levels among the working class, I tried to discuss my father's own advanced literacy, pointing out that he read academic journals. Similarly, I tried to discuss why illiteracy was not as disempowering as our readings made it sound by discussing my mother's productive role in society despite the "functionally illiterate" label so many would apply to her. Highlighting the alternate literacies she had—her ability to "read" power differentials in any social situation, or to interpret signs such as clothing, body language, and other indicators of privilege in order to verbally undercut their presumed authority—I attempted to demonstrate her adept rhetorical abilities in the contexts that "mattered" more in the social real. Yet, my responses fell on deaf ears as we quickly moved on to analyzing why the readings' perspectives were more generalizable than my experiences and, thus, more valuable. Most poignant is the American literature professor who authoritatively declared that "there is no working class that wants to identify itself as such in the U.S." When I tried to explain that my own working-class experience told me that Americans *do* place value in this community, his reaction was to move on as if I had not spoken, teaching me perhaps most clearly the value of silencing this perspective.

My lived experiences in another cultural scene were not considered a valuable source of knowledge in these contexts, so I stopped talking about them. I learned my lessons well. I learned to discuss for discussion's sake, rather than to win an argument; I began to value knowledge because it was new or prompted new thinking, not for the practical result it might have; I accepted my role as cultural sign—the proof of meritocracy at work, the working-class student who had made good and through her own intelligence had exceeded her class—rather than attempting to change the way that class was viewed. In accepting my own new middle-class habitus, however, I also sensed a loss of a part of self, a part of culture, an identification with people I value, a unique way of looking at problems that had been partially wiped away by my pursuit of "success." This nagging feeling insisted that this was not all there was: there was another way of living, valuing, and making knowledge that counted. Although I had become inscribed within the dominant because of my desire for autonomy and economic success, such a new self was never an easy fit. Ironically, the academy itself was finally what gave this feeling voice.

It was only late in graduate school, through reading Foucault, Marxist theory, and feminist theory, that I began to gain a critical vocabulary that could allow me to re-see myself and the "choices" I had made over the years. Without such languages, I have to wonder if I would have ever come to claim my working-class identity as something of value, to spend time trying to convince other educators that class is not simply economic status but as real and as lived as experiences of race, gender, and sexuality. To explain the anger I can no longer submerge when I read essays like Lynn Bloom's "Freshmen English as Middle-Class Enterprise" that presume she is talking to an audience with the same middle-class backgrounds and values as her own. The professorate, I am constantly reminded, is presumed to have always been middle class. Through critical theory I gained a new voice with which to object to such characterizations, a way to offer a critique of higher education and its classed biases in teaching and scholarship that was granted authority because it was couched in continental philosophy. But it took longer to admit, to write about, to talk about how such a critical voice did not, in fact, emerge from such scholarship. It was embedded in my everyday experiences of the past and the present; it was, in a sense, the autobiography I could never write as a student.

As I began to publish on identity politics, however, the "real" autobiography changed little; the masking I had learned so well in graduate school continued to operate most persuasively in professional contexts. I still ran away to bars, to pool halls, to any working-class environment I could find for the social connections that sustained me, but in the halls of academe, my well-dressed, soft-spoken body continued to signify an acceptance of the very hierarchies my writing sought to undermine. My writing had changed dramatically, but my life continued the pattern begun in junior high. It took longer to risk more—to risk the self in social interaction, the body of the teacher/professor and the congenial colleague. The fear of losing the safety I had finally found was formidable. Even now, I can't tell how much of my newfound ability to *be* working class in the academy derives from getting tenure. Or whether it was because letting the mask slip was finally conscious enough to be a deliberate action. What I do know is that my mom might finally be proud if she knew. I now perform both parts of self in contexts that need to hear/see them. Using something akin to her rhetorical acuity in "reading power," I have become once again truly classed as I attempt to insert my body and voice into contexts where it should probably be silent.

THE PRESENT: LETTING THE HYBRID SPEAK

While my narrative typically ends here when I've told it before—with the epiphany that theory provided for reevaluating the critical potential of my past—I've come to realize that this potential was always there. By valuing my early experience, by slipping so often and attempting to voice alternative material experiences, my past continually offered a critical perspective. What I tend to think of as the need for recovery is really a need for retelling, a need to see how even in junior high or in my M.A. program there was the possibility for class consciousness if only the context had allowed it to be heard. In other words, it is only this retelling, this narrative line, that allows me to understand that my past also makes demands upon my present.

As Amy Robillard has recently argued, we have had a lot of working-class autobiography in the academy: we working-class academics chronicle tales of our pasts in an attempt to highlight class politics, but we do so by remaining located in the past, in a time when our material conditions and being seemed more seamless. In Robillard's terms, "only once we've risen above our working-class origins do we grant ourselves the luxury of looking back. And by that point, it's a modern-day rags-to-riches story; we *know* how the story will end."[14] The trick, as Robillard tells it, is to reconceive of time, to imagine that any narrative is an interpretation, a way of ordering that helps us "understand our present by interpreting our past, analyzing its details and selecting the plot line."[15] The plot line I've chosen here is, then, deliberate; it is a line that allows me to recognize my working-class roots as not a thing of the past but a reality in all the presents I chronicle here. Something not to be recovered, but relived continually within structures that might exclude it. It is this process that brings about class consciousness rather than classed identity, and it is in this move where I find hope that schooling need not be the erasure of class but the prompt to a new way of being within a classed world that can address its oppressions and seek real social change.

I am not suggesting that everyone's research agendas need to turn in the directions my own have. Rather, my call to action is much simpler: that those of us from the working class need to speak and be heard in the academy. We serve as continual reminders of the meritocracy, our very presence seeming to speak for us. Yet our voices need not accord with that cultural significa-tion. We can be continual reminders of class politics rather than class mobil-ity, and we can create spaces for class consciousness rather than routes to classed habitus in our teaching. If my own past is any indication, we're prob-ably already doing that. As a student mentioned to me a few years back, "I knew you were from the working class the first day of class." Initially startled that perhaps I had unconsciously donned the wrong mask that day, I asked her why. "Because you actually mentioned how much our books would cost when you introduced the syllabus." That such a small thing could immedi-ately change the context of the course for this student is telling. She intro-duced class topics into her papers; she offered a critique of capital based in her lived experience. She lived my class differently for no other reason than that my body in the room indicated she could. She provided hope that higher education can work differently. It cannot avoid its implication in the pro-duction of class, but it can help foster class consciousness if we create class-rooms in which such difference can be heard.

NOTES

1. See Linda Brodkey, "On the Subjects of Class and Gender in 'The Literacy Let-ters,'" *College English* 51 (1989): 125–41.

2. See Pierre Bourdieu and Jean-Claude Passeron, *Reproduction in Education, Society, and Culture,* trans. Richard Nice (London: Sage, 1990).

3. David Seitz, "Keeping Honest: Working Class Students, Difference, and Re-thinking the Critical Agenda in Composition," in *Under Construction: Working at the Intersections of Composition Theory, Research, and Practice,* ed. Christine Farris and Chris M. Anson (Logan: Utah State University Press, 1998): 71.

4. See Penelope Eckert, *Jocks and Burnouts: Social Categories and Identity in the High School* (Carbondale: Southern Illinois University Press, 1989); and Victoria Anne Steinitz and Ellen Rachel Solomon, *Starting Out: Class and Community in the Lives of Working-Class Youth* (Philadelphia: Temple University Press, 1986).

5. Paul Willis, *Learning to Labor: How Working Class Kids Get Working Class Jobs* (New York: Columbia Press, 1977), 14.

6. Willis, *Learning to Labor,* 22.

7. Willis, *Learning to Labor,* 15.

8. Willis, *Learning to Labor,* 14.

9. Willis, *Learning to Labor,* 14.

10. E. P. Thompson, *The Making of the English Working Class* (New York: Pan-theon, 1963): 9.

11. Thompson, *Making of the English Working Class,* 11.

12. Paul Trembath, "Aesthetics without Art or Culture: Toward an Alternative Sense of Materialist Agency," *Strategies* 9/10 (1995): 133.

13. Trembath, "Aesthetics without Art or Culture," 136.

14. Amy E. Robillard, "It's Time for Class: Toward a More Complex Pedagogy of Narrative," *College English* 66 (2003): 87.

15. Robillard, "It's Time for Class," 84.

REFERENCES

Bhabha, Homi. "Cultural Diversity and Cultural Difference." In *The Post-colonial Studies Reader,* ed. Bill Ashcroft, Gareth Griffiths, and Helen Tiffin. New York: Routledge, 1997.

Bloom, Lynn. "Freshman Composition as a Middle-Class Enterprise." *College English* 58 (1996): 654–75.

Bourdieu, Pierre, and Jean-Claude Passeron. *Reproduction in Education, Society, and Culture.* Trans. Richard Nice. London: Sage, 1990.

Brodkey, Linda. "On the Subjects of Class and Gender in 'The Literacy Letters.'" *College English* 51 (1989): 125–41.

Eckert, Penelope. *Jocks and Burnouts: Social Categories and Identity in the High School.* Carbondale: Southern Illinois University Press, 1989.

Robillard, Amy E. "It's Time for Class: Toward a More Complex Pedagogy of Narrative." *College English* 66 (2003): 74–92.

Seitz, David. "Keeping Honest: Working Class Students, Difference, and Rethinking the Critical Agenda in Composition." In *Under Construction: Working at the Intersections of Composition Theory, Research, and Practice,* ed. Christine Farris and Chris M. Anson. Logan: Utah State University Press, 1998.

Steinitz, Victoria Anne, and Ellen Rachel Solomon. *Starting Out: Class and Community in the Lives of Working-Class Youth.* Philadelphia: Temple University Press, 1986.

Thompson, E. P. *The Making of the English Working Class.* New York: Pantheon, 1963.

Trembath, Paul. "Aesthetics without Art or Culture: Toward an Alternative Sense of Materialist Agency." *Strategies* 9/10 (1995): 122–51.

Willis, Paul. *Learning to Labor: How Working Class Kids Get Working Class Jobs.* New York: Columbia Press, 1977.

8

White, Working Class, and Feminist: Working within the Master's House and Finding Home Again

Julie Ann Harms Cannon

> I know that some things must be felt to be understood, that despair, for example, can never be adequately analyzed; it must be lived. But if I can write a story that so draws the reader in that she imagines herself like my characters, feels their sense of fear and uncertainty, their hopes and terrors, then I have come closer to knowing myself as real, important as the very people I have always watched with awe.
>
> Dorothy Allison, *Skin*

When I saw the call for papers at my favorite regional sociological conference, I was pleased to find that there was a session that called for the articulation of working-class experiences within the academy. From the time I moved from my local community college to the more elite state university I attended in the late 1980s and early 1990s I have been conscious of my class status—essentially, I did not fit in. It was not simply because I was "older" than my more traditionally aged peers (I looked like them in every way possible—I even maintained a large credit card debt to accomplish this), rather it was because we did not share the same social-class backgrounds. I never felt like I completely "fit in"—perhaps I even felt like a fraud. I never shared the same sense of entitlement as many of my peers. They always assumed that college was for them and others like them yet this was never the case for me. While I may looked the part, I was always waiting to be "discovered" (by whom I remain unsure). I still remember how lucky I was to be "allowed" to attend a university; I still think about the ivy-covered brick buildings on our campus and get chills. I was never supposed to be there, but there I was! I could walk along with what I considered to be "rich" people and no one would be the wiser. I had the feeling that perhaps I had made it, and yet I never felt as though I had truly arrived.

During my undergraduate years I learned about the possibility of attending graduate school—imagine, me a graduate student! Of course it was not until I learned about financial aid and funding for graduate students (from another working-class academic woman, I might add) that this dream became a reality. While financial aid at the undergraduate level made my bachelor's degree possible, funding at the graduate level was about much more than obtaining a master's degree or a doctorate (although these goals were ever present). When someone, some department, was willing to fund my education I realized that maybe, just maybe, I could find a way to belong in the academy.

However, while I realized that graduate school would be hard work, I did not realize that my social-class background would have such a major impact on my experiences. While a part of me longed to leave that part of my life behind, another part of me wanted to keep the security of my family and friends at home. Ironically, neither of these things was possible. I constantly found myself betwixt and between the two—I was not one of "them" and I was having difficulty connecting with those back home. I was entering the world of the privileged in some ways, and in some ways not, and now my family and friends could not relate to me (none of these people had attended college yet). In many ways I was alone—perhaps dealing with a "double consciousness" of sorts (although I'm not sure that it is appropriate to conceptualize my experiences of class in this way).

Now I am a full-time, tenure-track sociologist, and while I have the credentials to belong, I am constantly reminded of my social-class origins. I do not have the same cultural stock of knowledge as many of my peers; academically, and indeed intellectually, I can usually hold my own, but when it comes to "high culture" or travels, I cannot always relate. Furthermore, I have a daughter who is being raised in the middle class and has no understanding of poverty in terms of her own experiences. She does not understand me, and perhaps never can, as she herself (at age seven) already expects that college is a given—in fact, she hopes to attend Princeton! In this way she is much more like my students. I am pleased on one level (this means I "made it," right?), but on another level I feel afraid. She may leave me, much as I left my family, and enter a life to which I cannot fully relate.

As I pursue my writings on class for this project, I will attempt to examine the following components of my class experiences as related to my movement into academia and middle-class life. Beginning with a discussion of "double consciousness" (Du Bois 1989, 3) and the "outsider within" (Collins 2000, 11), I examine my early educational experiences of class shame and also my movement into the predominantly middle-class world of university life at both the undergraduate and graduate levels. Next, using the works of hooks and West in *Breaking Bread* (1991) and Peggy McIntosh in "White Privilege and Male Privilege: A Personal Account of Coming to See Correspondences through Work in Women's Studies" (1988) to frame my experiences, I address the impact of social class on my everyday work life. More specifically I discuss my experiences of community and privilege at work with my colleagues and students. Finally, once again relying on the strength of bell hooks (2000b), I discuss the difficulties of leaving the academy and returning home to working-class and poor family and friends.

LEARNING WITHIN THE MASTER'S HOUSE: UNVEILING THE EFFECTS OF "DOUBLE CONSCIOUSNESS" ON THE "OUTSIDER WITHIN"

> From grade school on I feared and hated the classroom. In my imagination it was still the ultimate place of inclusion and exclusion, discipline and punishment—worse than the fascist family because there was no connection of blood to keep in check impulses to search and destroy.
>
> bell hooks, *Where We Stand: Class Matters*

I can still remember going to school, from kindergarten through high school, and feeling as if I would never be good enough. These were really not happy times for me. First of all I was overweight, but even worse than this, I was a poor kid living with a single, alcoholic mother. Although we were never on public assistance, the shame of poverty was ever present. So many markers of poverty were evident in my life that I could never easily hide my socioeconomic status from my peers, their parents, or my teachers. Another sociologist, Lillian Rubin, describes a similar experience:

> Thus, long before I became a family therapist or a social scientist, I was born into a white working-class family. I experienced all the insecurity of poverty and the pain of discovering that my teachers looked upon my widowed, immigrant mother as ignorant and upon me as a savage child. I learned young to be ashamed of my mother's foreign accent, to devalue my family, and to disesteem the culture of my home. (Rubin 1976, 12)

From the clothing I wore (not enough designer jeans or tennis shoes) to the triplex I lived in on the edge of the "good" neighborhood, my social-class standing was obvious despite my best intentions to appear "normal" or middle class. Although kids can be cruel, teasing one another mercilessly for the slightest departure from the perceived middle-class, thin norm, I do not really remember being singled out for being poor. However, I always knew it could happen to me as it did to many others. I did have to avoid certain activities or hobbies because we could not afford them (skiing in the Pacific

Northwest is a good example) but I always had friends. In this way, I was not a complete outcast. But to remain unscathed in the classroom or on the bus ride home took a great deal of effort. I tried to "fly below the radar" as best I could and was typically successful, meaning that I remained somewhat, if not totally, invisible. It is this invisibility that becomes a major source of anguish, not just for the poor child, but also for those who manage upward mobility. This is a particularly dangerous existence that leads to many problems despite all outward appearances of having "made it" in the eyes of others. Getting out, while better than struggling within the confines of a life of poverty, comes at an emotional cost—one I have experienced firsthand. As an outsider within the academy I am glad to finally give voice to the poor kid who lives alongside Dr. Cannon (me—it is still a surprise to hear it!) every day.

Although Collins describes this outsider-within status as a positive characteristic in that it gives the stranger additional insight that those within the inner circle do not have, it also carries with it the pain of bifurcated consciousness, or double consciousness, in W. E. B. Du Bois's terms: "It is a peculiar sensation, this double-consciousness, this sense of always looking at one's self through the eyes of others, of measuring one's soul by the tape of a world that looks on in amused contempt and pity" (Du Bois 1989, 3). More specifically regarding socioeconomic status, one can observe the middle-class life and understand its requirements and at the same time realize that understanding the "other" does not guarantee acceptance or access to that world. That equal opportunity is a myth is a painful reality understood by many working-class children. This being said, these same children, myself included, often continue to work within the "master's house" (Lorde 1984, 12) to achieve some semblance of the American dream despite the fact that the tools necessary to achieve these dreams are placed out of the reach of the poor. The explicit rules of the game are clearly evident in our schools, media, religions, and so on; however, the outcomes are often beyond the control of the working class and the poor. Without knowledge of the implicit rules, information that is often taken for granted by those living and working within the middle class, the game cannot be won. Further, these outsiders are often blamed for their inability to succeed. It is this quandary that Du Bois wrote about (1989, 3). The game appears to be fair from the inside as the privilege system tends to be made invisible to the privileged (McIntosh 1988), but those on the outside know that their chances of succeeding are virtually nonexistent and yet they continue to try. This contributes to feelings of hopelessness and self-loathing that are at times actually exacerbated by increased knowledge of the system; it works both ways: at times the pain of double consciousness is most salient, while at others the second sight afforded to the outsider opens new and exciting doors.

I got out of poverty almost by accident. After graduation from high school I learned that working at the local mall or fast food establishment, besides being both physically and psychologically stressful, would never do much to increase my life chances. My mom suggested community college (I had never really considered college despite the fact that teachers often told me I was bright) and offered to pay for a quarter if I would try it out, so off I went. Of course I did not take school seriously at first—it made no sense to me, it just did not seem to be a part of the "real" world. I did not understand how an art history class would help my employment chances later on. Yet I stuck with it and eventually met the professor who literally changed my life. To this day, she is one of the toughest instructors I have ever had. She had just received her doctorate from a very prestigious university and was determined that we would receive a good education. Her standards were very high in comparison with those of her peers, yet she motivated us to perform at our best and we/I did. I earned an A in each of her courses, and from then on I knew that I could earn good grades as long as I worked hard. I didn't have to have the right car, clothes, parents, house, or friends. I just had to learn and work hard, which I was more than ready to do because school mattered to me. In other words, once the door was finally opened, I discovered that I indeed possessed the intellectual ability to succeed in an academic environment. Furthermore, I realized that school did not have to be a source of pain, it could become a site of empowerment (which I had always thought it should be despite the fact that it had not actually worked out that way for me; I was unable to apply this knowledge to my situation because I had no reason to trust myself and what I knew to be true, not yet anyway). Believe it or not, it was during this time that I decided to go to graduate school and become a professor (originally I thought I would teach anthropology, but that was to change later on). What a dream! Could a girl like me really become a person of such status? I was skeptical but determined to achieve this goal; I wanted to be "normal" and I thought this would be the best way to become "someone" in the eyes of others (I was not really doing it for me yet). I did not know where I would get the money to pay for graduate school, but I knew I would go some way, somehow. But first, I had to complete my undergraduate degree.

I never imagined that I would head off to the university; it was never considered or discussed while I was in high school, probably because I was poor and also because I had really given up and no longer made any effort to shine in school. Despite my best efforts earlier in school I was always put in the "average" reading group, the "average" penmanship group, the "average" art group. Even though I knew that these decisions were inaccurate, I could not keep others from coming up with this assessment of my abilities and then tracking me accordingly. (It was not until graduate school that I learned about tracking and that working-class children and children of color are disproportionately placed into the lower educational tracks. I had been right all along, but again didn't believe that I could be right.) Although bright, I think I gave up. It hurt too much to be found wanting by those I trusted to help me, my teachers. I desperately sought their approval and validation, but it really didn't come until high school, and by then it was too late; I no longer cared and it showed. I took easy classes, skipped school, focused on beauty and dating, avoided any serious schoolwork, and had fun—finally! If I could not be one of the smart kids, being popular would certainly do for the moment.

In addition to my scholastic apathy (despair?), I knew that the local private university was not for me; my family did not have the money for me to attend. The university was always present in our city, but it was never held out as a possibility (by my teachers or my parents). The guidance counselors at my school, overworked I am sure, did not tell everyone about college. They had one advanced program (which I self-selected myself into because of a friend and backed out of because I didn't think I was smart enough), and as far as I know (or recall), only these students were seriously groomed for college; the teachers and staff were content as long as the rest of us were not out wandering the halls or making trouble. Because of this, I never learned about financial aid. I never learned about student loans or grants and assumed that I was not smart enough to earn a scholarship—the only way for a student like me to finance an education. I do not argue that this would have been an option, given my attitude about school, but I never even had the opportunity to say no. Having the option might have made things seem fair somehow. Maybe it would not have made a difference, I do not know. I do know, however that it was not because of my lack of trying, not initially anyway. I wanted to be noticed and I wanted to succeed, but how many times can a child be overlooked or dismissed as "average" before she begins to believe it herself? I still asked myself that very question as I watched the "average" students in my daughter's first-grade class, students whose parents might not have had the opportunity to learn about the impact of social class or how to advocate for their bright but poor children. Do they assume, much as I did, that the teachers are there to protect and reward their children as long as they try hard? How long will it be before their children are worn down by the brutality of a system designed to reward only the "best" and the bright, or more accurately the upper classes?

But I did find out about financial aid (again, accidentally) and the doors to one of our finest state universities were opened to me—imagine that! I was slightly older than the average student and worked part time to pay for food and other bills accrued through my attempts to finance the good things in life (e.g., wardrobe, cosmetics, furniture). My mother paid my rent all but three months per year—loan checks only covered that much—or I would have been unable to meet my expenses. It was a lot of money for her at the time, but she managed (as she always did).

THE OUTSIDER ENTERS THE MASTER'S HOUSE:
WORKING CLASS AND WORKING WITH COLLEAGUES

Attending college was not immediately rewarding for me. I still had no idea of what a person like me could hope to become in such a place or how it was in any way relevant to my life. I passed my classes (at times by the skin of my teeth) and worked my way through the required courses, but I was merely drifting through community college life. But one person changed all of that for me—a professor who saw my potential and took the time to encourage me changed my life forever. I quickly became interested in earning high marks and demonstrating to the world and to myself that I could be more than what I was; I could become a professor.

Of course that required transferring to a "real" university and completing my bachelor's degree, but that all seemed possible somehow. With some assistance from my mother for living expenses and the promise of grants and student loans, I moved away from my family and began my academic career. Of course I was driven to succeed and did so, but I was unsure how one moved on to graduate school. However, I seemed to know that the right person would come along to help me with this as well, and she did. Once again a strong woman believed in me and took the time to explain the mysteries of the GRE, graduate school applications, and funding, and one year after earning my B.A. I was on my way to a large research university with full funding. I was getting paid to go to school—I had to keep pinching myself to make sure that it was reality and not a dream.

> Those of us who stand outside the circle of this society's definition of acceptable women; those of us who have been forged in the crucibles of difference—those of us who are poor, who are lesbians, who are Black, who are older—know that *survival is not an academic skill.* It is learning how to stand alone, unpopular and sometimes reviled, and how to make common cause with those others identified as outside the structures in order to define and seek a world in which we can all flourish. It is learning how to take our differences and make them strengths. *For the master's tools will never dismantle the master's house.* (Lorde 1984, 112)

Not surprisingly, the "veil" of poverty cannot be easily pushed aside to allow one to cross over into the middle-class life. In fact, the shame of poverty and the pain of double consciousness followed me into the middle class. For this reason I have had to rely on many forms of "beloved community" to see me through. "When we talk about that which will sustain and nurture our spiritual growth as a people, we must once again talk about the importance of community. For one of the most vital ways we sustain ourselves is by building communities of resistance, places where we know we are not alone" (hooks and West 1991, 17). Although hooks and West (1991) specifically refer to

African Americans, this quote captures the way I often feel as a feminist working-class academic. We need communities to resist the forces of traditional middle-class ideologies with the academy. This jargon of this omnipresent ethos is part of the language I have learned to speak, but it is one that does not speak to my growth as a scholar. My energy is increased by connections with others who *know* what life on the other side of the tracks is really like. This understanding, because it is a given in virtually any of our conversations, allows us to assume a particular worldview, and thus our energy is used more efficiently. Today's youth articulate this state in the expression "I feel you," and this expresses how I feel when I am in the midst of individuals with similar class origins.

It is difficult to express the taken-for-granted comfort I feel when I am in my element, so to speak. At these moments, and they can be few and far between, I can be myself without waiting for the other shoe to drop. At times it is easier to identify the feeling by articulating what my work life is like when I am *not* in this place. Now do not get me wrong, I still enjoy working and socializing with many of my academic friends and acquaintances, but it just is not the same. My guard is almost up in these situations, and the solace or safety I experience with my working-class peers disappears, leaving me feeling as if my social class is on display for the world to see and judge. That judgment, either real or perceived, is inevitably followed by the sting of shame that comes with not measuring up to middle-class standards of speech, dress, knowledge, wealth, and so on. I do not have easily at my disposal the reference to the right piece of literature, knowledge of "good" wine, or experience of traveling abroad. My car, while functional, new, and under warranty for ten years or one hundred thousand miles (a major source of security and pride in my life) pales in comparison with the latest sport utility vehicles, luxury sedans, or sports cars. I rent my home because we are not financially prepared to buy yet as we are still in debt from graduate school, among other things. I do not own my own regalia to participate in the numerous ceremonies I am asked to attend, nor did I even know how to wear it the first time I tried on my rental. I do not speak Latin or "Robert's Rules of Order" (which makes understanding a faculty meeting quite difficult). All of this leaves me feeling like an impostor waiting to be found out and dismissed (both literally and figuratively).

In addition to feeling out of place in social activities, I sometimes feel that my colleagues do not understand my need to write about the oppressed. Scholars working on social-justice-related research are often viewed with suspicion by their peers. This is true despite the fact that race, class, and gender studies have become more widely integrated into the sociology curriculum. But my experiences of classism and class shame have shaped my research interests. This was also true for Lillian Rubin, as she explains in her books *Worlds of Pain* (1976) and *Families on the Fault Line* (1994), Rubin writes:

> For many years now I have been writing about those in our society whose voices are muted or silent. The subject matter has been diverse—race, class, and gender—but always the intent has been to give voice to the voiceless. Scratch the intellectual preoccupations, however, and there's almost always a personal source. So although these issues have been at the heart of my professional concerns for nearly a quarter of a century, my interest and involvement in them grows out of personal experiences long before I was old enough to think about such concepts as "the voiceless." As a child whose first language wasn't English, I didn't have to *think* about not having a voice that could be heard. I experienced it viscerally each time I stepped outside the small, dark apartment my family called home. (1994, xiv)

My sociological training informs my research, much as it does Rubin's, and like Rubin I know firsthand what it is like to be poor and this experience shapes all of the work I do. It is what I know and it is what I want others to understand. When my colleagues overlook this need, despite the fact that they now know of my social-class background, I often feel hurt, rejected, and misunderstood. Again, I feel the pain of double consciousness as I once again realize that I am an outsider within my department.

But why do I feel such discomfort? My peers are certainly gracious, and given that they are sociologists, most recognize that social-class differences exist among us. For this reason, it is unlikely that my social-class location is ever mentioned. But silence, like invisibility, does not offer protection to the working-class academic. Rather, it seems to indicate only tolerance of a sort, not actual acceptance. You are tolerated until you learn to fit in or assimilate into the middle class. But here is the rub: I may learn to fit in, but I never feel welcome or understood. The working-class academic can at times cloak him- or herself in the garb of the middle class, but for many the cloak never actually fits comfortably, or it is removed to "go home" again.

But how does one slip into and out of class location—either past or present—with ease and grace? I find this transition to be very difficult, particularly with my students. While they enjoy my informality and use of slang (both remnants of my class background, I am sure), they are not always so kind when dealing with issues of privilege and poverty. In fact, the classroom is often a confusing mixture of joy and pain as my students and I traverse the boundaries and barriers of class.

PEDAGOGY OF THE PRIVILEGED: WORKING-CLASS ACADEMICS TEACHING PRIVILEGED STUDENTS

> By the early eighties the idea that sexism and racism had been eradicated, coupled with the assumption that the existing white supremacist capitalist

patriarchy could work for everybody gained momentum and with it the notion that those groups for whom it did not work were at fault.

bell hooks, Where We Stand: Class Matters

Many greedy upper- and middle-class citizens share with their wealthy counterparts a hatred and disdain for the poor that is so intense it borders on pathological hysteria. It has served their class interests to perpetuate the notion that the poor are mere parasites and predators.

bell hooks, Where We Stand: Class Matters

Teaching privileged students of any type (e.g., race class, gender, sexual orientation) can definitely be a challenge for the working-class academic; it certainly has been difficult for me at times. The central or defining issues appear to be related to assumptions of entitlement and deservedness. Many, perhaps even most, of my students come to the university from middle-class family backgrounds. This is overwhelmingly true when I consider the students in my honors courses. Not surprisingly, these more-privileged students know very little of the poor and the working class. Most of their information is derived from the stereotypical accounts gleaned from the media or their parents. Because of this I often hear rather hostile remarks regarding the parenting, work ethics, morality, and spending habits of the poor. So much of my students' own privilege is "hidden" to them that they do not yet realize that the so-called American dream is not as easily obtained as they have been taught to believe. The argument that anyone can do what they or their parents have done if they simply work hard enough is an emphatic belief that is held by many of my students. However, when these ideas are expressed in the classroom, I often feel alone and indignant because I know firsthand that this belief is both false and hurtful.

"The poverty I knew was dreary, deadening, shameful, the women powerful in ways not generally seen as heroic by the world outside the family" (Allison 1999, 15). But the students I meet typically do not understand the ability of a poor single mother to create a delicious meal for three out of some hot dogs, noodles, and a few vegetables. My mother made meager meals look like feasts and in that way did much to assuage the feelings of shame attached to our lives. She put on a brave face for us nearly every day and made my friends' mouths water for her delicious "tea biscuits" that were really nothing more than flour, shortening, baking powder, and a little milk. She knew how to make life special and fun because she remembered the importance of such moments from her own childhood. But this world, the everyday emotional and physical survival of the poor, is for the most part hidden from the lives of the middle class. Marks (2000) addresses the invisibility of privilege in the following discussion of his upper-middle-class upbringing:

Within this overall framework in which wealth was pitted against poverty as if in mortal combat, I learned a set of upper-middle-class entitlements presented almost as axioms about how my life would unfold. . . . I learned to assume the ultimate function of education is to prepare you for a prestigious profession; that work in your job will be stimulating, enjoyable, socially important, even fun; and that very ample income—far more than "enough to support your family"—is a mere byproduct of this important work you do. . . . Perhaps most important, I learned that there are no externally imposed constraints to arriving at your chosen profession. (616)

Intellectually, "the hidden nature of privilege" (McIntosh 1988) makes perfect sense to me in a purely academic way. I understand why my students have to be taught to actually see the effects of privilege in their own lives, but that does not always help during my initial encounters with them. More specifically, I have to acknowledge that I am frequently hurt and angered by the lack of compassion expressed about those whom they view as deserving to be poor or struggling. But why is it sometimes so difficult to forgive them their ignorance? I think it is because, albeit unknowingly, their hostility is aimed directly at me and my own.

During some moments I actually have a desire to retaliate with my own stereotypical accounts of spoiled "rich" kids. I know this is childish, but the pain often makes me feel irrational and unable to draw on my more intellectual or objective responses to such criticisms. At times I feel as though I am being personally attacked and publicly shamed. At times I feel as if I must defend myself. But this is really an attachment I feel to the shame of being poor and different as a child. The poor girl I was continues to be wounded by these remarks because the middle-class professional woman I've become is not comfortable enough in this new skin to relate to their ignorance of class privilege.

Of course some days are easier than others. When I watch my students grapple with notions of class and their attempts to understand the lives of the working poor, the unemployed, or the homeless, I am understandably more tolerant. But on those days when they are feeling superior and more deserving than the poor, I feel a rage that at times is nearly impossible to tamp down.

While any professor, even the most cynical, might be taken aback by the insensitivity of students regarding the poor, the feelings can be much stronger when you have lived the life of those they regard with such disdain. For me, it is a challenge to remain objective in my assessment of their discussions and their work. I must admit that at times I want to take my anger and frustration out on them. But of course this is not an option, nor would it be effective. Rather, I have to work very hard to find ways for them to walk in the shoes of the poor and gain insight into the workings of class privilege in our society. I can share my own experiences of poverty and social-class mobility so that they understand the capricious element in my making it out of poverty. Additionally, I can share with them the importance education holds for me and exactly why I become so angry when they take theirs for granted. I value beyond measure the education that I have been fortunate enough to receive. While I worked hard to earn each of my degrees, including my doctorate, I never allow myself to forget the alternatives that could just as easily become my reality today had I not been so lucky. I could have easily remained a retail sales associate, working slightly above minimum wage yet required to foot the bill for fancy clothes and accessories; or, better still, I could have returned to work as a fast food restaurant manager earning essentially a minimum-wage salary because of the typical fifty- to sixty-hour workweek required for those lucky enough to be salaried as opposed to hourly employees. Although sometimes health care is an option at such jobs, neither pays a high enough wage nor garners enough prestige to move one out of poverty or the working class. Additionally, both are such highly stressful jobs that the quality of life for the worker is quite low. The employee spends the vast majority of time, even time off, trying to devise new ways to earn a profit. Of course the profit never really trickles down to the employee, it may simply ensure employment for another month during which the employees must again prove themselves worthy of employment. I have done this work and I am able to let my students know how lucky we all are to be at the university.

But as one moves into the middle class and becomes even slightly more comfortable there, it is easy to lose sight of the discomfort the working class or the poor experience as they interact with those who are more privileged. While I may feel my working-class identity quite strongly, once you escape the confines of poverty you become one of "them," and it may actually become quite difficult for those you left behind to feel comfortable around you. I have experienced this quite frequently with my family and friends when I try to go home again. Home always looks different to me, and I always look different to the people there. Again, I have become the outsider within, although in a totally unexpected way.

BETWIXT AND BETWEEN BUT NEVER BELONGING: GOING HOME AGAIN TO WORKING-CLASS FAMILY AND FRIENDS

When I chose to attend a "fancy" college rather than a state school close to home, I was compelled to confront class differences in new and different ways. Like many working-class parents, my folks were often wary of the new ideas I brought into their lives from ideas learned at school or from books. They were afraid these fancy ideas like the fancy schools I wanted to attend would ruin me for living in the real world. At the time I did not understand that they were also afraid of me becoming a different person—someone who did not speak their language, hold on to their beliefs and ways. They were working people. To them, a good life was one where you worked hard, created a family, worshipped God, had the occasional good time, and lived day to day.

bell hooks, *Where We Stand: Class Matters*

While in graduate school I experienced the frustration of not being able to explain myself to my family and friends. They had no idea how hard I was working or why I would even put myself through such trials and tribulations. Additionally, my family and friends assumed that if I was willing to work so hard, I must have plans of becoming rich upon completion of my degree—hardly! It made no sense to many of them that I would struggle for so hard and for so long to make the same salary I could make working retail at home. It was lonely at times to be so far away from the ones I loved, but it was much more painful to know that they no longer understood my everyday life or what or who I was becoming. In addition, the social support they had to offer could no longer reassure me in times of crisis (e.g., my first graduate statistics exam, conducting research projects, teaching a college-level course). "It did not take long for me to understand that crossing class boundaries was not easy" (hooks 2000b, 144).

However, I made one serious miscalculation on my journey to the middle class: I assumed that those I left behind, particularly my family, would be understanding of the changes taking place in my life. I could not have been more wrong on this count. As long as I sounded like the old Julie they knew, things were good; "I could go home again. I could blend in, but the doors to that world threatened to close whenever I tried to bring new ideas there, to change things there" (hooks 2000b, 146). While they never stopped loving or missing me while I was away, they no longer knew what to do with me when I returned home during vacations from school. Yet for me, while "I was struggling to acquire an education that would enable me to leave the ranks of the poor and working-class, I was still more at home in that world than I was in the world I lived in" (hooks 2000b, 145). But what do you do when you go home again and the door is only grudgingly opened to you?

It would be bad enough if lack of acceptance was all that I experienced, but then came the anger. I can honestly say that this resentment and anger on the part of my family blindsided me. What had I done? Were they no longer proud of me? How had I failed them? I asked myself these questions and then finally had to ask my family. Although I am clearer now on why they responded as they did, at the time I was truly shocked. Essentially, they believed that I thought I was too good for them and thought less of them for their lack of advanced education. They thought I used big words to make them look foolish and that I no longer valued the work they did. They thought they were an embarrassment to me. Where did this come from? I thought they wanted me to go to school. I was still the same person I had always been, or at least I thought so. What had I said to hurt them in this way? Why did they feel so rejected by me when I was so glad to see them? Well, of course they wanted me to go to school and to become whatever my heart desired, but at the same time they were not expecting me to change so much from my experiences.

I somehow negotiated the boundaries of class; it became somewhat easier as my mother and youngest brother began to earn their way out of the working class (despite the fact that they both strongly identify as working class). However, some difficulties remain. These difficulties exist with all my family members "back home" and even with my newfound older brother. It seems that similar incomes do not make us equal—as a sociologist I should have understood this better! Although it seems somewhat obvious to me now, it took me some time to understand that my doctorate and also my academic career may always create some tension on the part of my family. My father and older brother hate it when I refer to my coworkers as "colleagues" because to them this sounds elitist (perhaps they are right on that one). My younger brother expresses both feelings of pride at my success and shame at his failings. His feelings of inadequacy are very real despite the fact that he has worked for a decade at the same job at a local cable company and that we both make about the same yearly salary. We are separated by my degrees.

CONCLUSION

Where does all this leave me? On many days I just feel caught in the middle. It is hard to find a way to please the many players involved in my everyday life, and at times it is even harder to figure out what it is I actually want and where I feel most comfortable. But what I try to remember, and it is not always so easy, is that struggling with issues of upward mobility is a luxury that most people from my background will never know. I am grateful that I have been given the opportunity to earn my doctorate, that I work in a job that allows me some autonomy, creativity, and respect, that I have the means to assist my father with his retirement so that he can live with me and live with more dignity than his Social Security income would allow, and ultimately that my daughter can move through the world without worrying about things like meals, new clothes, rent, and her future education.

However, being grateful for my current middle-class life does not mean that I do not struggle with my past and present lives. I still feel some distance between my family and myself at times. I still feel the stinging shame of poverty at times when my students or my colleagues refer to important works of literature, art, and so on that I know nothing about. On some days, I am still angry at my students' ignorance of privilege. But what I have come to realize is that every day I move through the world at work and at home, my double consciousness eases somewhat and I feel like less of an impostor or outsider in either of my lives. Further, I can also work with those around me to understand the intricacies of class privilege and the feelings that such a system generates for all of its members. In this way the dynamics of class are made visible, and the hate and shame so prevalent in our society can be diminished for some.

It has been a privilege to write this chapter. It has helped me both to understand my own experiences as a member of the working class and also to understand why I must continue my work as a feminist sociologist. "Simply being the victim of an exploitive or oppressive system and even resisting it does not mean we understand why it's in place or how to change it" (hooks 2000a, 21).

And when my seven-year-old daughter asks me about the type of essay I am writing and if I mentioned her in it, I can tell her yes, and so much more. I can also express to her some of the hidden injuries and benefits of class that I have come to know from living on both sides of the tracks. This way, when she leaves to attend college one day (which for her is a given, it seems), she will know that she is lucky to be sitting in that classroom and that such an opportunity cannot be wasted because there is someone just like her mother, uncles, cousins, and grandparents who will not be there with her.

REFERENCES

Allison, Dorothy. 1999. *Skin*. Ithaca, NY: Firebrand Books.

Collins, Patricia Hill. 2000. *Black Feminist Thought: Knowledge, Consciousness, and the Politics of Empowerment*. New York: Routledge.

Du Bois, W. E. B. 1989 (1901). *The Souls of Black Folk*. New York: Bantam Books.

hooks, bell. 1999. *Remembered Rapture: The Writer at Work*. New York: Henry Holt.

———. 2000a. *Feminism Is for Everybody: Passionate Politics*. Cambridge, MA: South End Press.

———. 2000b. *Where We Stand: Class Matters*. New York: Routledge.

hooks, bell, and Cornel West. 1991. *Breaking Bread: Insurgent Black Intellectual Life*. Cambridge, MA: South End Press.

Lorde, Audre. 1984. *Sister Outsider: Essays and Speeches by Audre Lorde*. Trumansburg, NY: Crossing Press.

Marks, Stephen R. 2000. "Teasing Out the Lessons of the 1960s: Family Diversity and Family Privilege." *Journal of Marriage and the Family* 62 (August): 609–22.

McIntosh, Peggy. 1988. "White Privilege and Male Privilege: A Personal Account of Coming to See Correspondences through Work in Women's Studies." Working Paper 189. Wellesley College Center for Research on Women, Wellesley, MA.

Rubin, Lillian B. 1976. *Worlds of Pain: Life in the Working-Class Family*. New York: Basic Books.

———. 1994. *Families on the Fault Line: America's Working Class Speaks about the Family, the Economy, Race, and Ethnicity*. New York: HarperCollins.

9

"Gimme That!": The Working-Class Student Meets the Working-Class Subject

William J. Macauley Jr.

> The vehicle merchant of Winesburg, like thousands of other men of his times, was an enthusiast on the subject of education. He had made his own way in the world without learning got from books, but he was convinced that had he but known books things would have gone better with him.
>
> Sherwood Anderson, *Winesburg, Ohio*

I remember waking that morning, after the last of the graduation parties, knowing that it was Monday, that I had to go to work. My mind was immediately there. I had to wonder whether I would be working that day as a driver or dispatcher. The Wednesday before, Janice and Milt had called me into their office yet again, for the fourth time in as many weeks. They sat behind their monolithic desk in chairs that were at least six inches higher than the one they expected me to take. I suspected they thought I hadn't noticed the distance and perspective they had intentionally created.

"We're getting complaints again, Bill. The drivers don't like the way you're treating them."

"What's the problem now?"

"You're pushing them too hard." I don't remember which of them was speaking to me, but I do remember thinking that I was close enough to graduation—just days away—that I didn't have to take it anymore. "They say you're acting like a . . . like a . . . well . . . like a smart-ass college kid."

Without a moment's hesitation, I replied, "I am a smart-ass college kid, the same one you both helped get to be a dispatcher before you were in charge." I paused, just long enough to realize that I had been outed, that I had suddenly made my first public claim to that title: college kid (even though I was

117

twenty-six-plus). We all recoiled a little, wide eyed, "taken aback," as my mother would have said.

"You know," I said, breathing in deeply, feeling my chest fill and expand, "I've been working here for seven years. I've been a dispatcher for three. There were never any complaints until you two took over. One week you haul me in here to tell me that I'm not pushing the drivers hard enough, so I push them harder. The next week, you call me in here to say I'm pushing them too hard, so I back off. And these meetings are never on the clock, either. Now, all of a sudden, my college education is the problem. For the extra 25 cents I get an hour to dispatch, put me back on the road if you don't like what I'm doing. It's a hell of a lot easier. Otherwise, leave me alone and let me do my job."

My ears warmed that morning as I replayed the scene, listened to what I had said again and again. At the open casement window facing my street, I took stock of where I was, what I had accomplished. I suppose I had never before really thought of actually having a degree, as opposed to working on one, but there I was. Graduated. As had been the habit of so many people in my life over the prior eight years, I was telling myself stories of the better life almost guaranteed by my brand-new, completed college degree. I said, quietly, toward the window and whatever lay beyond it, "Here I am world, a college graduate."

I waited for something to feel different, better. I waited there looking, scanning, staring, hoping for something camouflaged, moving carefully behind another thing, that would verify that I could see more and differently. I may have by then taken one too many fiction courses, but I could swear that I eventually heard a distant, small voice somewhere in the deep recesses reply. "Yeah? So what," it said. I knew, right then, that I would be late for work.

Even months later, the future still seemed to lie before me, but the life I could see seemed so uninspired, even after I had moved, started a new job, and begun abusing my first credit cards (for which I was preapproved as a new college graduate). The view of myself as the road warrior–intellectual had all but evaporated in the heat of a sixth week of seventy-plus unairconditioned hours behind the wheel of an airfreight delivery truck. The hotshots at night were just too lucrative to turn down, even though it meant that I would only see my bed momentarily and the shower twice each day, once to wind down and once to wake up, before I worked again. I became much more sensitive to the lives of my parents, even if I lost something in sympathy and tact. "Dad, how can you stand to go to that factory day after day, year after year?" I asked after my mother forced him to drive her the half hour to my apartment. "Why don't you want more out of life than . . . just . . . *this*, Ma?"

I had been duped by deferred gratification. I had been played like a Woolworth's guitar without the chord book. I was a junkie with a desperate physical addiction to schooling and no means by which to quell my craving. "Nobody ever told me I couldn't go back to my life," I often complained from my Sunday afternoon stool on the long side of Mulligan's bar. And, besides all of that, I felt like a fake, like a K-tel college graduate.

My malaise was at least partially attributable to senioritis, to separation anxiety. Having a long-term goal yanked out from in front of you is hard. However, my assumed departure from academe and desperate alienation in life outside of it resulted from the cultural distances between academe and the working-class life I was leading, as well as the barriers constructed to discourage border crossings between them.[1] At school, I had been part of the crowd, one unremarkable face among many; away from school, I was consistently saying the wrong thing, constantly suspect, frequently accused of judgments that had not even occurred to me but sounded reasonable when they were pointed out. I seldom feel quite so desperate now because I have a regular fix, so to speak (a tenure-track job), but I continue to wonder about why my education made life feel so miserable then.

The best evidence of these border skirmishes I experienced were the family stories told around schooling, and how those stories changed over time. When I went off to college the first time, my parents were filled with pride and excitement, as far as I could tell, because I was going to have a better life. They weren't sure how that would happen or when, but they were willing to trust that a college education would improve my life significantly (I was not as trusting but preferred college to a full-time assembly-line job). Not much later, I was accused of avoiding my responsibilities. Soon, my family told me and themselves that a college education made my life easier, too easy, and they found that I was harder to get along with because I wasn't satisfied to just be educated. My friends at school told me that I only drove a truck for a living because I wanted to collect characters for my stories, and speculated that I worked because my parents could but wouldn't pay for my schooling. Later, they were traveling, telling Europe and Colorado stories in letters and postcards. My supervisors, at one time, told themselves that I was reliable and responsible. Later, I was "that smart-ass college kid." I had continually told myself that, after graduation, I would have options. From June on, I could only see that I no longer belonged anywhere; my trucking job was the only thing that seemed to make sense, and only because I was never anywhere long enough to care about belonging.

These stories, these experiences are far from unique for a blue-collar kid trying to better himself. Even so, and maybe because they are so usual, they have had a profound impact on my professional work. Only continual schooling and ongoing critical inquiry have quieted any of the displacement I felt. And, it doesn't go away, at least not for me. It only subsides periodically, when I can bring who I was into who I have become. Because of this, I have wanted to enable students' bringing with them into academe in overt, informed, and critical ways, familiar stories, narratives, literacies, rhetorics, and paradigms for learning and knowing, in the hope that a bridging can occur. Critical analysis earlier might have enabled me to navigate those stories more successfully.

I would like my working-class students to feel a little less isolated and polemical, a bit less like cultural traitors. At least first-year composition could become a space where students could learn an academic culture within which, as Bartholomae suggests, they can "work closely with the ways their writing constructs a relationship with tradition, power and authority—with other people's words."[2] A greater academic openness to the incorporation of currently alternative rhetorics, narratives, and paradigms would, as Elbow hopes, "get there by a path where the student is steering, not me."[3] The path lay ahead—and it is opening more and more as we explore the power and importance of this negotiation.

In some ways, Sophistry is not dead in that so many of us teach from a range of social-constructionist perspectives. Williams writes that "although we know little about the philosophies the Sophists taught in conjunction with rhetoric . . . we do know they tended to be relativists, believing that the truth concerning any issue depends on one's point of view."[4] Early iterations of our active role in creating knowledge and reality are available here. Academics, it might be said, prize logic, reason, and clarity in writing because we agree that there are few if any capital-T truths, that it really is a matter of perspective to one degree or another.

This idea of construction dovetails nicely and not coincidentally with the progressive ideas of John Dewey, who wrote that "education in order to accomplish its ends for both the individual and for society must be based upon some experience—which is always life-experience of some individual."[5] Our interest in personal writing, especially in freshman comp and especially in academically reified forms, might be a good example of our efforts to make that connection between the individual and the societal, bringing the personal into the public and vice versa. This agenda also foreshadows much of the current interest in community-based and service learning. However, the reasons this has been an uphill battle are not entirely theoretical.

We academics have created and perpetuated a culture of transience, a system of enclaves for people from somewhere else. We move around a lot. Seldom do we live and work where we came from. This shapes us in some peculiar ways that influence directly how we work.

As we consider who we are, what our culture is, it is not difficult to find contrasts with the cultural backgrounds of many working-class students. Because we are less thoroughly (or extensively) anchored in particular communities or neighborhoods, we have fewer opportunities to develop deep narratives of our lives there. There may be reasons other than physical ones that our campuses feel separate from the communities within which they exist. Because there is always a chance that we could move again, our relationships with communities are less entrenched than they might be for those born and raised there. Even when we do feel settled, within our academic communities there is so much coming and going that we have difficulty feeling any sense of stability. And this has a very direct and significant impact on how we think about teaching writing.

We are transients, we academics. Because we are transients, we need portable work, including our writing assignments. We don't want our work to be contextually bound because it means that it won't work elsewhere. This doesn't just mean our teaching; our scholarship reflects this interest as well. When we read our journals and newsletters, we look for consideration of unique contextual factors to be discussed and reviewed only after the more theoretical (and thereby more widely applicable) discussions have been completed. We look for the knowledge, thinking, argument that is applicable beyond a particular context, what some refer to as the transcendent. In other words, we don't want to read about what happened there, to them, unless we can take it with us, too. Portability.

A working-class student comes to English 101 and is asked to write an expository essay about an experience that changed her life. The student thinks hard about this assignment, completes several free-writing sessions, works with a writing tutor on identifying workable ideas, and she even does the readings for class that should help her to get it all going.

Her motorcycle accident is the life-changing event on which she has written. She crashed the bike when a gust of wind blew through a gap in the dunes and pushed her off Lakeshore Drive near Camp Kiwanis. She shattered her hip—three steel pins—and spent the summer in the hospital. She can probably never have kids naturally. She bought the motorcycle because it was cheap and because her father had always spoken so lovingly about that BMW he owned while he was in the service in Germany.

Her mother has always been opposed to the motorcycle because motorcycles are so dangerous, but that seems more about Mom's boyfriend in high school who may or may not have wooed her into trouble after a long motorcycle ride to Jones Beach. Tony, the boyfriend, was killed a month later when a drunk crossed the median on the Long Island Expressway and wiped out Tony, his motorcycle, and four cars under a bridge. Mom and Dad married less than three months later, in July. The author, their first daughter, was born the following January. The bike was fun while it lasted, though.

The professor reads the paper and marks it up as he goes. "Where is your thesis?" he asks at the bottom of the first page. "What does your mother's boyfriend have to do with your motorcycle? Explain," he writes after the third paragraph.

You have a good start here. There are lots of good ideas and interesting details. However, I'm not sure what you are after. What's the point of your paper? What points are you trying to argue or demonstrate? If you don't make the connections and points as clearly as possible, the reader would have to know you and your family very well to understand what you are writing about. As a reader, I want to understand so I can know something about who you are and what matters to you.

As thoughtful as this response appears to be, writing students, especially those whose home cultures are further removed from the academic, may too often learn to conform rather than explore or discover. This is what Finn refers to as "learning for domestication."[6] Most teachers have seen too many students fade into the woodwork, pass from the teacher's attention.

Students whose class affiliations are neither enviable nor obvious often struggle because they can "pass." There are advantages in passing, to be sure. However, there are also liabilities. These students are at risk because they experience significant and unique struggles in college, because they are trained to believe that they are "middle class, just like everyone else," because others have had it so much harder, because their "otherness" is hidden.

Passing, in this context, is overtly heteroglossic. Working-class students can pass their courses, meaning that they can do the required work. Passing also means that they have succeeded in not calling attention to their status as "other," in becoming academically opaque. These students can also pass in the sense that they move along, that they only come near to "it" as they are moving by it. This suggests that they may be only peripherally involved. Thus, working-class students often go unnoticed and end up as I did: angry, disengaged, displaced, and confused.

A focus on working-class students in the composition classroom has caused problems for those who reject the notion that there is class differentiation in the United States and, by extension, argue that issues of class are not important to the teaching of writing. Also troubled are those who cannot see that working-class students come to their writing courses with different ideas and concerns than do the children of academic parents, managerial-class parents, or those whom Michael Zweig refers to "the capitalist class."[7] Others just want to say that we Americans are all middle class, or that the working class includes everyone from the optometrist with her own practice to the illegal migrant worker traveling with his family. If there is no differentiation, there is no problem, right?

Class differences are particularly troubling in the postsecondary classroom because higher education, whatever shape it takes, is theoretically the great equalizer, the societal device that levels the playing field for everyone. If you just get an education, you will succeed. Through education, many believe, people can overcome class barriers even when they can never transcend race, gender, or other social markers. I am not so sure that class ascendancy is possible, other than in material terms; neither am I convinced that it is always or even more frequently the goal of working-class students. Neither am I convinced that ascendancy is the real issue. Regardless, assuming ascendancy as *the* goal is a necessarily flawed and narrow view of class.

So, the question becomes, what do we do? Some would advocate focusing on issues of class and economic status as the subject matter of courses, as a way to bring these issues to the fore. Firsthand and recent experiences tell me that too many working-class students experience this as *their* being studied, examined, and pigeonholed. Others would advocate reading and writing about work and labor, focusing on what is familiar to these students. This is a fine idea except that many working-class students have come to college to get away from those issues, from those futures and histories. Still others would invite students to investigate power relations, to critically review how power is distributed, used, and abused. Working-class students are all too familiar with power relations; it is seldom long before these students recognize the incongruity of a teacher forcing students to question power without questioning his application of said power. Some questions must be addressed.

First, about whom are we talking? This is an important question for a number of reasons. If we do not put some boundaries on the population with which we intend to work, any clarity that would have come from that work will be compromised. We simply cannot address the needs of all people each time we try to inquire into these socially determined issues. There is at least one other, less obvious reason for definition as well. The way we describe and define this group tells us something not only about where we are looking but also about the vantage point *from which* we are looking. We can use this description to interrogate our own assumptions.

A second essential question is, what do we want to know? Many of the discussions of working-class lives and students get caught in the web of definition, to the exclusion of other, more important discussions. One such discussion might be about what the unique literacy practices of working-class students are, particularly practices that we do not find in the academic setting. One example is the wishing song, an Irish tradition of developing ad-lib verses fit to a particular tune, about people and issues of common interest. For example:

> Oh, I wish I had written this chapter before
> The time is so short, I could write so much more.

A Puerto Rican student told me about her home country's "trobas," rhyming, sung stories improvised on the day's events. African American scholars and students have discussed in a number of venues the importance and frequency of signifying in black culture.[8] These are all literate practices, acts of linguistic skill that have no place in academia. What purposes do they serve outside the academy? What might they teach us within it?

As Neil Postman writes in *Technopoly,* curricula are technologies for information control, for limiting what counts as knowledge and what does not.[9] Interrogating what counts as knowledge in and out of that curricular system would enable not only further understanding of what we are missing out on but also what we have assumed about students and their needs that may not be valid.

Another part of this discussion might revolve around the orientations of working-class students to literacy; how is literacy part or not part of their lives outside of college? How are we assuming it is or should be within the campus? Walter Ong enabled our ignoring this question by differentiating between primary oral and primary textual cultures, in some ways releasing us from working inclusively with members of those so-called primary oral cultures in our literacy education.[10]

Having said that, we may very well find that some of our students do come from cultures that value the oral over the textual. We might find, for instance, a culturally reified suspicion of the written word among certain members of American Indian tribes. How might this suspicion shape differently a student's ability, even her interest, in learning to write successfully? If we were to inquire into these positions, we might more readily identify our own assumptions and hegemonic projections as well.

A third essential question, after we have identified our target group and what we would like to learn, is, what will we do with our results? This is probably the most difficult decision to make at the outset of the research. However, speculating about the expected results is a useful tool because it allows us to, again, interrogate our own thinking.

I am not advocating this approach for everyone, even though I find it very useful, very informative, and very engaging. It is often very clumsy and very cumbersome, too. At the same time, this participatory narrating of research processes enables an understanding of the study and the researcher that would not otherwise be possible. It both enables and complicates the process. And that seems to be just what we are seeking.

Before we descend into a discouraging discussion of narrative as personal writing or as story, let me clarify what I mean when I point to narrative. As we know, Joseph Campbell made it his life's work to explore not only narrative as a cultural phenomenon but also the extensive commonalities among the narratives embedded in seemingly unique, socially isolated, and physically distant cultures. Campbell's *Hero with a Thousand Faces* focuses exclusively on the myth of the hero's journey, a story we can see repeated in so many forms throughout the world and history.[11] This is not an artifact but a living critical tool for investigating and querying the world around us. But it is not only the proliferation and commonality of narrative that makes it so appealing.

Aristotle, in *Poetics,* recognized the power of narrative: "The narrative form makes it possible for one to describe a number of simultaneous incidents; and these, if germane to the subject, increase the body of the poem."[12] If we pursue a kind of cultural awareness that will enable multiple readings and understandings, certainly, according to the classical founder of rhetoric, narrative would prove most useful. Homi K. Bhabha, in *Nation and Narration,* carries this idea along further into our present considerations by explaining what those multiple, simultaneous incidents can be, including the roles that working-class students and we academics must play in the exchange:

> The ethnographic demands that the observer himself is a part of his observation and this requires that the field of knowledge—the total social fact—must be appropriated from outside like a thing, but like a thing which comprises within itself the subjective understanding of the indigenous. The transposition of this process into the language of the outsider's grasp—this entry into the area of the symbolic of representation/signification—then makes the social fact "three dimensional."[13]

In short, narrative can enable participation in the stories of others' lives. It can and does enable one to become aware of and sensitive to another. Martha Nussbaum says it best when she writes, "The ability to tell ourselves the story of a parent or a lover or a child who has angered us can often help us avoid selfish vindictiveness."[14]

Freire illuminates this important next step when he advocates that people must be enabled to "develop their power to perceive critically *the way they exist* in the world *with which* and *in which* they find themselves; they come to see the world not as a static reality, but as a reality in process, in transformation."[15] And academics are not exempted from this process. In other words, we should engage with our students in the critical investigation of the roles we all play in generating our own realities while simultaneously activating recognition of the malleable nature of that constructed reality. This means that options must be available, from academe and elsewhere. Ideally, rather than simply receiving what is presented to them, our students are enabled and encouraged to question what they see, wherever they see it, and make reasoned decisions about what those images mean. In the mix, we academics are enabled to participate in worlds and communities outside of the campus, to become a part of something larger than ourselves.

Nussbaum has illuminated at least one way that narrative and story can be the medium through which this negotiation occurs. She writes that narrative

> has the power to make us see the lives of the different with more than a casual tourist's interest—with involvement and sympathetic understanding, with anger at our society's refusals of visibility. We come to see how circumstances shape

the lives of those who share with us some general goals and projects; and we see that circumstances shape not only people's possibilities for action, but also their aspirations and desires, hopes and fears.[16]

But, this calls for some displacement of traditional approaches to the teaching of writing. It means that we, teachers and professors, must be willing to discuss literacy and meaning-making beyond the safety of multicultural readers, the essay, and the research paper and move toward a genuine interaction with the lives, priorities, and meaning-making activities of the students we encounter and the cultural contexts that our teaching serves. In many ways and in overtly Freirian terms, it is we who must be freed by the students whose heritages and training our discussions have excluded. Our work becomes much, much messier.

Linda Flower, in her article entitled "Intercultural Inquiry and the Transformation of Service," writes that we need not fear this complication but, to genuinely engage with others who are unlike ourselves, to avoid the pitfalls of only enacting that culture that perpetuates itself and protects us from getting our hands dirty, we must engage in active discourse. Flower writes,

> My argument is this: the conflicts and contradictions of community outreach call for an intercultural inquiry that not only seeks more diverse rival readings, but constructs multivoiced meanings in practice. . . . Transformative understanding is an activity, not a statement. It is a form of praxis—a kind of knowledge making that names problems in the world and transforms our representations both of them and ourselves, opening the door to informed action.[17]

Beyond these more extended cultural concerns, there are those who would argue that narrative writing is not as extracurricular as we might think. Candace Spigelman argues "that the telling of stories can actually serve the *same* purposes as academic writing and that narratives of personal experiences can accomplish serious scholarly work."[18] Anne Ruggles Gere supports this idea and carries it yet further:

> Asking [students] to draw upon their own lives allows students to see themselves in conscious ways, to enjoy knowing *that* they know. That visibility enables students to claim their own lives and become protagonists in their own stories. Certainly, pleasure lies here.[19]

This approach might also enable us, those who provoke these stories, to move toward more contextualized and culturally responsive methods of teaching writing or any other subject.

I have never been accused of being subtle. Plato's "Allegory of the Cave" is not hard to see here. More germane to this discussion than the allegory itself is Socrates' charge to those who move out of that world of shadows:

Each of you, when his turn comes, must go down to the general underground abode, and get the habit of seeing in the dark . . . you will know what the several images are, and what they represent, because you have seen the beautiful and just and good in their truth.[20]

We almost reflexively assume that we are they who have ascended and stood outside of the cave, but our students are equally viable candidates for that role. Even so, we too frequently miss Plato's admonishment that all who have stepped away from the projections must work toward explicating the "first principles" of the higher ground within the shadows of the lower. Instead, we academics may never look back. This makes our culture of academic transience easier to handle but creates real problems for our students who intend to return to and look for the good in the projections of their lives outside of college. If students reject the dissociation inherent in academic culture, they must "pass" with us in the sense that they mislead us into thinking they capitulate. Meanwhile, they must also minimize differences with or questions from their home cultures because schooling too often makes them suspect.

We identify the college degree as a token of separation, and a back-formation follows that we are no longer "them," even if it means that students' options have been severely curtailed by our assumptions. Much of my own experience was a result of this epistemological phenomenon. Aronowitz writes that "we seem to be permanently wedded to the idea that the credentializing system of public and private education is the primary vehicle through which any student, regardless of race, class, gender, or even physical handicap, may succeed in achieving professional or technical status."[21] This credentializing becomes a self-fulfilling prophecy in many ways because, believing this, we build systems of education and advantage to reflect these assumptions. Culturally, higher education has recently become much more available to professional training at least in part because the other segments of what we academics teach have been so successfully distanced from the shadows they might have explored.

Herein lies the rub (a phrase to which I admit an unnatural allegiance). If our systems of reason and foundational academic philosophies revolve around the ability of the individual to construct, critique, and question his reality, however fragmented, are we not violating Plato's admonishment by doing so in a way that alienates that student from his culture? How is education guiding individuals toward clarity of vision and, simultaneously, discouraging them from applying that vision to the constructs that would have otherwise constrained them? Where does that leave students whose sociocultural status conflicts with the academic credentials they have acquired? How do we, as teachers, overcome the boundaries between academe and "the real world" if we are culturally predisposed to reifying them?

Finn writes that a contrast between two distinct kinds of education rests squarely in affluence and class.

> The *least* we can do is face facts. Our schools liberate and empower children of the gentry and domesticate the children of the working class, and to a large extent the middle class as well. You may want to argue that that's all right, or at least it's all that's possible—fine. But let's stop denying it.[22]

This contrast, though not always consciously available, is embedded in many working-class parents' attitudes toward education. They assume a disparity and are infrequently dissuaded from that assumption. An example:

Every student in my high school was assigned an adviser for scheduling. I told mine that I wanted to take typing. I enjoyed writing and thought taking typing would be a good idea, just in case I ever decided to go to college. "Well," Mr. Camphor started, looking up over his football clock, "what's your old man do for a living . . . uh . . . William?" I had to think about what to call it, not because I was unsure or concerned about how it might sound, but because he did so many different things in the factory where he worked.

"He's a machinist, at Life Savers," I replied, only barely wondering how that was relevant.

"Oh . . . well . . . you don't want typing then. You'll want industrial arts."

"I will?"

"Sure you will."

"I don't know. I think I might like to go to college sometime, so typing seems like a good . . ."

"Naw, industrial arts'll give you and your old man something to talk about." I said nothing as Mr. Camphor signed me into co-op for yet another semester. I was neither inclined to argue nor able to articulate why I should. I knew I had tried to "reach above my station," and I got caught! "Just let it go," I thought. I knew, and Finn confirms, that "'border crossers' are likely to be censured by their own as traitors and they are not likely to be fully accepted by the dominant group."[23]

Had I told my parents, they would have certainly acknowledged the wrong, but they would have done nothing. They would have recognized the futility of arguing with a system that so clearly disfavored us. They were well versed in the futility of getting my hopes up. We were not college people, not any of us. Like other working-class families, my "parents *said* they wanted their children to go to college, but they didn't *do* anything to make it happen, and looked on with equanimity when their children did not make any moves to actually enroll in college."[24] What might seem laziness was an act of kindness and acknowledgment of a wrong. No one should tell a kid he can't go to college, but the kid shouldn't be led on a wild-goose chase, either.

Bhabha points to not only the power of narrative to join a people but also the inability of a colonizer to use that story toward control, not unlike the inability of the academy to appropriate cultural narratives toward its own sustenance as the dominant narrator of values. When one tells a story,

> as narrator, she is narrated as well. And in a way she is already told, and what she herself is *telling* will not undo that somewhere else she is *told*. This narrative inversion or circulation . . . makes untenable any supremacist, or nationalist claims to cultural mastery, for the position of narrative control is neither monocular or monologic. The subject is only graspable between the telling/told, between "here" and "somewhere else," and in this double scene the very condition of cultural knowledge is the alienation of the subject.[25]

The story becomes the vehicle by which both narrator and narrated become, evolve, develop. The listener is transformed as much as the teller.

One side, the academic, is encouraging an "up-and-out" mentality that disables working-class/first-generation students (as well as other "other" students) from readily and constructively participating in their home cultures. The academic has inadvertently distanced itself from lives outside of the campus other than those lives affluent and academic. The working class relies on the inherent elitism in the system to encourage fatalism, to deny the opportunities of higher education, and to rationalize those choices by locating the power "out of my hands." Both want better things for themselves and students but neither has found a safe way of reaching out. "Perhaps more than any other factor, this reluctance to come to terms with more serious and entrenched forms of privilege is why most diversity programs produce limited and short-lived results."[26]

In order to change, the academic has to acknowledge the reified otherness of higher education. The working class must assert the validity of its cultural epistemologies as cooperative with and available to inquiry. Both must acknowledge and address the privileges they assign to their own paradigms. The academic must be open to nonacademic inquiry. The working class must be willing to not only trust but allow inquiry to challenge its assumptions, to question its reasoning. This is essential.

One semester, I taught two courses at a very blue-collar, urban, satellite campus of a well-known university system. Students were commuters, most were full-time workers somewhere, and many had homes and families to contend with outside of class. ENGL 103 was an advanced first-year composition course. ENGL 231 was an introductory literature course for sophomore non-English majors. Neither course was one that students would have probably chosen voluntarily and both fulfilled general education requirements. However, the students in 103 were probably a little less jaded because of their newness to college and their better writing skills. Class was a focus for both courses, but in very different ways. Owing to the time constraints here, a down and dirty representation will have to suffice. I will say at the outset that neither the success of the one nor the failure of the other was predominantly my doing—I take only partial credit for both.

ENGL 103 did not focus on class, but I knew identity would come up because the course would force that. I never expected that class identity would become so important so early, though. The major projects for the course were

- Together, the class planned, wrote, and produced a book.
- Each student created an extensive literacy portfolio that included a thematic autobiography, an annotated literature review, and a short research paper on that reviewed topic, which he or she then presented to the class.
- A "choice" research project allowed students to pursue their own interests, write about them, and, again, present their work to the class.
- There was also a final portfolio.

We kept coming back to ideas of identity in 103, to individual concerns and interests, because these issues were built into the work of the course. Students would have had to work very hard to remain detached or disengaged from that course work because it was built on such a "generative theme."[27]

The students in 103 wrote a book about being nontraditional students. This opened up a number of discussions revolving around their having the right to be in college, their awareness that many thought they should not be there, and their collective conclusion that circuitous routes to that education were well worth the trouble. The 103 students frequently and collectively said no to my assignments, but they were also willing to discuss and develop appropriate (and usually better) alternatives.

In ENGL 231, things were different. Labor and the working class seemed like a good theme for an introduction to literature because of its familiarity for those steel mill and refinery students and their families (not to mention the myriad materials available in multiple genres). The readings for the course included Ben Hampers's *Rivethead,* Rebecca Harding Davis's *Life in the Iron Mills,* Arthur Miller's *Death of a Salesman,* and Jim Daniels's *Punching Out.* The work of the course, beyond the readings, included

- a five- to seven-page literary critique of an approved work
- a student-authored creative piece
- a collaborative genre presentation
- an individual creative presentation
- a final portfolio

These students, too, resisted the assigned work of the course, but there was no discussion of alternatives—only conspicuously missing papers and presentations.

The 231 students were generally no different from their 103 counterparts in terms of background, but most of the 231 students were committed exclusively to earning engineering degrees. They had never liked reading and I saw them do nothing voluntarily, even when it was directly related to their majors. ENGL 231 was a waste of time for them, and they were generous in sharing that perspective. Beyond that, they simply despised the selections I had made. "I came to college to get out of that; why would I want to spend a whole semester reading about it?" one student complained later.

Student evaluations reflected this same general sense among the students. Each item on the evaluation form would be most favorable when answered in the most affirmative (e.g., This professor is knowledgeable; I would recommend this course to a friend; etc.). On a scale of 0 (strongly disagree) to 5 (strongly agree), the overall ratings of 103 and 231 were 4.7 and 3.3, respectively. Particularly interesting was the differentiation on two prompts about the learning in and content of the courses. Statement 4 said that students felt they had learned a great deal in the course; 103 and 231 reported 4.9 and 3.6 respectively, even though the students in 103 had done much less traditional course work. On statement 7, 103 and 231 students were prompted with the idea that the course was relevant, interesting, and the assignments well integrated: 4.8 and 3.1, again respectively, even though 231 involved much more familiar and predictable kinds of academic work.

There are any number of possible explanations for these differentiations. It is possible that I was a great teacher in one class and lousy in the other, but it is less likely that my teaching alone accounts for such huge differentiations within the same semester in such closely related courses. After much consideration, I attribute these variations at least partially to the way class identity was involved.

In 103, identity came from less-remote work that opened doors for student inquiry, resistance, engagement, and construction. The 103 students made the work of the course, and the course work. In 103, I taught as though the students knew something I wanted to learn. The subject of class in 231 was problematic because it was a synthesized version of the students' own experiences. It was too rarefied to be discursive. My approach there was that the literature and assignments would do all of the talking, that the materials could drive that course and those students to some deeper understanding.

So, "what's the frequency, Kenneth?" In order to really invite the "other," working class, first generation, or another "other" into academe, we must learn to see in the dark again. We must be willing to invoke our own philosophies and continue to adjust our perceptions of the shadows by learning the values and reason our students bring to us. Otherwise, the unilateral character of our work, a "what we have is better than what you have" mentality, will only continue to alienate diverse students, isolate the humanities, and verify working-class suspicions.

Meanwhile, working-class students, as well as others, must be willing to trust that higher education will, in fact, benefit those who pursue it. They must set aside their enculturated suspicions and fears and actively pursue that which we intend to share. They must be willing to resist the trend toward vocation and preprofessionalization in undergraduate education, as must we. On neither side will tolerance be sufficient, and both must constantly support choices built on trust. We all stand to gain and lose a great deal if we aren't more careful. If we pay attention, we may yet see what is moving, back there, behind that desk.

NOTES

1. Patrick J. Finn, *Literacy with an Attitude: Educating Working-Class Children in Their Own Self-Interest* (Albany: State University of New York Press, 1999), 47.

2. David Bartholomae, "Response: David Bartholomae, University of Pittsburgh," in *Cross-Talk in Comp Theory: A Reader,* ed. Victor Villanueva, 503 (Urbana, IL: National Council of Teachers of English, 1997).

3. Peter Elbow, "Response: Peter Elbow, University of Massachusetts–Amherst," in Villanueva, *Cross-Talk in Comp Theory,* 509.

4. James D. Williams, *Preparing to Teach Writing: Research, Theory, and Practice* (London: Lawrence Earlbaum Associates, 1998), 7.

5. John Dewey, *Experience and Education* (New York: Collier Books, 1968), 89.

6. Finn, *Literacy with an Attitude,* 123.

7. Michael Zweig, *The Working Class Majority: America's Best Kept Secret* (Ithaca, NY: ILR Press, 2000), 15–17.

8. Molefi Kete Asante, *The Afrocentric Idea* (Philadelphia: Temple University Press, 1987), 47; Valerie Balester, *Cultural Divide: A Study of African-American College-Level Writers* (Portsmouth, NH: Boynton/Cook Heinemann, 1993), 35; Geneva Smitherman, *Talkin' and Testifyin': The Language of Black America* (Detroit: Wayne State University Press, 1977), 82.

9. Neil Postman, *Technopoly: The Surrender of Culture to Technology* (New York: Vintage Books, 1993), 75–76.

10. Walter Ong, *Orality and Literacy: The Technologizing of the Word* (New York: Routledge, 1982).

11. Joseph Campbell, *The Hero with a Thousand Faces* (Princeton, NJ: Princeton University Press, 1949), 245–46.

12. Aristotle, *The Poetics,* in *The Rhetoric and the Poetics of Aristotle,* ed. Edward P. J. Corbett, 1459*b*: 26–28 (New York: Modern Library, 1984).

13. Homi K. Bhabha, ed., *Nation and Narration* (New York: Routledge, 1990), 301.

14. Martha Nussbaum, *Cultivating Humanity: A Classical Defense of Reform in Liberal Education* (Cambridge, MA: Harvard University Press, 1997), 97.

15. Paulo Freire, *Pedagogy of the Oppressed,* ed. and trans. Myra Bergman Ramos (New York: Continuum, 1994), 64.

16. Nussbaum, *Cultivating Humanity,* 88.

17. Linda Flower, "Intercultural Inquiry and the Transformation of Service," *College English* 65 (2002): 182, 186.

18. Candace Spigelman, "Argument and Evidence in the Case of the Personal," *College English* 64 (2001): 64.

19. Anne Ruggles Gere, "Revealing Silence: Rethinking Personal Writing," *College Composition and Communication* 53 (2001): 210.

20. Plato, "The Allegory of the Cave," in *Greek Philosophy: Plato, The Allegory of the Cave, The Divided Line, The Republic, Book 6,* ed. Richard Hooker. www.wsu.edu/~dee/GREECE/ALLEGORY.HTM.

21. Stanley Aronowitz, "A Different Perspective on Educational Inequality," in *Education and Cultural Studies: Toward a Performative Practice,* ed. Stanley Aronowitz, 179 (New York: Routledge, 1997).

22. Finn, *Literacy with an Attitude,* 189.

23. Finn, *Literacy with an Attitude,* 46.

24. Finn, *Literacy with an Attitude,* 71.

25. Bhabha, *Nation and Narration,* 301.

26. Allan G. Johnson, *Privilege, Power, and Difference* (Mountain View, CA: Mayfield, 2001), 27.

27. Ira Shor, *Empowering Education: Critical Teaching for Social Change* (Chicago: University of Chicago Press, 1992), 46.

REFERENCES

Anderson, Sherwood. *Winesburg, Ohio.* New York: Viking Press, 1960.

Aristotle. *The Poetics. The Rhetoric and the Poetics of Aristotle,* ed. Edward P. J. Corbett. Modern Library College ed. New York: Modern Library, 1984.

Aronowitz, Stanley. "A Different Perspective on Educational Inequality." In *Education and Cultural Studies: Toward a Performative Practice,* ed. Stanley Aronowitz. New York: Routledge, 1997.

Asante, Molefi Kete. *The Afrocentric Idea.* Philadelphia: Temple University Press, 1987.

Balester, Valerie. *Cultural Divide: A Study of African-American College-Level Writers.* Portsmouth, NH: Boynton/Cook Heinemann, 1993.

Bartholomae, David. "Response: David Bartholomae, University of Pittsburgh." In *Cross-Talk in Comp Theory: A Reader,* ed. Victor Villanueva. Urbana, IL.: National Council of Teachers of English, 1997.

Bhabha, Homi K., ed. *Nation and Narration.* New York: Routledge, 1990.

Campbell, Joseph. *The Hero with a Thousand Faces.* Princeton, NJ: Princeton University Press, 1949.

Dewey, John. *Experience and Education.* New York: Collier Books, 1968.

Elbow, Peter. "Response: Peter Elbow, University of Massachusetts–Amherst." In *Cross-Talk in Comp Theory: A Reader,* ed. Victor Villanueva. Urbana, IL: National Council of Teachers of English, 1997.

Finn, Patrick J. *Literacy with an Attitude: Educating Working-Class Children in Their Own Self-Interest.* Albany: State University of New York Press, 1999.

Flower, Linda. "Intercultural Inquiry and the Transformation of Service." *College English* 65 (2002): 181–201.

Freire, Paulo. *Pedagogy of the Oppressed.* Ed. and trans. Myra Bergman Ramos. New York: Continuum, 1994.

Gere, Anne Ruggles. "Revealing Silence: Rethinking Personal Writing." *College Composition and Communication* 53 (2001): 203–23.

Johnson, Allan G. *Privilege, Power, and Difference.* Mountain View, CA: Mayfield Publishing, 2001.

Nussbaum, Martha. *Cultivating Humanity: A Classical Defense of Reform in Liberal Education.* Cambridge, MA: Harvard University Press, 1997.

Ong, Walter J. *Orality and Literacy: The Technologizing of the Word.* New York: Routledge, 1982.

Plato. "The Allegory of the Cave." In *Greek Philosophy: Plato, The Allegory of the Cave, The Divided Line, The Republic, Book 6,* ed. Richard Hooker. www.wsu.edu/~dee/GREECE/ALLEGORY.htm.

Postman, Neil. *Technopoly: The Surrender of Culture to Technology.* New York: Vintage Books, 1993.

Shor, Ira. *Empowering Education: Critical Teaching for Social Change.* Chicago: University of Chicago Press, 1992.

Smitherman, Geneva. *Talkin' and Testifyin': The Language of Black America.* Detroit: Wayne State University Press, 1977.

Spigelman, Candace. "Argument and Evidence in the Case of the Personal." *College English* 64 (2001): 63–87.

Williams, James D. *Preparing to Teach Writing: Research, Theory, and Practice.* London: Lawrence Earlbaum Associates, 1998.

Zweig, Michael. *The Working Class Majority: America's Best Kept Secret.* Ithaca, NY: ILR Press, 2000.

10

Critique of Domination: The Pain, Praxis, and Polemics of Working-Class Consciousness in Academia

Daniel D. Martin

My task within this chapter is not simply to delineate the contours of academic life for working-class scholars. Rather I wish to theorize instances in which the relations of ruling that they find themselves in with professional-managerial-class colleagues are revealed and shaped within the academy. Consequently, I intentionally avoid issues such as why some working-class academics may feel obliged to enact a working-class role, or how that role-playing separates them from other working-class academics; other analyses have admirably provided insight into these processes.[1] The questions guiding this paper are (1) How do sociologists and other academicians experience and negotiate class relations within both the academy and the profession of sociology? (2) What are the biographical and experiential sources that either make class salient or ensure its invisibility? and (3) What definitions of professionalism do working-class and professional-managerial-class sociologists operate by and what are the consequences of these?

METHOD OF INQUIRY

My theoretical insights are speculative, drawn from personal experiences acquired during the first six years of a career in academia begun at Miami University in Oxford, Ohio. Using the Department of Sociology, Gerontology, and Anthropology as a case study, I have relied upon content analysis and "autoethnography" in exploring what Dorothy Smith has termed "the relations of ruling."[2] Interrogating relations of ruling within sociology has a long and venerable history, including Robert Lynd's *Knowledge for What?*[3] and Irving Louis Horowitz's subsequent explanation of the Camelot Project;[4]

Alvin Gouldner's essay "Anti-Minotaur: The Myth of Value Free Sociology" along with his book *The Coming Crisis of Western Sociology*;[5] Howard Becker's query, "Whose side are we on?";[6] and more critical interrogations of sociology by feminists beginning with Dorothy Smith's "Women's Perspective as a Radical Critique of Sociology" in 1974.[7] Two years after the publication of Smith's article, Don Martindale's book *The Romance of a Profession: A Case History in the Sociology of Sociology* appeared with chapter titles such as "The Power Brokers" and "The Arrogance of Power."[8] Martindale named names, rendering a critique of the Department of Sociology at the University of Minnesota. When I entered as a doctoral student at Minnesota ten years later, *Romance* was considered an exotic and deviant book to have on one's shelf because a substantial number of the faculty whom Martindale had characterized in less-than-flattering terms were still employed by the department. For other faculty, as well as for most graduate students, the book was a curiosity written in advance of their arrival, serving as both the repository and the purveyor of institutional memory. In it, Martindale detailed the intellectual brutalization of students in a department where, among other ills, sexual harassment ran unchecked. Martindale's account of a lawsuit filed by a graduate student combating an arbitrary dismissal served as a stock of knowledge to which graduate students added other known tales of consensual, sexual exploits between professors and students, or professors and secretaries, in departmental lounges and library offices.[9] Like Martindale's method of inquiry, mine relies upon both document analysis and autoethnographic detail. Unlike Martindale, however, I do not feel the need to reveal professional identities to establish the veracity of my claims concerning the contemporary history of Miami University.[10]

IDEOLOGICAL AND DISCURSIVE FORMATIONS

The doctoral training of sociologists resembles the professional socialization of medical students in at least one significant respect: in neither group is the meaning or knowledge of managing emotions or conflictual relations formally dispensed.[11] Graduate training does not usually include information on how to resolve, negotiate, or survive conflictual relations with colleagues, though the topic may be discussed in either graduate assistant orientations or "Teaching Sociology" courses where relations between graduate instructors and undergraduate students are more generally discussed. Instead, any knowledge obtained about how one should maneuver through the vast field of potentially problematic relations in academia must be derived either vicariously—watching professors, mentors, and other graduate students—or by trial and error in the course of direct experience. The latter option in gaining this necessary stock of knowledge is likely to be experienced as the most problematic, especially when poor relations are exacerbated by unacknowledged differences such as class, race, gender, age, or theoretical or political-economic ideology that serve as a subtext in interaction. While teaching as a graduate student, I received two admonitions related to enacting a working-class style in the classroom and in my relations more generally: I had been cautioned to "quit playing working-class hero." The first time was by my adviser and mentor, the progeny of Hungarian immigrants who carved out a living as small shopkeepers once they made it to the United States. The second admonition was issued by a radical scholar who grew up in New York and ended up teaching at a private liberal arts college in Minnesota where I held a one-year teaching appointment. After quietly acquiescing in both situations, I later reflected upon the phrase that was used. The trope "working-class hero" is a label referencing the class-based interaction style of an individual that may contain unseemly performative elements. Yet, this is the pedestrian meaning of the term. For working-class academicians, the phrase bears a deeper meaning, one that is decidedly political: it refers to enacting working-class interests.

Disapprobation of both working-class interests and the attendant performance through which those interests are enacted implicates the social context of academia as one that is decidedly professional-managerial class. It is a context within which class relations are invisible though continually reproduced through discursive as well as institutional practices. One never hears "Quit playing upper-middle-class hero" or "Quit playing middle-class hero," even though members of the professoriate are notorious for occasionally feigning personal friendships with well-published and, hence, well-known colleagues, or unabashedly letting it be known that they were on leave in Europe all year. In 1997, my first year on tenure track at Miami University, I went to lunch with two upper-middle-class colleagues, one of whom "highlighted" her experiences during the past summer spent in Tuscany while the other feigned identification and sympathized with the discomfort of long-distance travel. Such disclosures would seem to serve as conversational markers of upper-middle-class-hero status. So, why can't upper-middle-class professors play the role of "hero"? The answer has to do with social location. Those born into upper-middle-class families who end up assuming positions of power and privilege are simply reproducing an institutional order (and broader political economy) within which their own occupancy is viewed as normative. Tout court, suffering the unpleasantnesses of long-distance travel is not suffering at all, at least not from the perspective of working-class families where putting up with the indignities of the laboring process is preferred over factory closings and the possibility of bank foreclosures.[12] Discursive formations found within the academy are deeply embedded in the institution and reproduced in interaction between faculty; at both levels they reveal the deep structure of class. In marketing their programs, universities and colleges tout the accomplishments of their faculties, highlight their international programs abroad, and pay homage to diversity on campus, hoping to enlarge their pool of potential students and realizable resources. In the interaction orders among faculty, and throughout the organization of the institution, privilege is taken for granted in the natural attitude of everyday life; the consciousness of most faculty, including sociologists, has been "colonized."[13] By contrast, enacting working-class interests within this same institutional order entails highlighting class relations, indicting class structure, and resisting its social reproduction. The institutional performances through which working-class interests are advanced, then, serve as residual markers of former class membership. Enacting working-class interests bears *identification with* and *identification of* the station in life that one has transcended—an accomplishment that is seldom understood, regarded, or reciprocally expressed by one's upper-middle-class counterparts, or even one's own family.[14] At most, playing the role of working-class hero can disrupt the taken-for-granted assumptions regarding pedagogy, critical thinking, and collegiality and threaten bourgeois program development that is based upon the maintenance of the status quo. Of course, to threaten the established order of institutional privilege places one at risk of being marginalized, disenfranchised, or, in the case of untenured faculty, terminated.

A BRIEF HISTORY OF INSTITUTIONAL CONFLICT, 1999–2003

Anterior Relations

Until 2002, the program of sociology at Miami University existed in a combined department with gerontology and anthropology. In 2002, anthropology was decoupled from the other two programs by the administration in an attempt to quell interminable conflict. While the potential for intradepartmental rivalry between the gerontology program and the two social sciences might logically be expected, alliances had formed between sociology and gerontology faculty, the latter field regarded by most sociologists as a substantive specialty within the discipline, even though gerontology, given the composition of its faculty, was correctly identified by its members as an interdisciplinary program. As in the case of other alliances, the bonds of solidarity between gerontologists and sociologists that I witnessed and experienced in the first three years of my stay had been forged through informal socializing and the recognition of mutual, objective interests. While these relationships did not necessarily translate into joint political or programmatic agendas, they were solidified by the realization that the anthropology component was dominated by primatologists whose work on chimpanzees bore little or no relation to anyone else's in the department. While political cleavages in many departments often reflect paradigmatic changes occurring in the field—as graduate schools train the next generation of scholars to supersede their predecessors with new stocks of theoretical knowledge, pedagogies, research, and teaching technologies—the political differences within the department appeared to display a peculiar mix of preestablished political, theoretical, paradigmatic, and personal tensions.

The Cauldron Brews

Tensions within the department were first curiously stirred in 1997 as the department faced hiring a new chair, a process eventuating in the selection of a person whom the administration had transferred from the department of social work after she had destroyed it and another program on campus. Allegedly, the faculty in both programs hated her and hated each other. Finding her hiring unacceptable, one member of the department created a petition to rescind the administration's selection of the new chair and collected several signatures in a recall effort. The vast majority of the department eschewed, abstained from, or was ignorant of the recall effort. Questions of the new chair's competency began to grow during her first week in office as she drained $30,000 out of a discretionary departmental fund, repatriating it back to the College of Arts and Science in hopes of ingratiating the department with the administration. The strategy backfired. When moneys were later needed by the department, the administration refused to hand over additional funds, surprising no one except the chair. In the second semester of her first academic year, details of how the chair had micromanaged previous departments began to circulate among faculty, who now found themselves under a deluge of her daily e-mail. Yet, in spite of this communicative morass, she revealed little of her intentions to hire a visiting anthropology professor whose specialty was hydrology. At the behest of the hydrologist's friends, two senior-level primatologists (a husband-wife team), the chair engineered the hiring without a national search, communicating to the dean (whose retirement was imminent) that the faculty supported the hire. In fact, the faculty had not been notified. At the following departmental meeting, the chair announced that the dean approved of the hire and that the department faced forfeiting a tenure line if it passed on the deal that she and the primatologists had brokered. The hydrologist, a friend and now political ally of the primatologists, was hired, representing the deciding vote on issues of annual leave, occupancy of the "anthropology" chair, and other programmatic concerns. Three months later the dean retired and was replaced by an associate dean.

Deteriorating relations between faculty rapidly turned hostile. Activist (and working-class) anthropologists who had been outspoken critics of the "illegal" hire within the anthropology group were quickly disenfranchised as the pri-matologists and their new hire enlarged their sphere of support among other anthropologists. They rewrote policy, beginning with the decision rule for holding the "anthropology chair." Voting now replaced the long-standing tra-dition of rotating occupancy of the chair, a tradition that had ensured that eventually all members would share responsibility and power. The maneuver ensured that the person slated to serve as the next anthropology chair—a working-class, activist anthropologist—was completely disenfranchised. Moreover, the actual vote occurred while the activist anthropologist was out of town tending to a death in the family—a death that had occurred while he was consulting with the Tigua tribe, which was attempting to reclaim sacred lands from the federal government. The chair of Sociology, Gerontology, and An-thropology (SGA), "Dr. Brevis," was consulted by the primatologists during the coup d'état but refused to halt the vote or require notification and representa-tion of the out-of-town activist anthropologist. Notably, it was the same working-class anthropologist whose name had been tendered as the only al-ternative candidate when the chair was first hired. Indeed, not long after this event, Chair Brevis awarded annual leaves to the primatologists. The decision effectively shifted the burden of teaching the now-vacated courses to the group's remaining members, some of whom interpreted the award as payment for political allegiance to the chair. Within the department as a whole, the po-litical cauldron reached the boiling point. The departmental chair was viewed by half of the department as a micromanager who played favorites, incompe-tently managed the affairs of the department, and displayed little regard for fairness. The other half viewed her as a benevolent colleague who duly re-warded team players who supported the university and thought she should be given more autonomy in decision making unfettered by the criticisms of mal-contents. Levels of resentment, desperation, and hostility passed all former wa-termarks. Where political alliances had formerly existed as three shifting and tenuous coalitions, they now crystallized into two competing groups, repre-senting a cross section of all three disciplines and age cohorts (see table 10.1). Those without apparent political commitments (Free-Floating Nodes) shared the political definitions of other community-action researchers, viewing the chair's decisions as ill informed and biased. While the Scientists had been in the department the longest and had formed strong ties of in-group solidar-ity, the more tenuous coalition of "community-action" anthropologists, soci-ologists, and gerontologists equaled their number. But could the coalition be held together?

Mobilization

The working-class sociologists, senior-member gerontologists, and two outcast activist anthropologists mobilized. We held meetings off campus to

Table 10.1. Number of Faculty by Discipline Comprising Political Factions in the Department of Sociology, Gerontology, and Anthropology

Scientists	Critical Social Science and Community Action Research	Free-Floating Nodes*
6 Sociology	3 Sociology	2 Sociology
2 Primatology	3 Gerontology	2 Gerontology
2 Archeology	2 Cultural Anthropology	
1 Hydrology		
4 Females, 7 Males	2 Females, 6 Males,	3 Females, 1 Male
5 Full professors	2 Full professors	3 Associate professors
2 Associate professors	4 Associate professors	1 Tenured assistant professor
1 Assistant professor	2 Assistant professors	1 Working-class female
1 Working-class male	5 Working-class males	
N=11	N=8	N=4

*Free-Floating Nodes are sociologists and gerontologists who were *apolitical* (operationalized as those who recurrently abstained from voting or whose voting was mixed).

discuss grievances and possible solutions; we sent a petition to the newly appointed dean expressing discontent over distortions in decision-making processes, misallocation of departmental resources, and the general demise of department morale, requesting administrative intervention. Finally, we sent a group of representatives comprised of senior faculty to meet with the dean to discuss these concerns in depth. At the beginning of the new chair's second year, the dean called for an evaluation. Several weeks later the dean visited the department and announced the results: 50 percent of the department evaluated her performance in absolutely glowing terms; 50 percent of the department evaluated her as the worst chair they had ever had. Unsurprisingly, the reasons cited in her negative evaluation replicated the complaints allegedly heard from faculty located in the two previous programs that had fallen apart under her administration. Subsequently, the dean announced that he had asked for the chair's resignation, allowing her, however, to specify the date upon which she would vacate office—one year later. Unsubstantiated rumors filled the hallways, the most notable being that the new dean was fearful of litigious behavior on the part of the exiting chair, who had threatened a lawsuit the last time she was removed from the position. Moreover, speculation abounded that the chair and her supporters would seek "payback." The intensity of hostility quickly escalated. In November 1999, a departmental meeting was held to discuss the evaluation and replacement of the chair, issues that were hotly contested as her supporters demanded that she should remain in the meeting while her evaluation was discussed. Her supporters proceeded to voice their indignation at those who had engineered her removal, claiming that the entire situation had been carried off behind their backs. One full professor within the ranks of the community researchers—a previous departmental chair who was well respected by the administration—reminded them that they had engineered her hire by sending their own cadre of full professors to the dean's office in an attempt to exert pressure, and this after an official letter had been sent by the former dean insisting that he would not give audience to any member of the department on the issue. Additionally, the matter of the hire without a national search was provided as testament to the chair's incompetence, evoking a response from the newly hired hydrologist who was in attendance. The invective that followed began as he first mumbled, "Goddamn Marxists," and then proceeded to yell, "This is bullshit, you are all chicken shits."

Another full professor, a sociologist known by his colleagues for race-baiting, began to reaffirm the sentiment, shouting, "Bullshit, bullshit, bullshit! This is bullshit!!!"

The first comment was later deemed amusing by those of us who were working-class scholars: we had never identified ourselves as "Marxist" in theoretical orientation or professional identity, only as *critical sociologists.* The latter exclamation was a harbinger of hostility that was yet to spiral completely out of control; it was issued by the chair of the Retention, Promotion, and Tenure Committee.

Pereunt et Imputantur—*The hours pass away and are reckoned against us*

Prior to the meeting, a confrontation had occurred between the hydrologist and one of the critical working-class sociologists. On the day of the meeting, the medical sociologist in whose office the confrontation occurred was conscripted by the hydrologist into filing a complaint with Chair Brevis, both reporting that the critical-theoretical scholar had referred to them as "mountain niggers." The hydrologist claimed his ancestral lineage as Afghani and was reportedly born in New York to parents who were diplomats. His fellow plaintiff was Nepalese and allegedly claimed that he would "someday return to Nepal as its prime minister." Chair Brevis responded. Without interviewing the alleged perpetrator, gathering any additional information, or requesting that the parties meet with either her or the dean in mediation, she ushered the plaintiffs to the office of the Equal Employment Opportunity Commission (EEOC) to file a grievance. The EEOC referred the plaintiffs to the Committee on Faculty Rights and Responsibilities, where they filed a formal grievance on the matter. At the end of a long, grueling process of investigation and series of testimonies, the committee found the charges against the working-class sociologist to be without merit. It did establish, however, that the hydrologist had (1) threatened to physically assault the sociologist, telling him "Take your tie off, we're going outside"; (2) violated ethics of submission in professional journals, plagiarizing his own work by publishing the exact same material in multiple journals (an activity for which he was reprimanded though not terminated by the graduate school); and (3) attempted to physically intimidate at least two other faculty members with whom he had disagreements. The hydrologist responded by filing a petition with the president's office stating that the entire committee, some of the most respected senior professors on campus, were all racists. The Rights and Responsibilities Committee presented its findings to the provost's office, which reviewed the committee's findings but refused to accept them. In the process, the language within the grievance document was changed; the working-class sociologist was no longer being charged with "racial" harassment but "workplace" harassment, a charge upon which the provost's office anticipated a conviction might more easily be found. The committee was compelled by the provost to reconsider its findings under the new language used by the provost's office, and did so, reissuing another statement that the claims against the defendant still remained groundless. This finding again was rejected by the provost's office, which issued a memorandum to the Rights and Responsibilities Committee that its responsibility now was to issue penalties to the defendant. The Rights and Responsibilities Committee refused. At the time of this writing, the matter is still unresolved, the Rights and Responsibilities Committee having found the charges against the working-class sociologist to be without grounds, and the provost's office refusing to ratify its findings. Four years have elapsed since the initial incident and filing, two years since the grievance committee heard all of the evidence and collected testimony from all relevant parties. Yet, no one in the administration nor the faculty senate has ensured due process protecting the rights of the sociologist who was falsely accused. Nor has any committee or office in the administration proceeded with the grievance filed against the hydrologist for threatening physical assault, even though the incident was established during testimony.

Concurrent with the grievance filed against the working-class sociologist for racial harassment, two junior-level sociologists, both working-class scholars, were seeking tenure and became the subjects of a "retention review" in the fall of 1999. The Committee for Retention, Promotion, and Tenure (RPT) convened to review the two junior members, a process during which the supporters of the dethroned chair hoped to retaliate. As one of the primatologists characterized the context, "This is war." And in wars there are casualties. Drs. "Smith" and "Jones," both junior faculty members, were retained by the narrowest of margins. The political alliances that had formed around the chair's recall were replicated in the retention hearing of the two junior sociologists, both of whom had favored removing the chair. Having lost the battle to remove the junior scholars from the department, the Scientists, in a required committee report to the dean, issued statements of "uncollegiality" for both faculty. The statement was written outside of the RPT Committee behind closed doors so that neither the junior scholars nor the other half of the committee could discover the authors' identities, contest the secrecy of its construction, or ask for evidence upon which its claims were made. The statements, in part, read:

> Collegiality—Prof. Smith stubbornly advocates borderline positions. He is frequently mean spirited and displays a self-righteous intolerance of others' viewpoints. There is a pervasive cynicism and political one-dimensionality that often is reflected as arrogance to those who differ philosophically, intellectually, or scholarly. . . . [W]hile the department has a history of fragmentation, the stance, attitude or behaviors of Dr. Smith have only served to aggravate these tensions. Finally, Prof. Smith, on a number of occasions, has been unwilling to support or work with individuals whose positions differ. In conclusion . . . [we] evaluate Dr. Smith as being uncollegial.
>
> Collegiality—Dr. Jones frequently attempts to circumvent departmental processes and procedures. He has been particularly criticized for helping to foster an atmosphere that was not conducive to teaching and research within the department. Dr. Jones has been described as being mean spirited, arrogant and seemingly unable to value the positions of others. Dr. Jones is often dismissive of those ideological positions that he does not agree with. . . . [W]hile the department has a history of fragmentation, the stance, attitude or behaviors of Dr. Jones has only served to aggravate these tensions. In conclusion . . . [we] evaluate Dr. Jones as being uncollegial. Retention.

While locutionary differences exist in the text of the letters, the essential content is nearly identical. Receiving the letter, and proceeding to read it in his office, one of the junior scholars began quietly sobbing. Crushed by the characterization, he determined to fight it, eventually filing a grievance. Both junior working-class scholars contested the committee's letter as an unfounded character assassination that provided no evidence of "uncollegial behavior" and sent letters of protest to the dean, one of which read:

> I am formally asking that you investigate the process that was used in evaluating collegiality for both Dr. Smith and myself. I consider the statement issued by the committee and Dr. Brevis to be an acute *misrepresentation* of relations and actions I have maintained in the department. I was told by "Dr. White" [chair of the RPT Committee] that the process of evaluation *DID NOT* take place when the entire committee met but that statements were privately submitted to Dr. White. Moreover, neither Dr. White, nor Dr. Brevis, nor any members of RPT have ever told me what specific behaviors I engaged in which constituted "uncollegiality." When I asked repeatedly for such feedback during the meeting (which was attended by Professors Dr. Brevis, White, "Johnson," myself and Associate Dean "Ladoux"), I was told by Dr. White that the information was "confidential." I believe that the process used by RPT is not only unfair, but that it also violates MUPIM [Miami University Policy and Information Manual]. . . . I am

concerned that full professors in my own component have intentionally and strategically constructed a statement to ultimately force me out of the university. The statement includes no facts, provides no details, nor cites specific behaviors to substantiate the judgement of uncollegiality. I regard the statement to be nothing more than a character assassination and ask that you fully investigate it so that an impartial, fair process might prevail in the future. I ask this not only on behalf of myself and Dr. Smith, but also for those junior scholars who may follow us on the tenure track. (Emphasis in the original)

In addition to letters sent by the junior working-class scholars, other letters were sent by the full professors and dissenting faculty who saw the statements of uncollegiality as nothing more than retaliation. Petitioning the dean of the College of Arts and Science, faculty wrote:

Dear Dean "James":
We write this letter in response to the recent departmental retention process and letters concerning Smith and Jones. Our concern with the process and the letter surrounds the issue of non-collegiality. As you are well aware our department is in the middle of turmoil that involves personal, ideological, and structural issues facing the department. The collegiality vote, which was divided on factional lines, is just the latest example of our organizational difficulties. [We] the undersigned believe that the collegiality decision is invalid and in fact find these two individuals to be collegial and supportive. We view this decision by the department as a symptom of our organizational dysfunctional behavior, rather than a valid criticism of these two individuals.

A letter authored by one of the dissenting, senior faculty—the past chair of the department before the arrival of Chair Brevis—was sent to the entire department. It urged:

In my 15 years in this department (5 as chair) we have never found a colleague to be non-collegial during any retention, promotion or tenure decision. The fact that we had two negative votes in one year, during a period when department political conflict has reached new depths, is very disturbing. The fact that a committee could have a vote without any discussion is deeply troubling. Would we do this in our review of teaching or research? Surely we would find the lack of professional and collective consideration of this issue unacceptable. Having individuals outside of the meeting anonymously give comments to the committee chair deprives the committee of meaningful participation and does not allow any of us the ability to discuss or examine the legitimacy of the concerns raised. As I have observed the teaching and research commitment of these two individuals, the statements produced in the letter seem worse than inaccurate. . . . This is particularly troubling this year because of the inclusion of selected anonymous comments of an inflammatory and personal nature, which in my 15 years had never been done before. . . . I realize that we are deeply divided and that there is anger and mistrust across the department. But voting on collegiality in this environment seems like a bad decision.

However, members of the RPT Committee ignored the appeal and refused to reconvene. Months later, one of the junior faculty filed a grievance with the Committee for Faculty Rights and Responsibilities against Dr. Brevis, the chair of SGA, and Dr. White, the chair of RPT, compelling all of those who signed the initial statements on uncollegiality to produce direct and tangible evidence or delete language regarding uncollegiality from all departmental documents referencing Drs. Smith and Jones. Members of the RPT Committee who had strategically maneuvered to remove the two working-class junior faculty summarily purged passages citing uncollegiality from all documents in the personnel files of the two. Had the two junior scholars decided to file, and then won, "grievances of retaliation"—a much more serious charge—those RPT members bearing false witness in their accusations would have potentially faced the penalty of unpaid leaves. It is, perhaps, ironic that the anthropologists who were instrumental in organizing the failed expulsion of the two junior scholars were rewarded as the anthropology group was institutionally decoupled from sociology and gerontology, eventuating in the promotion of one of the primatologists to chair of the new department. By contrast, both junior scholars, disgusted with the university, with the apathy of the administration in protecting their rights, and with the full professors in sociology—Scientists—who contributed inflammatory statements behind closed doors, resigned their tenure-track positions at Miami University.

Drown All Voices

Not only faculty, but students as well, found themselves targets of retaliation by the Scientists. Following "the meeting" in November 1999, some of the Scientists began to penalize students for "conceptual spillover" into their classrooms. Using the language of postmodern sociology, critical-feminist sociology, and critical theory to frame issues within sociology and anthropology rather than that of traditional, value-free, bourgeois social science, students raised questions and contested the knowledge paradigm of the Scientists. Paradigmatic challenges by students were, of course, cast in the same critical-theoretical language that they had learned in our courses. The students' understanding of the critical-knowledge paradigm provided them with cognitive and discursive ammunition. The Scientists had heard this language before and they were not going to allow it within their own classrooms. Students were humiliated in the classroom, told they were not engaged in true "critical thinking" but in ideologizing. The students reported that, upon one occasion, when asked about postmodern forms of knowledge and the politics of its production, the hydrologist chastised the students and then joked that he was going to flunk them because they had not learned a thing about "real" or "valid" knowledge. Eventually the students were silenced in the classroom. However, students refused to be silent outside of the classroom and contested their treatment by posting protest signs around campus and throughout the sociology building. One such poster displayed three Nazi soldiers bearing the names Sociology, Anthropology, and Gerontology interrogating an elderly Jewish man. The accompanying caption read,

> How Many More in SGA Will Be Silenced . . . Before someone Speaks Out?? Stop the tyranny, voice your concern! One Department should not be allowed to trample over rights guaranteed in the constitution. Remember what happens when we turn our backs on fascism? Please do NOT direct your concerns to the SGA office . . . no one there gives a damn!

Hearing of the treatment being endured by junior faculty, and angry over their own subjugation, students distributed myriad other songs, poems, limericks, and posters, satirizing relations between the Scientists, who now appeared to dominate the department, and everyone else. One such poster displayed three monkeys assuming the poses "See No Evil," "Hear No Evil," and "Speak No Evil," encapsulated in text reading:

> Look at what's going on around you. Listen to the silenced voices. Speak out! What is oppression? When a professor cannot speak freely for fear of losing his/her job is that oppression? When students are pulled into departmental politics and cannot speak out with out fear of reprisals is that oppression? When professors and/or administrators intimidate those who disagree with them, using their power and influence is that oppression? When free speech as we know it does not exist and is subject to censure, backlash and silencing is THAT oppression? Why is it that we can have bleeding hearts for every injustice except those that occur in our own classes? Who wants a real education? Who wants to be able to formulate their own thoughts and opinions and not have to be spoonfed the privileged knowledge of a few tyrannical individuals? Make no mistake there are many honest and decent faculty and staff in the SGA department, these people are also at risk of being oppressed by the few. Help them help themselves. Stand up and say, "We refuse to allow ANYONE to be silenced in this class and in this department!" *Disclaimer*—The phrases "oppressive" and "tyrannical" only refer to a few people in the SGA department, people who would tear this sign down for example. If you feel that these words do not apply to you then you may be one of the honest and decent people in the department.

Through these emergent forms of protest, students had effectively created, presented, and maintained an injustice framework, which, albeit briefly, became part of their idioculture. It is notable that they remained undeterred by the fear of being failed—a possibility bandied about by the hydrologist. By the end of the term, the Scientists faced no other challenges from students.

The most vociferous students prepared for imminent graduation; for all others, the prospects of summer without the requirements of classes—or intermittent harassment—superseded all other concerns.

RELATIONS OF KNOWLEDGE PRODUCTION

In a critical, structural analysis of organizations, Fischer and Sirianni point out that all bureaucratically organized entities—including universities—are very limited in their potential for democratic participation.[15] Instead, they are forms of "friendly fascism," to use Bertram Gross's term, socially reproduced by two classes of workers.[16] *Political laborers* are members of the professional-managerial class whose job it is to control the work of "productive labor." Within the academy, productive labor is most recognizably embodied in the activities of junior faculty, secretaries, and student workers responsible for the creation of value in the form of education. Within SGA, critical, working-class sociologists provided most of the productive labor, teaching the largest classes, advising most of the majors, and ensuring the existence and operation of most of the extracurricular activities such as the Sociology Club and the student contingent of Democratic Socialists of America. By contrast, the scientists (1) reserved for themselves the smallest classes, including the applied sociology course (n = 6 students) and the sociology capstone (n = 12), and refused to share courses; (2) evaluated all junior faculty; and (3) evaluated and voted on the promotion of associate faculty who had applied for full professorships. The Scientists—all full professors—decided who stayed or was terminated, who received tenure, and who advanced to the highest levels within the department. Participation of associate and assistant professors was limited to program evaluation, course changes, and the departmental hiring of job applicants. What the ensuing departmental conflict revealed, then, was not just pedagogical differences between interest groups but also tensions in class relations that were embedded institutionally.

Class relations are institutionally formulated in the activities and rights bureaucratically incumbent upon those who find themselves in positions of relative control or subordination within the laboring process.[17] Within the academy, class is determined by the reification of organizational positions through which differential rights to participate in evaluation, regulation, and processes of termination are guaranteed (see table 10.2). This places full professors and administrators together in what Dahrendorf terms the "control class," assistant and associate professors, along with secretaries and student workers subordinated in the process.[18] Within the Department of Sociology, Gerontology, and Anthropology at Miami University, the social process of class was manifest in the distribution of leaves, course assignments, merit increases, and even summer teaching assignments.[19] Yet, there are also informal processes of class that accompany formal, organizational processes,

Table 10.2. Systems of Labor within Formal Organizations

Productive Labor	*Political Labor*
Work done to produce services, commodities, or achieve organizational goals Carried out by: Obey class Main interest: Efficiency of production	Work done to maintain the administrative apparatus and control labor Carried out by: Command class Main interest: Managerial control over workers*

*Relations are exacerbated by autocratic as opposed to democratic leadership styles.
See Fischer and Sirianni (1984).

lending the latter institutional legitimacy. That senior faculty are encouraged to serve as mentors in both research and teaching legitimates the formal processes by reifying the assumptions that it is they whose experience produces a superior educational experience for students. Yet, within Sirianni sociology, student evaluations revealed exactly the opposite. And conversations initiated by students, within the private enclave of my own office, confirmed the "objective" indicators provided in course evaluations.

Within sociology, as well as the department as a whole, the ideological constructs used in legitimating the social organization of class relations were those differentially defined by the "scientists" and "critical, working-class" scholars within the department (see table 10.3). Having already suggested

Table 10.3. The Organization of Class Relations in Academia

Ideological Constructs in Sociology as a Profession
Civility/Professionalism
Philosophy of Science
Critical Thinking

Class: The Structure of Responsibilities and Privileges
Civility/Professionalism
Philosophy of Science
Critical Thinking

Class: The Structure of Responsibilities and Privileges
Teaching Load
Course Assignments
Committee Assignments
Awarded Leaves
Merit Increases
Summer Teaching Money
Internal Grants

Relationship to the Knowledge Production Process
Rank of Employment (Formal)
Supervision of Labor (Formal & Informal)
Evaluation of Labor (Formal & Informal)
Termination of Labor (Formal)

paradigmatic differences in the philosophies of science between Scientists and the Critical Scholars, in at least cursory fashion, I turn now to a more thorough examination of two other elements within the ideology of both the department and sociology as a whole: civility and critical thinking.

IDEOLOGICAL CONTOURS

Civility as Ideology and Discourse

Three significant developments marked the collective experience of the department by fall 2002. First, the dean of the College of Arts and Science split up the combined SGA department, creating a Department of Sociology and Gerontology separate from a new Department of Anthropology. Second, he also replaced former chair Brevis with a new interim chair from the English department. And, finally, former chair Brevis retained a position within the gerontology group but eventually refrained from participation. Posterior to these developments, talk of the need for civility—especially among members of the scientific sociologists, who now found themselves the numerical minority within a reconstituted department—increased. This discourse was still present as I departed the university in spring 2003. One member of the department, Dr. White, was apparently upset when, after he entered the main department office and issued a loud salutation, one colleague did not respond. Dr. White, the former chair of the RPT Committee, then sent an e-mail to the entire department, lecturing all of us on civility:

> Civility, defined by Webster as courteous behavior, politeness, a courteous act or utterance, is a basic assumption of any social community. As a citizen in the department, such courteous behavior is part of what we normally refer to as collegiality. Please be advised, as both a Christian and a citizen in this department, I will continue to treat each and every member with civility. Speaking, recognized even among combatants on the war field, fights, hell even by opposing gangs on the street. . . . therefore anything else constitutes not only disrespect but can only be understood to violate the [tenets] of collegiality.

What is ignored in the lecture on civility is a basic sociological understanding of the meaning of silence. Silence can be regarded as an "indexical expression" deriving its meaning and illocutionary force from relations found within the social context.[20] Quite simply, there are as many meanings of silence as social contexts within which it occurs. Within church sanctuaries, silence represents the sanctification of both physical and social space. Silence within Amish communities may indicate that one is being shunned. Silence between "combatants on the war field" represents the need to avoid detection. "Grandmother's Rule" admonishes that if one cannot say anything nice, then one should not say anything at all. Dr. White's estimate of the occasion as one that "can only be understood to violate the [tenets] of collegiality" is both ironic and decidedly incorrect. As Dr. White was the architect of a process that ultimately drove the junior scholars from the department, elevating already high levels of conflict, silence here *was* civility. Moreover, Dr. White's own presentation of self was marked by common, bellicose displays including the proclamation, "Jesus has blessed me," loudly announced as he traversed the hallways. His intermittent insinuations that white racism on the part of faculty marked departmental decisions with which he disagreed, along with his confrontational, bellicose style, became the basis of interpersonal avoidance by more than one faculty member. The unresponsive faculty member harangued by Dr. White in the sociology office, was a working-class, critical sociologist who had formerly sought mediation under the auspices of the dean's office. During mediation, he requested that Dr. White cease race-baiting and simply leave him alone. Within this context, it is surprising that the meaning mobilized about silence by Dr. White is one premised on a lack of civility in the department, as opposed to other available meanings. What then is "civility"? While the Scientists in the department defined civility as being courteous and well mannered in face-to-face interaction (a tenet that they themselves violated during the infamous November department meeting), working-class, critical scholars defined it in terms of democratic ideals that ensured representation and fairness (see table 10.4).

In his book *A History of Manners*, Norbert Elias observes that through the late seventeenth century and into the early eighteenth century the German bourgeoisie began to "practice" civility.[21] As Elias notes, the practice itself was guided by an ideology of civilizing that exalted French customs and language over native German culture. This ideology preserved the cultural hegemony of the French nobility even as members of that class found themselves being displaced by an ascendant (revolutionary) class. The ideology of civility found within sociology and other professions likewise serves several purposes: first it extends hegemonic influence to the degree that it is practiced on terms established by those in power. It exists as both a set of cultural expectations and a meaning structure that can be invoked as challenges to relations of ruling are orchestrated on other grounds. Second, as norms of civility come to be shared, they "democratize good manners" even as they mystify relations of ruling; they insist that challenges to power are addressed within the established institutional frameworks privileging those relations. Civility as an ideology, then, eschews disruption, open conflict, dissent, and noncooperation in favor of manners, courtesy, and etiquette. Within the confines of academia, the resources of the relatively powerless—criticism, protest, and noncompliance—are defined as "uncivil."

Let us return to Dr. White and the unresponsive critical sociologist. The question of sociological significance is not what a single "speech act"—or a

Table 10.4.   Ideological Differences between Scientists and Critical, Working-Class Scholars

Scientists' Definition of the Situation

Mobilizing for change is "acting ideologically" and bad.

Activism in any form is not sociology but ideology. Ideology and Science are antipodal. Science and scientific knowledge are "value-free" and disinterested forms of observation.

Those who undermine the administration's appointed leaders are circumventing the system and are not real "team" players.

Civility means "being friendly" to all people, demonstrating good manners and etiquette in interaction.

Critical thinking entails seeing the same phenomenon from multiple viewpoints in order to promote understanding.

Critique: Critical Sociologists are ideological not scientific or disinvested of interest in outcomes. Critical sociologists who avow and engage in organizational, institutional, and programmatic change are the source of all conflict.

Critical Scholars' Definition of the Situation

Mobilizing for change in support of workplace democracy is ideological and good.

All science is teleological and ideological. All knowledge and knowledge production is value based. "Disinterested sociology's" prescription against praxis is itself a form of ideological action that reproduces the relations of domination/subordination.

Administrators are "political labor" whose job it is to control productive labor (faculty), not ensure democracy.

Civility means ensuring the autonomy of all workers, guaranteeing due process and rights to all, staying out of each other's way.

Critical thinking entails applying historical and comparative (multiple) perspectives in order to promote change while remaining self-reflective of one's own position.

Critique: Scientists are ideological though unaware of their own ideological bias. Their avowed disinterest in outcomes ensures social reproduction of the present system of inequality from which they derive privilege. Sociology departments that fail to acknowledge and strive for humanizing change are nothing more than country clubs supporting individual hobbyists.

refusal to speak—*really* means; rather, it is who gets to decide the basis upon which both utterances and silence are judged to be legitimate. What is revealed in such an analysis is the power relationship between colocutors and the "illocutionary force" of utterances where rules of civility serve as a professional-managerial-class resource. This point is made precise in the work of both Michel Foucault[22] and Jürgen Habermas:[23] discursive formations reveal and reproduce power relations.

The ideological contours of civility bear similarity to other political ideologies. As Martin Selinger indicates, all ideologies are action-based systems of coherent beliefs based upon moral prescriptions.[24] These prescriptions become salient as people blend them in everyday analysis, trying to make sense out of situations. Moreover, ideologies deny the plausibility and/or relevance of alternative beliefs, meanings, and definitions. Civility as an ideology operable within the academy contains class-based premises that negate possibilities for understanding action or promoting change. To define the critical analysis of power relations within the department as ideological, and the actions taken by working-class and other scholars to democratize them as forms of incivility, serves to ground power/knowledge relations in the dominant paradigm. Claims for the need to restore "goodwill," speak when spoken to, act with civility, and resolve crises according to the rules of the dominant ideology ensure its reproduction.

Critical Thinking *Em-bourgeois*

Another formative element in the discourse of liberal, bourgeois sociology is the claim to critical thinking.[25] This ideological construct at Miami University, as well as within the profession, is one defined as a series of cognitive shifts allowing students to view the same phenomenon from multiple perspectives in order to promote understanding. Commonly, thinking is considered "critical" if it effectuates a cognitive shift from clinical or individualist perspectives to one that is structural. Yet, the deployment of critical thinking—its use in interrogating relations of ruling within one's own department, or the relations between professors and students within the academy—is defined as untoward behavior when it potentially subjects power holders to discreditation before an audience of others. As Goffman points out, performers in everyday life are commonly compelled "to take seriously the performance that is fostered before them."[26] We are obliged to regard as sincere those "individuals who believe in the impression fostered by their own performance."[27] Yet, the preeminent task of both sociology and critical thinking is "to penetrate the smoke screen of official versions of reality,"[28] allowing us to locate ourselves within the nexus of biography and the political, economic, and social forces shaping history.[29]

After ushering in removal of SGA chair Brevis and protesting other injustices within the department, working-class Critical Scholars found themselves the target of retaliation on the part of Scientists. Levels of trust having plummeted, Critical Scholars engaged in collegial discourse with scientists over programmatic concerns in the meetings of the new department but increasingly withdrew from everyday interaction with Scientists. Charges of incivility and refusal to be "real team players" were leveled against the Critical Scholars by the Scientists remaining in the new department. From the perspective of the Critical Scholars, attempts to normalize interaction on the part of Scientists were viewed as "suspect," as a denial of culpability, and as a "whitewash" of the damage that the Scientists had perpetrated.

Performative as well as ideological orientations may be mistakenly assumed as similar among sociologists sharing the same work context. Moreover, similarity in consumptive patterns, professional training, and occupational demands among upper-middle-class and working-class sociologists may lead to the presumption of a common identity, biography, and set of professional experiences. This image of commonality congeals when basic sociological terms such as "critical thinking" or "civility" are used by all, their ubiquity mistakenly taken as a sign of common pedagogy and philosophy. It is sociologically intriguing that presumptions of commonality do not seem to be made as readily among working-class sociologists as they are among their professional-managerial counterparts.

CONCLUSION

Civility and critical thinking are ideological components enacted as class-based vocabularies of motive. Hence, these components are defined very differently by professional-managerial-class and working-class scholars. Definitions of civility constructed by members of the professional-managerial class at Miami University included norms of courtesy, etiquette, and manners. However, for working-class scholars, civility meant constructing social relations upon the basis of equality, democracy, and autonomy. Performances that embodied dominant norms of etiquette while enforcing relations of ruling were defined as cynical performances by working-class scholars. Working-class academics can, of course, forsake their own ideology of civility. Granfield's research on working-class law students reveals the strategies that many students use in covering their former class membership in order to become "social climbers."[30] The adoption of such strategies is always a possibility for working-class faculty and administrators as well. Moreover, as social climbers become "locationally secure," they may tout their working-class identities even as they forsake the interests and ideals of other working-class members who look to them for help.

While critical sociology demands self-reflective interrogation of one's own theory and practice, critical analyses of class relations with other sociologists are rarely made. Indeed, "critical thinking" itself has now become the legitimating discourse of bourgeois sociology. Paying lip service to the intellectual heritage of critical education, represented in the work of scholars such as Paulo Freire[31] and Henry Giroux,[32] bourgeois sociologists depart from critical pedagogy's insistence on democratization, constructing a meaning of critical thinking in line with corporate ideology and marketeering. Bourgeois sociology accepts critical pedagogy's insistence on a reflective, skeptical posture that relies upon multiple perspectives but fails to embrace its mandate for social change. In a world inhabited by 6.3 billion people, 60 percent of whom live in poverty, one must ask those questions abandoned by sociology's bourgeois impulse: "Knowledge for what? Whose side are we on?" Because bourgeois sociology neglects teaching critical theory that is anchored in radical analyses of political-economic history, it can offer no philosophical anthropology or teleology that can serve as the basis for humanistic intervention in the world. By contrast, critical, working-class scholarship mandates that the reason to "do sociology," to engage in critical thinking, is to create the conditions and strategies for meaningful intervention in the world. Intervention is "meaningful" to the degree that it humanizes and democratizes the lives of people, empowering them as agents of change within the local contexts of their own existence. In so doing, critical scholarship is of necessity steeped in a historical understanding of production relations, social relations, and political economy.

The case study presented in this analysis highlights the differences between working-class and professional-managerial-class scholars, especially with regard to the meaning and mission of social science. My own working-class experience, reflected within this chapter, suggests that simply adhering to norms of bourgeois etiquette will not secure the rights to full citizenship within the academy or elsewhere. In historical moments of conflict, class relations are often revealed in compelling fashion. Within academia, enacting the operative values to which members of the professional-managerial class commonly pay homage rarely threatens a social order based upon privilege and inequality. In the absence of critical analysis, bourgeois civility provides little more than a performative gloss over relations of ruling. By contrast, a civility grounded in structural processes ensuring autonomy, equality, and democracy leads to both mutual survival and full citizenship. To produce a world of civility based upon these values means that we construct ourselves, fully, as subjects.

NOTES

1. Robert Granfield, "Making It by Faking It: Working-Class Students in an Elite Academic Environment," *Journal of Contemporary Ethnology* 20 (1991): 331–51.

2. Dorothy Smith, *Texts, Facts, and Femininity: Exploring the Relations of Ruling* (New York: Routledge, 1993).

3. Robert S. Lynd, *Knowledge for What? The Place of Social Science in American Culture* (New York: Grove Press, 1964).

4. Irving Louis Horowitz, "The Life and Death of Project Camelot," *Trans-Action* 3, no. 1 (1965): 3–7, 44–47.

5. Alvin W. Gouldner, "Anti-Minotaur: The Myth of a Value-Free Sociology," *Social Problems* 9 (1962): 199–213; and Alvin W. Gouldner, *The Coming Crisis of Western Sociology* (New York: Basic Books, 1970).

6. Howard S. Becker, "Whose Side Are We On?" *Social Problems* 14 (1967): 239–47.

7. Dorothy Smith, "Women's Perspective as a Radical Critique of Sociology," *Sociological Inquiry* 44 (1974): 7–13.

8. Don Martindale, *The Romance of a Profession: A Case History in the Sociology of Sociology* (St. Paul, MN: Windflower, 1976).

9. These tales were shared among secretaries as well, some of whom served as "priests" of the institution's underlife, sharing stories and tales with graduate students. One story, of contemporary vintage, included a tryst carried on between a secretary and a professor in one of the obscure offices of Wilson Library. The story reported the involved secretary exclaiming, "And he gave me the best oral sex I've ever had!" at which point some of the graduate students began to call the professor "Doctor Long-Tongue" behind his back.

10. All names appearing in the text have been changed to protect the guilty. Identities are easily enough discerned through material from both the American Sociological Association and files at Miami University. Miami University files are subject to open disclosure under the Public Records Act established by Ohio state legislative fiat and published through the office of Attorney General Betty D. Montgomery: *An Ohio Sunshine Laws Update: March 2000*.

11. Allen Smith III and Sherryl Kleinman, "Managing Emotions in Medical School: Students' Contacts with the Living and the Dead," *Social Psychology Quarterly* 52 (1989): 56–69.

12. See Barbara Ehrenreich's recent autoethnography, *Nickel and Dimed: On (Not) Getting By in America* (New York: Metropolitan Books, 2001).

13. The term "colonized" is one I have appropriated from Jürgen Habermas, *Communication and the Evolution of Society* (Boston: Beacon Press, 1979). and bears his intended usage. Gouldner (1970) emphasizes that for most sociologists, colonization is methodological; my point is that the process is molded by social class.

14. I have adopted the distinction between "identification of" and "identification with" from Gregory Stone, "Appearance," in *Social Psychology through Symbolic Interaction,* ed. Gregory P. Stone and Harvey A. Faberman, 101–13 (New York: Macmillan, 1986*).* The issue of how working-class academics negotiate relations in their family of origin is one given full treatment in Janelle Wilson's chapter in this book.

15. Frank Fischer and Carmen Sirianni, *Critical Studies in Organization and Bureaucracy* (Philadelphia: Temple University Press, 1984).

16. Bertram Gross, *Friendly Fascism: The New Face of Power in America* (Boston: South End Press, 1982).

17. Erik Ohlin Wright, *Classes* (London: New Left Books, 1985).

18. Ralf Dahrendorf, *Class and Class Conflict in Industrial Society* (Stanford, CA: Stanford University Press, 1959).

19. During the course of my employment, the basis of teaching assignments within sociology was changed to a rotation basis. Violation of this norm was occasionally attempted by one full professor, a Scientist.

20. Harold Garfinkel and Harvey Sacks, "On Formal Structures of Practical Action," in *Theoretical Sociology: Perspectives and Development,* ed. John C. McKinney and Edward A. Tiryakien (New York: Appleton-Century-Crofts, 1970).

21. Norbert Elias, *The Civilizing Process,* volume 1, *The History of Manners* (1939; reprint, New York: Pantheon Books, 1982).

22. Michel Foucault, *Discipline and Punish: The Birth of the Prison* (New York: Vintage, 1979); and Michel Foucault, *The History of Sexuality,* vol. 1, *An Introduction* (New York: Vintage, 1990).

23. Jürgen Habermas, *Communication and the Evolution of Society,* trans. and with an introduction by Thomas McCarthy (Boston: Beacon Press, 1979).

24. Martin Selinger, *Ideology and Politics* (London: George Allen & Unwin, 1976).

25. By the term "bourgeois sociology," I mean sociology practiced by people who have no intention of changing relations of production or distribution either in society or within the profession.

26. Erving Goffman, *The Presentation of Self in Everyday Life* (Garden City, NY: Doubleday Anchor, 1959), 17.

27. Goffman, *Presentation of Self,* 18.

28. Peter L. Berger, *Invitation to Sociology* (Garden City, NY: Anchor, 1963), 35.

29. C. Wright Mills, *The Sociological Imagination* (New York: Oxford University Press, 1959).

30. Granfield, *Making It by Faking It.*

31. Paulo Freire, *Pedagogy of the Oppressed* (New York: Seabury Press, 1970).

32. Henry A. Giroux, *Schooling and the Struggle for Public Life: Critical Pedagogy in the Modern Age* (Minneapolis: University of Minnesota Press, 1988).

REFERENCES

Becker, Howard S. "Whose Side Are We On?" *Social Problems* 14 (1967): 239–47.

Berger, Peter L. *Invitation to Sociology.* Garden City, NY: Anchor, 1963.

Dahrendorf, Ralf. *Class and Class Conflict in Industrial Society.* Stanford, CA: Stanford University Press, 1959.

Ehrenreich, Barbara. *Nickel and Dimed: On (Not) Getting By in America.* New York: Metropolitan Books, 2001.

Elias, Norbert. *The Civilizing Process.* Vol. 1, *The History of Manners.* New York: Pantheon Books, 1982.

Fischer, Frank, and Carmen Sirianni. *Critical Studies in Organization and Bureaucracy.* Philadelphia: Temple University Press, 1984.

Foucault, Michel. *Discipline and Punish: The Birth of the Prison* (New York: Vintage, 1979).

———. *The History of Sexuality.* Vol. 1, *An Introduction.* New York: Vintage, 1990.

Freire, Paulo. *Pedagogy of the Oppressed.* New York: Seabury, 1970.

Garfinkel, Harold, and Harvey Sacks. 1970. "On Formal Structures of Practical Action." In *Theoretical Sociology: Perspectives and Development,* ed. John C. McKinney and Edward A. Tiryakien. New York: Appleton-Century-Crofts, 1970.

Giroux, Henry A. *Schooling and the Struggle for Public Life: Critical Pedagogy in the Modern Age.* Minneapolis: University of Minnesota Press, 1988.

Goffman, Erving. *The Presentation of Self in Everyday Life.* Garden City, NY: Doubleday Anchor, 1959.

Gouldner, Alvin W. "Anti-Minotaur: The Myth of a Value-Free Sociology." *Social Problems* 9 (1962): 199–213.

———. *The Coming Crisis of Western Sociology.* New York: Basic Books, 1970.

Granfield, Robert. "Making It by Faking It: Working-Class Students in an Elite Academic Environment." *Journal of Contemporary Ethnology* 20 (1991): 331–51.

Gross, Bertram. *Friendly Fascism: The New Face of Power in America* (Boston: South End Press, 1982).

Habermas, Jürgen. *Communication and the Evolution of Society.* Trans. and with an introduction by Thomas McCarthy. Boston: Beacon Press, 1979.

Horowitz, Irving Louis. "The Life and Death of Project Camelot." *Trans-Action* 3 (1965): 3–7, 44–47.

Lynd, Robert S. *Knowledge for What? The Place of Social Science in American Culture.* New York: Grove Press, 1964.

Martindale, Don. *The Romance of a Profession: A Case History in the Sociology of Sociology.* St. Paul, MN: Windflower, 1976.

Mills, C. Wright. *The Sociological Imagination.* New York: Oxford University Press, 1959.

Selinger, Martin. *Ideology and Politics.* London: George Allen & Unwin, 1976.

Smith, Dorothy E. "Women's Perspective as a Radical Critique of Sociology." *Sociological Inquiry* 44 (1974): 7–13.

———. *Texts, Facts, and Femininity: Exploring the Relations of Ruling.* New York: Routledge, 1993.

Smith, Allen C., III, and Sherryl Kleinman. "Managing Emotions in Medical School: Students' Contacts with the Living and the Dead." *Social Psychology Quarterly* 52 (1989): 56–69.

Stone, Gregory P. 1986. "Appearance." In *Social Psychology through Symbolic Interaction,* ed. Gregory P. Stone and Harvey A. Faberman, 101–13. New York: Macmillan, 1986.

Wright, Erik Ohlin. *Classes.* London: New Left Books, 1985.

11

Working-Class Values and Life in Academe: Examining the Dissonance

Janelle L. Wilson

Over the past several years, I have attended and sometimes participated in sessions at the annual meeting of the Midwest Sociological Society that had as their focus experiences associated with being an academic originally from the working class. These sessions have been characterized by stories, insights, and theorizing that speak to central sociological issues and topics, such as stratification, social justice, prejudice, and alienation. These sessions also have produced, for me, the comfortable feeling of being understood—that is, of not being so alone in some of my perceptions, feelings, and observations. Indeed, lasting friendships have formed from participation in the sessions.

I am a sociologist whose teaching and research is best described as following a sociology-of-everyday-life approach. I work in the areas of self and identity, deviance, collective memory, and nostalgia. It seems that research undertaken by sociologists who use this approach often has autobiographical roots. My interest in the self (or "selves") and identity reflects my own trajectory of trying to know and understand the self—the selves—that I am creating (realizing that the self called for in my hometown among relatives is a very different self than that called for in my professional life). My interest in the sociology of nostalgia reflects knowledge of where I came from—never wanting to forget those humble roots. I desire to hold on to pleasant memories of growing up with extended family all around me. Much of my research has focused on the study of popular culture. That I am attracted to the study of popular culture—an area that demands that the researcher study culture (and history) from the bottom up—fits with my own feelings of being an underdog in academe and my identification with how it feels to not belong among the elite.

Writing a chapter on the topic of working-class academics is both cathartic and empowering. Knowing that many of the experiences about which I write are shared and familiar to others and knowing that there is an audience for a book like this makes insecurities, doubts, and frustrations related to what is felt as a marginal position all the more bearable.

Academics from the working class tend to experience a great deal of cognitive dissonance. Admittedly, many of us have the proverbial chip on our shoulders. Thought processes, emotions, and behaviors that were appropriate given our class location prior to becoming professors are not accepted as legitimate or advantageous in the academic setting. Lacking many of the resources that others in academe take for granted, the working-class academic perpetually feels out of place. Professors from working-class backgrounds do not initially have the kind of social and cultural capital that they eventually acquire en route to a position in the academy. For most of us, this is a source of dissonance—a constant reminder that we are living and working in a place far from our origin.

Many of the values that those of us from the working class have internalized are quite different from the types of values that characterize life in academe.[1] Hence, dissonance is a fairly normative experience for working-class academics. In this chapter, I present some specific examples and consider the implications of this clashing of values.

COMMUNICATION

With regard to communication, a prominent working-class value is "telling it like it is," which can result in one being quite direct. This collides with the rhetoric and diplomacy of the academy. In departmental or committee meetings, how often do academics *truly* tell it like it is? Keeping thoughts and emotions in check is the normative expectation. Parsimony is not typically a characteristic of scholarly writing or speaking. Scholarly articles are lengthy, jargonized, complex. "Succinct" is not often used to describe academic speaking or writing. As Dews expresses, "My background taught me that thinking or talking for the sake of thinking or talking is show-boating, a waste of time in a world where time clocks matter."[2]

Another trait of the working-class individual is that she is probably quite passionate. It seems that being passionate—in meetings, in the classroom— is not typically looked upon favorably by administrators. This is an emotion that needs to be managed, and the results can be quite stifling, as it is disingenuous to hide or try to ignore what triggers our passion. David Wellman notes that, for what he calls "border academics," being too passionate is unacceptable; so is "being committed to principles which university insiders call being 'inflexible,' or 'unreasonable.'" He continues:

We discover that survival in the academy depends upon learning that it is inappropriate to argue from the heart, or from a position of principle. The appropriate method is to invoke "empirical evidence," or remain silent until sufficient "data" have been collected. Border academics find out that direct talk, "telling it like it is"—or speaking "truth to power" is counterproductive.[3]

The professor is supposed to exemplify value freedom—to objectively explain and describe phenomena but not necessarily express that she *cares* or is *passionate* about issues. She is expected to be thorough (which does not allow for spontaneity) and prudent (which does not allow for emotional expression). Such academic qualities as prudence and thoroughness are admirable, but are they qualities to a fault? The working-class academic brings to the university setting qualities that have more applicability, relevance, and potential for enacting positive change. Because working-class academics have at least one foot in "the real world," their presence can lessen the general tendency to reify social problems and issues.

Humor is another aspect of communication where we see key social-class differences. The kind of humor that is deemed appropriate among academicians is humor that relies upon clever puns and witticisms. For those from the working class, humor is apt to be more direct. Humor is valued, for it provides us with a sense that we can make it through hard times. In the academic setting, working-class academics commonly use humor to poke fun at themselves and, indeed, at the academic enterprise altogether. There is a tendency to not take oneself too seriously and to make fun of those who do. Yet, we know that scholars are expected to take themselves and their work quite seriously, and failing to do so might be viewed as an insult or even a threat to the profession.

The way in which conflict is handled calls upon different communication techniques based upon one's class background. In the academic setting, conflict is managed by keeping your cool, managing your emotions, and addressing the issue in a professional manner such as writing a respectful memo or setting up a formal meeting. A fellow working-class academic told me, after he had been in an intense argument with an administrator, that he was not that far removed from the jungle, and he would "kick some ass" if he had to. He genuinely seemed tempted to "take it outside." That kind of raw emotion is not allowed in the academic setting.

Another area where we can see differences in communication is in the vocabulary of individuals from different social-class backgrounds. While academics can be viewed as "equal" in the sense that they have all gone through graduate programs in order to receive advanced degrees, the academics with working-class roots did not enter those programs on an equal footing in terms of cultural experience and elegant vocabulary. As an undergraduate student, I sent for a set of cassette tapes (actually, just half of the set of tapes because that was more affordable) that were intended to increase vocabulary. Every night I listened to those tapes, rehearsing the words—their pronunciation, spelling, and definitions. The working-class academic always feels that she is "behind" and must try to "catch up" with the skills, abilities, and experiences of colleagues. Even when we feel that we have acquired a command of the vocabulary and vernacular that indicate our membership in the academic group, we might find ourselves uncomfortable employing this knowledge. As Dews says: "I find myself using words like *hegemony* against my will. I just can't shake it. So what happens is that I shift back and forth between these styles . . . between my old way of talkin' and the new discourse of the academy."[4]

The topics of conversation among academics from different social-class backgrounds also highlight differences in experiences and resources. For the upper-middle or upper-class academic, travel to exotic places, for example, has probably been a way of life. Those of us with working-class roots are not likely to be well traveled. When colleagues talk about previous or future trips over seas, we feel alienated from this experience. Even if we reach a time in our career when our salary would allow such travel, there may be hesitancy to take advantage of it. After all, this is a whole new experience and the skills associated with this kind of travel are underdeveloped. I had never been on a plane until my second year of graduate school, when I was invited to give a presentation at Vanderbilt University. My professors told me what to expect, how early to get to the airport, and so on. They seemed surprised that this was my first experience with air travel.

Arrogance pervades academe. In conversations with fellow professors at the university where I teach, I take umbrage at their criticism of many of the students. These professors comment on the lack of preparation and intelligence among students. While this group of professors may have been given the opportunity to attend private schools and universities and receive private tutoring if they were having difficulty in a subject, this is an experience far removed from that of many of the students who attend this public university.

For many of us, it is as Nancy LaPaglia describes:

> I like academics as a group: They are smart, funny ("witty"), reasonable, and they usually talk rather than hit people. But I still think of them as "them," although I have graduate degrees and have been on a college faculty for decades. I am not comfortable with middle-class gentility, for one thing. My upbringing did not equip me with polite (which I often read negatively as "passionless" or "distanced" manners) . . . the great majority of academics come equipped with middle-class manners.[5]

FAMILY

Some of the family values that typify the working class include loyalty and mutual support, staying close to home, and sacrificing. Those of us who choose careers in academe may end up living far away from our family of origin. And our families may not understand what it is we do, why we had to go so far away, or why we are not able to get back to the hometown. My first tenure-track job was in a state different from where I had lived all of my life. At least for the first few years, my mother never failed to notify me whenever she heard that there were openings in a university closer to home. Though the positions may have been in specializations different from mine, they were viewed as jobs for which I ought to apply so that I could "come home." The tenure process does not make sense to my family of origin. My family did, however, pick up on the fact that getting tenure typically means that you stay at that university for life. When I got tenure, my dad responded, "So that means you can never leave, huh?" What for me was a big milestone was viewed as more of a burden or obstacle by my parents. In the vernacular of a factory worker, I appeared destined (or doomed?) to be a "lifer."

In some cases, working-class academics have been the beneficiaries of a great deal of family sacrifice, getting them to where they are. In my case, this meant my parents paid for the bulk of my undergraduate education. Although my parents never earned high wages, they were very thrifty, committed to making sure that my brother and I had the opportunity to go to college so that we wouldn't end up, as my dad used to say, having to work in a dirty factory like he did. My going to a community college for the first two years and receiving scholarships helped to alleviate some of the burden of the cost of the undergraduate education.

In some cases, the kid in a working-class family who shows promise of making something of himself gets the support and sacrifice of parents and also siblings. Families mobilize resources, support, and emotion for children who appear to be able to escape the cycle and do something and be something. Colleagues in the university who come from higher social-class backgrounds are not likely to understand these kinds of values and experiences. The paradox is that, even as working-class families may make it possible for children to leave home, they may not fully realize or accept the implications of departure. The working class is wedded to stable community, while academics are wedded to their profession. My sense is that academics from a higher social-class standing *expect* to be geographically mobile. And, further, since travel has likely been a normative part of their lives, geographical mobility is not viewed as unusual. It is assumed that there will always be resources that enable family members to get together—money for plane tickets or a new SUV for road travel.

Relationships with members of working-class families can become strained because of generational differences in education. The further I went in school, the more distance there was between my parents and myself. Going directly to graduate school following my B.A. degree was a move that invited labeling as a "professional student." The combination of *still* being a student and majoring in a field misunderstood by my family (sociology) contributed to the chasm. It is still felt today. Law recalls that, when she was about to enter a Ph.D. program, her mother said to her: "Education destroys something." Law understands what she meant; as she says:

"In my trajectory from working-class family of origin to the threshold of middle-class professional status, I have suffered a loss my present context doesn't even recognize as loss; my education *has* destroyed something even while it has been re-creating me in its own image."[6]

COMMUNITY

For the working class, idealistic images of community contain a sedimentation of basic values: Everyone looks out for everyone else, people are treated fairly, community members cooperate with one another, and there is personal responsibility to look out for "the little guy" (i.e., root for the underdog). The values of democracy and egalitarianism are manifested. All of these values potentially clash with life in the university. The underdogs, adjunct and nonregular faculty, are invisible, devalued, pressed upon, and exploited. Indeed, exploitation becomes normative. People are not on an equal footing with each other in the university setting. Stratification is seen and experienced at all levels. Consider, for example, the bureaucratic structure of the university; the varying income levels among professors in different disciplines regardless of expertise; the income levels of staff compared to those of professors; resource allocation based on discipline; the professor's authority over the students. Many working-class academics find it uncomfortable and awkward to exert their authority over students. There seems to be a reluctance to be judgmental and an attempt to democratize the classroom. Yet, we are instructed that if we do not display our authority, we will lose it. Treating students with respect and downplaying the hierarchical dimension of the student-professor relationship might be viewed as trying to gain favorable teaching evaluations. Attempting to "go to bat" for an adjunct faculty member could threaten one's tenure bid.

Certainly, in any work setting we can see stratification and its effects, inclusion and exclusion as well as competition and disloyalty. But we also expect more of the university, a setting anticipated to be open, tolerant, and diverse, employing highly educated individuals. Yet, where is the community in this setting? Are people looking out for one another? Community in the academic setting is more likely to be formed on the basis of social class and ideology. Thus, the divisions continue.

WORK

In the realm of work, members of the working class may display variable commitments to the work ethic. Work itself is defined as that which produces some tangible result. Work is practical and functional. Thus, while the commitment to work may be potentially variable, its nature and character are likely to yield a strong work ethic. This type of work ethic is not applicable in academe. One of the frustrating aspects of teaching is that the instructor is unable to gauge whether he or she is having an impact. Typically, it is only when students come by our office and tell us that they are engaged with the material that we get the kind of feedback that comes close to something tangible. Talking about ideas and theories and writing articles for other academics are not practical, useful, functional activities from the standpoint of the working class. Academics from the working class struggle with reconciling the differing definitions of work.

In the world that I had been accustomed to, hard work is defined as involving sweat, body aches, tangible results, a clear beginning point and a clear end point, as well as the idea that a certain amount of work is equal to a certain amount of money. In the academic world, however, hard work is defined as tenacity, intangible results, an emphasis on the "process" (not necessarily an end point). Michael Schwalbe, a working-class sociologist, expresses greater attraction to research than teaching. He explains it this way:

> I need to see a tangible product in order to believe I'm doing real work. . . . I learned that real work is done with the back and hands and results in things you can see and touch and use. . . . At least if I write a paper I can heft it. I can see that something exists where nothing existed before. And if I write lots of papers, I can see lines add up on my vita. All this is evidence of my ability to produce, which I also somehow learned is an important measure of a person's worth.[7]

Another way in which academic work differs from the working-class definition of work is that it may not be compensated with money but rather with personal pride or public recognition. Consider how output is defined in academe as opposed to most other occupations: In our capitalist system, output is directly related to remuneration. Within the university, on the other hand, professors are encouraged to publish articles and books that are not in any direct way related to salary. With the exception of textbooks, many academic books generate little or no income. And writing textbooks is not considered "research." In academe, there is no direct payment for many of the professional activities we are expected to perform, such as presenting papers at conferences, reviewing articles for a journal, or writing and publishing articles and books. While such activities may slightly boost merit pay, there is no direct, "piecemeal" payment. Viewed from the working class, this seems rather strange.[8] My adviser in graduate school told me that, when his first book came out, he called his mother and told her about it. Her immediate question was, "How much money did you make writing that book?" Getting a mere $2.95 in royalties each year was not understandable to her. When I go to conferences to present papers, family members and friends outside academe assume that all of the expenses are covered by the university. In fact, we must apply for grants to help cover some of those costs.

Much of what is expected of (tenure-track) faculty might be viewed as game playing. Senior colleagues may offer advice on how to "play the game," but having gainful employment has not, for working-class academics, been viewed as a game. In fact, it feels unsettling to refer to it as such. Work-related functions (social or professional) demand a presentation of self that does not feel very authentic for the working-class academic. Most individuals deeply rooted in the working class do not feel comfortable with or adept at activities such as networking, "sucking up," and self-promotion. And yet, these are activities both common at such functions and often necessary for success (or even survival). Social gatherings of academics often seem fake and haughty to me. At the same time, I feel ashamed for not fitting in better and am envious of those who are better able to play the game. I have been at social gatherings where there is a mix of academics and laypersons. Quite often, I find that I enjoy talking with the laypersons much more than with the academic types.

The very different conception of work between the social classes also contributes to misunderstanding and conflict with my family of origin. If my teaching schedule is such that my classes meet only two or three days a week, my family automatically assumes that those are the only days of the week that I work. It does not seem to help when I try to explain that there are other aspects to the job—writing, advising, committee work. This misunderstanding leaves me feeling that my family thinks I truly have a gravy job, and, if I complain about the stress associated with being a professor, this is viewed as whining. After all, how can I complain when I have a job with so many perks!?

IMPLICATIONS

In these various areas, then, we see how the working-class academic faces misunderstanding and resistance in academe, if not directly, then at least indirectly. (In addition, it is clear that misunderstanding and resistance are experienced with family members and friends who are not familiar with life in academe.) The constant clash of values inevitably creates dissonance for working-class academics. But what strategies are available to help reduce the dissonance? One option might be to buy into the professional set of values—that is, embrace being resocialized into academe. Another strategy is to compartmentalize life so that we can go on without constant tension. We are not likely to experience *role-person merger*, where our academic role is salient in all situations.[9] Rather, we are likely to exercise *role distance*—separating ourselves from our academic role. As Goffman points out, when exercising role distance, one can achieve distance from a role by rejecting, not the role itself, but the virtual self implied by the role.[10] We may also improvise our roles by engaging in *role making*, whereby we carry out our "professor" role in a way that may be different from what is expected but that helps us to stay truer to who we are.

With regard to classroom implications, the armchair theorizing of academicians is not taken all that seriously within the classroom. Philosophizing about the real world by those who live in the academic world is seen as lacking sincerity and applicability. Students seem to appreciate real-life applications of the material they study in their classes. I find that I often allude to jobs in the "real world" that I had as a college student, or that my relatives have, in order to illustrate a concept or idea. The majority of college students today must work while enrolled in college. They can relate to examples coming from the world of work. The current generation of college students is, in general, less respectful of the traditional hierarchical relationships that are prevalent in our social institutions. And why not? The members of Gen X and Gen Y have witnessed the fall of political and religious leaders; they rely less upon traditional authority figures in their own socialization processes, depending more upon extrafamilial relationships. Students' disinclination to blindly follow authority meshes well with the working-class academic's egalitarian and democratic values. Lessening the distance between student and professor is perhaps more natural for the working-class professor. Rapport may be established more easily. Students may feel freer to ask questions, debate, and truly engage with the subject matter in such a class.

I have suggested elsewhere that the working-class academic occupies a marginal position, recognizing that this has emancipatory potential.[11] In some ways, marginality is a default condition; it is always there, as if a stable aspect of my identity. In Georg Simmel's portrayal of "the stranger," the marginal person is an emancipated individual. Indeed, as Simmel described, the stranger is "freer, practically and theoretically. . . . [H]e is not tied down in his action by habit, piety, and precedent."[12] To the degree that the marginal person is not bound by a certain society's (or status's) rules and traditions, he or she is free.

Institutes of higher education tout their ideological tolerance and social inclusiveness. Yet, incidents of discrimination on the basis of sex, race, and class are embedded within them as in other social institutions. Increasing the diversity among personnel and within the student body should reduce such discrimination and bring about greater understanding. It seems that social class is a relation that has been understudied in this context, even though class is important and shapes lives in myriad ways. Assumptions are made about those who work in higher education; we know the stereotypes—professors as well-traveled cosmopolitan intellectuals who appreciate the finer things in life. Yet, invisible are those of us who have very different backgrounds and who fight against feeling like impostors in a work setting that is "so far from home." When we realize that we bring a more diverse and fresh perspective to the academic setting, we can move from a position of self-doubt to security. Indeed, we can embrace the ways in which we clash with what is accepted and expected, realizing that our experiences contribute to a broader, richer perspective.

NOTES

1. "Some General Values of Working Class Culture," http://members.aol.com/_ht_a/lsmithdog/bottomdog/WCValuespost.htm.

2. C. L. Barney Dews, afterword to *This Fine Place So Far from Home: Academics from the Working Class*, ed. C. L. Barney Dews and Carolyn Law, 332 (Philadelphia: Temple University Press, 1995).

3. David Wellman, "Red and Black in White America: Discovering Cross-Border Identities and Other Subversive Activities," in *Names We Call Home: Autobiography on Racial Identity*, ed. Becky Thompson and Sangeeta Tyagi, 38 (New York: Routledge, 1996).

4. Dews, afterword to Dews and Law, *This Fine Place*, 332–36.

5. Nancy LaPaglia, "Working-Class Women as Academics: Seeing in Two Directions, Awkwardly," in Dews and Law, *This Fine Place,* 177.

6. Carolyn Leste Law, introduction to Dews and Law, *This Fine Place,* 1.

7. Michael Schwalbe, "The Work of Professing (A Letter to Home)," in Dews and Law, *This Fine Place,* 320.

8. Janelle L. Wilson, "Blue Ring around a White Collar: An Application of Marginality," *ETC: A Review of General Semantics* 59, no. 1 (2002): 25–31.

9. Ralph Turner, "The Role and the Person," *American Journal of Sociology* 84 (1978): 87–110.

10. Erving Goffman, *Encounters: Two Studies in the Sociology of Interaction* (Indianapolis: Bobbs-Merrill, 1961).

11. Wilson, "Blue Ring."

12. Kurt H. Wolff, ed. and trans., *The Sociology of Georg Simmel* (New York: Free Press, 1950).

REFERENCES

Dews, C. L. Barney. Afterword to Dews and Law, *This Fine Place*.

Dews, C. L. Barney, and Carolyn Law, eds. *This Fine Place So Far from Home: Academics from the Working Class*. Philadelphia: Temple University Press, 1995.

Goffman, Erving. Encounters: Two Studies in the Sociology of Interaction. Indianapolis: Bobbs-Merrill, 1961.

LaPaglia, Nancy. "Working-Class Women as Academics: Seeing in Two Directions, Awkwardly," in Dews and Law, *This Fine Place,*

Law, Carolyn Leste. Introduction to Dews and Law, *This Fine Place.*

Schwalbe, Michael. "The Work of Professing (A Letter to Home)." In Dews and Law, *This Fine Place.*

Turner, Ralph. "The Role and the Person." *American Journal of Sociology* 84 (1978): 87–110.

Wellman, David. "Red and Black in White America: Discovering Cross-Border Identities and Other Subversive Activities." In *Names We Call Home: Autobiography on Racial Identity*, ed. Becky Thompson and Sangeeta Tyagi, New York: Routledge, 1996.

Wilson, Janelle L. "Blue Ring around a White Collar: An Application of Marginality." *ETC: A Review of General Semantics* 59, no. 1 (2002): 25–31.

Wolff, Kurt H., ed. and trans. *The Sociology of Georg Simmel*. New York: Free Press, 1950.

III

STOKING THE FIRES OF RESISTANCE: LONGTIME WORKING-CLASS ACADEMICS SPEAK

The final section of this text traces the way social class continues to affect academics who have spent years working in and confronting the systems of higher education. As is the case in the first two sections of the text, similar themes arise. Readers of this text should not discount this phenomenon. This phenomenon is, in fact, the point of the text. Those who come from a particular class experience *will have to face* similar experiences on the road toward, and during, a life in academe.

In his aptly titled essay "Teaching from the Wrong Side of the Tracks: Questioning Privilege and Authority in the Classroom," Kent Sandstrom begins by identifying the ways in which education serves the status quo. In the tradition of Bowles and Gintis, Giroux, and others in the areas of critical pedagogy, Sandstrom theorizes that the education system in the United States, contrary to its self-promoting rhetorical flourishes about fostering critical thinking and sparking the imagination, instead rewards unquestioning submission to authority, irrational jingoism, and self-serving careerism. He draws upon his own experiences as a student to illustrate the costs of challenging authority and how these experiences provided him with valuable lessons about not only school policy but the realities of class privilege as well. However, rather than leave the reader with a sense of fatalism, Sandstrom, like Visano, also focuses heavily on how his own experiences provided him with valuable lessons about the importance of ideas, relationships, and solidarity networks that enabled resistance to, and neutralization of, some of the system's more oppressive elements. The piece concludes with a discussion of how these experiences lead him to adopt a critical pedagogical style that emphasizes solidarity, egalitarianism, and democracy in the classroom. Ultimately Sandstrom provides us with strategies to foster a

171

social consciousness in students that can help them see and challenge prevailing forms of social privilege.

In her essay "The Meaning of Class Differences in the Academic World," senior scholar Bonnie Berry addresses the complications of being less than middle class in an academic society peopled by the middle classes. Most notable among these difficulties, according to Berry's narrative, is the legacy of practical and social deficits attached to being from a working-class background, leaving her with the feeling that she's not worthy and will never be. Berry recounts her realization as a young teen that having aspirations was pointless, painful, and humiliating. Hence, not unlike Mike Presdee's experience a continent away, Berry was disabused early on of the notion that she might one day enjoy a wealthy and luxurious life. Berry's narrative contrasts her sense of self with that projected by her middle- and upper-class students and colleagues: inadequacy versus entitlement. The piece concludes with a theoretical overview of social stratification and ties together structural and interpersonal alienation.

As the title implies, Phyllis Baker's essay "Trajectory and Transformation of a Working-Class Girl into an Upper-Middle-Class Associate Dean" focuses upon transformative class experiences. However, contrary to what one might expect, Baker does not provide support for the notion of meritocracy and the myth of upward mobility. Rather, her narrative is framed within materialist and interpretive frameworks. In the structural realm, like Wilson and Kauzlarich, some of the other contributors to this volume, and most working-class students who pursue education beyond the high school level, Baker first attended community college. Baker, like Berry, was able to pursue higher education largely because it was a time in the 1970s and early 1980s when financial assistance to working-class kids was much more readily available than it is now. She also contends that interpersonal factors, such as her activist leanings, her appropriation of cultural capital from her middle-class hippie roommates, and the personal-political dynamics of University of California–San Diego sociology department, were tremendously influential. Ultimately, Baker concludes that class is simultaneously rigid and flexible, transformative and reproductive.

In "Making the Grade: Impostors in the Ivory Tower," Lyn Huxford, a long-time sociologist from the working class, describes how the coping mechanisms required to become part of academe also serve to silence those people who choose to become professors. Finding one's voice, Huxford argues, takes time and the presence of mentors, friends, and specific life experiences to rebuild a sense of legitimacy lost through persistent attacks from the white, middle-class hegemonic imperative.

In his essay "An Unwashed's Knowledge of Archaeology: Class and Merit in Academic Placement," full professor Michael Shott contends that, contrary to public images of open access and the paramountcy of merit, higher education remains both internally and externally stratified. He argues that admission to and placement within a university setting is determined as much, if not more, on the basis of one's social capital and pedigree than on scholarship. According to Shott, inherited sensibilities, academic origins, research interests, and locales are paramount; in short, the professoriate's version of unwritten codes of class identity and conduct ultimately determines where a person falls on the academic hierarchy. Shott provides readers with an overview of the data on external stratification and then presents his own data on internal stratification. He concludes with a discussion of the possibilities of class-based remedies.

Livy Visano's "Class Enriching the Classroom: The 'Radical' as Rooted Pedagogic Strengths" addresses the process of teaching as learning. He stresses the equal importance of intrapsychic "reaching in" and intersubjective "reaching out." Following a rich and detailed narrative that addresses his working-class family's multiple victimizations at the hands of both violent corporate entities and criminal states, he addresses how this informs his teaching and learning. For Visano, working-class identities and experiences are at the core of dynamic counterhegemonic struggles and resistance. He concludes with arguments for emancipatory and transformative pedagogies grounded in struggles (race, gender, sexual orientation, and other, in addition to class) as a means to overcome the judgmental and colonizing shackles of the disciplinary canon.

12

Teaching from the Wrong Side of the Tracks: Challenging Privilege and Authority in the Classroom

Kent Sandstrom

What happens to people as they participate in the process called "education," particularly if they come from a working-class background? In reflecting upon this question, I found myself thinking about Bowles and Gintis's (1976; 1988) critical analyses of the nature and consequences of higher education in the United States. One of their key arguments is that a structural correspondence exists between the social relations of the educational system and the social relations of production in capitalist America. According to Bowles and Gintis, American schools serve primarily as training grounds that prepare students, as future workers, to fit smoothly into the corporate workplace. Through the schooling process students get exposed to both formal and hidden curricula, grounded in elaborate systems of social control, that teach them the "values" necessary to be productive workers and good corporate citizens. These values include:

1. Punctuality and compliance with clock-oriented, bureaucratic regimens.
2. Submission to authority and acceptance of one's place in existing systems of hierarchy and inequality.
3. Conformity to the practices, standards, and styles of the dominant culture.[1]
4. Achievement through individual competition rather than cooperative relationships.
5. Productivity for the sake of extrinsic rather than intrinsic rewards.

In many respects, classrooms function as miniature workplaces in which time, space, goals, and ideas are fixed by others, rewards are extrinsic in nature, and interactions are mediated by hierarchical structures (Giroux 1981). Thus, through their classroom experiences students learn to embrace passive and subordinate roles and to see school as a place where they have relatively little power. This is particularly true for students from working-class backgrounds. As Bowles and Gintis (1988) observe, "Predominantly working class schools emphasize behavioral control and rule-following" and allow for less student participation and decision making than schools in well-to-do suburbs. Thus, working-class students are socialized into outlooks and behavior patterns that encourage them to embrace and reproduce their own subordination.

My own experiences as a student attending working-class schools fit in many ways with Bowles and Gintis's rendering of the nature of education in America. I was clearly taught the importance of obeying authority and conforming to prevailing cultural standards. On those rare instances when I challenged those in power at my schools, I paid a steep price. For instance, in eighth grade I decided to disregard our principal's insistence that we "stand at attention to show our respect" when he walked down the hallway. (For some reason, I didn't think that we, as students attending a public school, should feel obliged to treat the principal like a general.) One day when he walked by I opted not to stand at attention, instead leaning up against my locker while talking with my friends. For this transgression, the principal grabbed me by my shirt, smashed me up against my locker, and ranted at me for not displaying a "respectful posture" toward him. After that experience, I shied away from expressing antiauthority sentiments at school for a while. However, as time passed I grew a bit bolder, and while attending an assembly in high school, I decided to take the risk of asking a mildly critical question of a speaker championing the merits of "patriotism" and the Vietnam War. I paid for that offense when the assembly ended and a teacher walked up behind me, lifted me off the ground by my hair, and harangued me for my display of "insolence." In the process the teacher hammered home a lesson to me and my fellow students: the costs of disobedience, even in mild form, are high.

In addition to instructing me in the virtues of obeying authority, my experiences in high school taught me about the privileges accorded to those from "the right side of the tracks." While this lesson was reinforced daily in a variety of ways, it was brought home to me most keenly by an event that took place during my junior year. I was a member of the school newspaper staff, and, after some lobbying, the staff convinced the journalism teacher that we should have the right to choose the newspaper editor for the next year. The teacher said that she would allow us to do this, but only if she got to pick one of the two candidates who would run for the position. She subsequently told us that her candidate of choice was a girl who belonged to one of the town's most affluent families. The student staff, in turn, nominated a bright and popular girl who was "one of us"; that is, who lived on our side of the tracks. We also coordinated a whisper campaign in which we all agreed to vote for this girl, especially since it would mean so much for her to be selected as editor. The election was held and, predictably, the journalism teacher informed us that her preferred candidate, the girl from the affluent family, had won. Of course, the teacher would not tell us the actual vote tally and we all knew who had *really* won the election. Some of us protested the outcome and refused to reenroll in journalism for our senior year, but this had no effect on the election results. The girl from the right side of the tracks walked away with the editorship and we walked away with yet another lesson in class privilege and the unjust use of authority.

Experiences like these clearly left my working-class friends and me feeling cynical about, and oppressed by, our school and its systems of power and privilege. Still, I have to admit that we didn't only experience school as a site of oppression and class reproduction. Our experiences in school and school-related activities (e.g., athletics) also provided us with some empowering bases of knowledge, skill, achievement, and connection. The schooling process, then, had complex and contradictory features. It did not simply impose legitimating ideologies, hierarchical structures, and alienating behavioral routines on us, as implied by Bowles and Gintis. Rather, it also provided us with ideas, experiences, relationships, and solidarity networks that enabled us to avoid, resist, and neutralize some of its more oppressive features. We found that school offered us activities, opportunities, and networks through which we could experience at least some moments of efficacy, equality, and community. We also discovered that we could use certain ideas and tools we acquired through the schooling process to challenge and penetrate, albeit partially, prevailing structures of social reproduction (see also Willis 1977).

After graduating from high school, a few of my classmates and I went on to attend the local university, where we had a chance to experience a less constraining and regimented form of schooling. While our general education classes were sometimes impersonal and stultifying, we found that we had more room to think imaginatively and critically on a college campus than we did at our high school. This freedom was promoted in part by dynamics occurring in the larger society, particularly protests against racism, sexism, the Vietnam War, and the corruption of the Nixon administration. In the classroom, however, it was also fostered by the relationships that a few of our professors were willing to form with us. I was particularly lucky as a sociology major because I had a couple of professors who were truly student centered and thus took time to get to know us as people as well as students. One of these professors, Denny Brissett, was an especially inspiring teacher and friend. Denny was from a working-class background and took special interest in those of us from the same side of the tracks. He encouraged us to embrace rather than conceal our class heritage and to recognize its merits.

He also exposed us to a uniquely different experience of education. Denny designed his classes in a way that prompted (and required) us to think creatively, to question our taken-for-granted assumptions, to engage each other in dialogue, and to refine our understandings of ourselves and the surrounding social world. Although this was challenging and sometimes frustrating, it left us—or at least me—feeling empowered. It also gave me a sense of how transformative education could be and, consequently, inspired me to want to become a professor. Through my experiences in Denny's classes (and a few other sociology and philosophy courses), I came to see that education and teaching could be used to interrogate privilege, challenge oppression, and promote empowerment.

Fortunately, the experiences I had in Denny's classes were reinforced in some of my graduate courses, most notably in classes taught by another professor from a working-class background, Ron Aminzade. Indeed, Ron intentionally designed his courses so that we, as his students, were exposed to theories, readings, and teaching strategies that contested traditional ideas and practices, particularly in regard to the structure and purposes of higher education. He also used a pedagogical approach that promoted democracy, cooperation, egalitarianism, and solidarity in the classroom, inciting and supporting the active involvement of students.

HOW CLASS INFORMS MY PEDAGOGY

Fostering Solidarity, Democracy, and Engagement in the Classroom

Through my schooling experiences, both positive and negative, I learned the importance of "taking the role of," and building a sense of solidarity with, the people you want to teach. Given the alienating experiences I had endured as a younger student attending working-class schools, one of my goals as a professor was to challenge and transform the hierarchical and somewhat distant relations that so often characterized the classroom. Moreover, given the rewarding and inspiring experiences I had in some of my college and graduate classrooms, especially in Denny's and Ron's courses, I wanted to offer students the pleasure of learning in a context where they had a sense of solidarity with their classmates and their teacher. My desire to build community and connection with my students was also reinforced by the fact that a number of them had biographies similar to my own—that is, they were "first-generation" college students from working-class families who had to pay their own way through school. This motivated me to see how we could establish a connection in the classroom that would help them not only to get a "useful" education in terms of their vocational goals but also to develop ideas and skills that would provoke them to question and transform existing social arrangements.

Guided by a desire to build solidarity with students, I have committed myself to using pedagogical strategies that offer them safe opportunities to share their perspectives and build alliances in the classroom. For instance, I begin each of my courses by asking students to break into small groups and talk with each other about four themes: their personal interests and backgrounds, their goals for the course, their expectations of me as a professor, and their ideas about evaluation procedures (e.g., tests, grades, papers, and styles of feedback). After the students complete this group task, I ask them to summarize their discussions for the larger class. This exercise works well because students openly discuss their interests, goals, expectations, and perspectives on evaluation. In the process, they raise some interesting issues and learn that I will listen to them in designing class sessions and assignments. They also learn that it is acceptable to challenge traditional and hierarchical structures in the classroom. Moreover, they get to know one another better, thereby building a foundation for higher levels of dialogue, engagement, and community to exist in the class.

Using this first-day exercise as a springboard, I draw on other strategies that enable the students and me to get to know one another better and to build a sense of solidarity. These strategies include involving the students in role-playing exercises, classroom experiments, interactive games, small group discussions, dramatic skits, and group analyses of case studies. In addition to using these classroom-based strategies, I design assignments that allow students to share their perspectives more privately. For example, at the beginning of each course I ask students to write a personal essay about a central theme addressed in that course, such as the "nature of individuality" in social psychology or the meaning of "health" in medical sociology. Through reading these essays and subsequently discussing them with the students, I gain a better understanding of their outlooks. I also feel more connected to them in my teaching endeavors. When lecturing, leading discussions, or planning course sessions, I can keep specific individuals in mind, such as Greg, the contemplative thinker who hopes to become an ethicist, or Kai, the witty extrovert who wants to become a counselor in student services, or Michelle, the cynical marketing major who doubts she can learn much useful in sociology. This is far more engaging than trying to teach to a sea of anonymous faces (see Beidler 1986).

Most important, through employing these pedagogical strategies I try to offer my students opportunities to participate actively and meaningfully in my courses—opportunities that are not as dull, problematic, or threatening for them as discussions in more traditional, lecture-based classrooms. In the process, the students can build a sense of solidarity with me and each other and get used to hearing the sound of their own voices (see also Muzzatti and Samarco's chapter in this book). In turn, I can better draw upon and highlight their voices and experiences in the classroom. As Henry Giroux (1988a) has proposed, this is a critical component of teaching, particularly for those who want to use radical and democratic pedagogies. We fail to truly teach if we do not include and celebrate students' voices, recognize the meanings they give to their experiences and selves, and make them a central part of our pedagogical endeavors (Freire 1970). By focusing on how students construct meaning, what categories they draw upon in this process, and how they bring these categories into play in their encounters with us, we can become their collaborative allies in the practices of teaching and learning (Freire 1970, 1995; Giroux 1988b, 1993). We can also help them to develop a form of critical consciousness that is grounded in their own experience—a consciousness that can help them to see and challenge prevailing forms of social privilege.

Another important benefit of using student-centered and group-oriented strategies is that they can foster more cooperative and democratic relationships in the classroom. When carefully designed, these strategies give students the experience of learning with and from each other and provide them with a context that stresses social responsibility and solidarity. These dynamics, in turn, help the students to counteract the effects of the hidden curriculum—obedience, conformity, competitiveness, and mistrust—they have learned through the schooling process. (For an insightful and more extensive discussion of how group work is an integral aspect of a critical and democratic pedagogy, see Giroux 1981.)

Encouraging Reflexivity and Developing Insight into Self

In using pedagogical strategies geared toward promoting solidarity and democracy in the classroom, I try to help my students build stronger alliances with me and each other and to gain better insights into themselves and their social practices. Through involving them in a nurturing, challenging, and sociologically minded "learning community," I encourage students to see how their outlooks and actions are shaped by their class background, cultural context, and social relationships. In the process, they gain helpful insights into who they are and want to be as students and people. At the same time, I gain insights into them and I learn more about who I am and want to be as their teacher. This helps my students and me to build a stronger sense of trust, connection, and solidarity in the classroom. However, our efforts to build community and deepen our self-understanding are not smooth or linear; instead, they are characterized by ongoing struggles and challenges. For instance, my understanding of who I am as a teacher is influenced not only by the struggles I encounter as I interact with some apathetic or resistant students, but also by two key pedagogical challenges: (1) what teaching style to employ in my classes, and (2) how to use my authority as a teacher.

When I talk with colleagues about the issue of teaching style, they often assert that I, like other teachers, should simply use a style that "fits my personality." This advice is not very helpful, and it clearly shows a lack of sociological mindfulness. In offering it, my colleagues assume that the issue of pedagogical style is essentially a psychological matter. They make the mistake of downplaying the significance of the social context of teaching. Through my experiences as a student and teacher, I have learned that the question of style cannot be separated from one's teaching context. The appropriateness and effectiveness of a particular style depends on a number of widely varying factors, including the nature of one's cultural and institutional settings as well as the social characteristics and aspirations of one's students.

As I have taught for more years and grown more aware of how contextual factors influence the effectiveness of one's pedagogical style, I have recognized the importance of not getting locked into a specific style. By cultivating a flexible repertoire of teaching styles, I can adjust my methods in response to the particular characteristics of my contexts and students. In turn, I can find varying ways to pursue and realize the pedagogical goals I regard as essential—active learning, critical thinking, and democratic classroom relations.

In experimenting with various styles and methods, I have learned that a certain consistency exists between pedagogical means and goals. Lectures are unlikely to foster classroom democracy. However, I have also learned that teaching is a dialectical process that works best when it involves students in divergent and sometimes contradictory moments. That is, "good" teaching not only encourages students to think critically and creatively but also offers them moments to "let their guard down" and uncritically "fall in love with" a subject (Elbow 1986). Guided by this insight, I try to use a teaching style that gives students opportunities to engage in both of these dimensions of learning.

Ultimately, through grappling with the issue of pedagogical style, I have discovered that I need to show students, above all else, that in teaching them from and about "the other side of the tracks," I am committed to teaching them in the best ways I can. For me, this means using methods that tell the students I am interested in both teaching and learning from them and am willing to help them pursue or develop their "itch" for learning. It also means adopting an approach that tells students I am ready to take the time to evaluate their learning efforts carefully, holding them to high standards; however, I am *not willing to coerce them* into learning, even if they want me to do so. This brings up the complex issue of authority.

Grappling with the Issue of Authority

When I started to teach, I thought of authority as primarily negative. As noted earlier, I had suffered under a number of teachers (and administrators) who "played the heavy," priding themselves on intimidating students inside and outside of the classroom. I didn't want to act or teach like them. Instead, I wanted to emulate the student-friendly teachers, such as Denny and Ron, who had inspired me and others to learn. They had invited their students to join them in exploring challenging questions and in thinking imaginatively. They had also listened thoughtfully to students' ideas and treated them more like allies than adversaries. Because of this, students rarely thought of them as exercising authority.

I began my teaching career with the assumption that if I adopted a similar approach I could simply sidestep the issue of authority. But my experiences in the classroom quickly revealed the flaws in this assumption. Even though I used a democratic pedagogy and had a friendly demeanor, students rightly saw me as an authority figure who had the power to evaluate their classroom participation and academic performance. Whether I liked it or not, I was located in an institutionalized power relationship with them and I carried the weight of authority. To try to avoid or deny this was to be naive and deceptive (Elbow 1986; Giroux 1988a).

In turn, rather than evading the issue of authority, I have embraced a broader and more positive conception of authority, recognizing how it can serve as an enabling force in student-centered and critical pedagogies. I realize that I can use my authority as a teacher to expose students to readings, videos, theories, and other materials that broaden their sociological imaginations and self-understanding, especially by showing them (1) how to interrogate prevailing systems of power and privilege, and (2) how to discern the consequences of class, race, and gender inequalities. In the process, I try to motivate students to reflect critically upon their own social experiences, particularly within systems of privilege and inequality, and to develop the skill, confidence, and desire to question or challenge these systems.

Drawing on my own biography and social experiences, I also use my authority as a teacher to encourage students to be mindful of their capacity for agency. I remind them of the key sociological insight that they are not pawns or passive victims of "society." Guided by the sociological imagination, they need to be conscious not only of how their actions are influenced by others but also of how they influence others, particularly as they engage in joint action with them. Above all, they need to consider the privileges they derive, as well as the costs they incur, through their social relationships and interactions. They must also recognize that they have to take responsibility for these consequences. This means that they must work not only on changing their attitudes but also their practices. More specifically, it means that they will need to bring themselves into difficult interactions with others—in the workplace, at school, at home, and elsewhere—to learn more about the consequences of their actions and to find out how to engage in more just social practices. In some cases, this will mean joining a larger group of others, perhaps even in a social movement, to work for changes in society or in larger social arrangements (Sandstrom, Martin, and Fine 2003).

Of course, in using my authority as a teacher to promote students' awareness of their capacities for agency and their responsibilities to work for change, I do not try to transform the classroom into an arena where I proselytize for specific political perspectives or social changes. Instead, I try to offer students models of how to present and defend sociological arguments with logic and evidence; how to understand the intersection of history, society, and biography; how to ask critical questions of prevailing arrangements; and how to create and sustain democratic relationships and beneficial social changes. In addition to this, I try to exercise my teaching authority in a way that encourages students to participate actively in classroom discussions, to grapple with challenging issues, to think creatively and independently, to understand and appreciate diverse perspectives, and to form thoughtful and just relationships with one another.

One of the biggest questions I face in exercising authority as a teacher is how to serve as both a nurturing ally and challenging evaluator of my students. In addressing this problem, I have adopted a "solution" offered by Peter Elbow (1986); that is, I have chosen to become an ally to my students in meeting the challenging standards of thinking, writing, and communicating I hold them to in my courses. In forging this alliance, I clearly communicate my standards as a teacher and offer students more than one chance to meet them (e.g., by allowing them to submit preliminary drafts of papers before getting a graded evaluation). I have also found ways to negotiate and share authority with students in the evaluation process. This means engaging them in reflection and dialogue about what criteria should be applied in assessing their exams, papers, or classroom participation. By asking students to evaluate each other's ideas and to identify and explain the criteria they used in these evaluations, they become more aware of what standards to aspire to in presenting their own ideas. They also have a chance for some input in the evaluation process, and they gain insight into the difficulties and limitations that characterize processes or assessment (Elbow 1986).

CONCLUSIONS: MODEST HOPES AND RADICAL PEDAGOGY

The most vexing issue I grapple with as a teacher, especially given the current political and economic climate, is how to sustain a sense of hope. When I started teaching, I held very ambitious visions of and goals for teaching, defining it as a true vocation that, at its best, "calls" practitioners to be involved and dedicated, inquisitive and creative, critically reflective of themselves and their world, and willing to promote understanding that contributes to the construction of a more humane world. Inspired by Paulo

Freire (1970, 15), I also believed that teaching should be a "practice of free-dom"—a means that enables people to "deal critically and imaginatively with reality and to discover how to participate in the transformation of their world." I thought that one of the key goals of teaching should be "citizenship education" (Dewey 1918), or the fostering of political visions, social hopes, and critical thinking skills that would prepare students for active and socially responsible citizenship. I wanted to enhance students' abilities to understand and participate effectively in the decision-making processes that affected their lives. I also wanted to assist them in developing the intellectual and emotional resources that would allow them to transform oppressive social practices and to create more just, nonviolent, and democratic forms of com-munity life.

As the years have passed and I've taught a growing number of courses, I've become painfully aware of how difficult it is to realize these teaching ideals. This has not led me to abandon my visions or hopes, but it has forced me to come to terms with some of the key obstacles I've encountered in pur-suing them—obstacles such as class privilege, the power of the hidden cur-riculum, and the influence of cultural and economic factors that encourage students to place a premium on conformity, predictability, and conflict avoidance rather than creativity, critical reflection, and social transformation.

As I've taught more courses and continued to encounter these and other obstacles, I've clearly modified my pedagogical ambitions. While I haven't given up my visions of teaching as a practice of freedom, I've discovered how difficult it can be to engage in this practice. I've also learned to appre-ciate the unpredictable and sometimes fleeting moments when my students and I successfully enact freedom (with all its limits) in the classroom. In ad-dition to this, and perhaps most essentially, I've become more aware and ap-preciative of other worthy goals I can strive for as a "radical" teacher. These goals include:

1. Get to know your students and build connections with them. Be will-ing to listen to your students, to explore common questions, to befriend and mentor them, and to find out about their hopes, dreams, joys, tri-als, and tribulations. Above all, be willing to nurture and challenge your students, particularly through being honest.

2. Reward your students for being curious, imaginative, and passionate about learning. Expose them to creative and critical thinkers who have the courage to interrogate systems of privilege and authority and to tackle the "big questions" about social life and arrangements. Also, give your students opportunities and encouragement to develop this courage and to tackle these questions themselves.

3. Be aware of how your own social background and experiences inform and guide your teaching. Don't buy into or hide behind the delusions

of "value neutrality." Instead, be as aware and honest as you can be about your biases and offer your students insight into how pedagogies are always, in some sense, grounded in social and political judgments. Moreover, if you come from a working-class background, embrace it and recognize how it can be an asset in your teaching, especially in asking critical questions about social arrangements and in building solidarity with students.

4. Help your students to recognize and appreciate the fact that social reality is a human construction and thus is open to change. In a related vein, teach your students that they face a critical ethical choice: they can willingly collaborate in the reproduction of the social world, with its systems of privilege and inequity, or they can join with others who will strive to change that world in beneficial ways.

5. Finally, and perhaps most crucially, embrace modest hopes and take joy in the "small accomplishments" that you realize as a professor. Cherish those moments of joy, grace, and wonder when your students fall in love with an idea, gain an interesting insight, ask a provocative question, feel excited about learning, or look at themselves and their world in a new way. These moments are perhaps the best evidence that you are enacting a liberating pedagogy.

NOTE

1. Schools often see conformity to the dominant cultural practices and standards as evidence of the development of "good citizenship skills." Ironically, students who rate high on these skills also rate "significantly below average on measures of creativity and mental flexibility" (Bowles and Gintis 1976, 41). Thus, schools define citizenship in a way that measures how well they serve as agents of social control rather than how well they enable students to think critically and act ethically in their daily worlds.

REFERENCES

Beidler, Peter. 1986. *Distinguished Teachers on Effective Teaching*. San Francisco: Jossey-Bass.

Bowles, Samuel, and Herbert Gintis. 1976. *Schooling in Capitalist America: Educational Reform and the Contradictions of Economic Life*. New York: Basic Books.

———. 1988. "The Correspondence Principle." In *Bowles and Gintis Revisited*, ed. Mike Cole. London: Falmer Press.

Dewey, John. 1967 [1918]. *Democracy and Education*. New York: Free Press.

Elbow, Peter. 1986. *Embracing Contraries: Explorations in Learning and Teaching*. New York: Oxford University Press.

Freire, Paulo. 1970. *The Pedagogy of the Oppressed*. New York: Seabury Press.

————. 1995. *Pedagogy of Hope: Reliving Pedagogy of the Oppressed*. New York: Continuum Publication Group.

Giroux, Henry. 1981. *Ideology, Culture, and the Process of Schooling*. Philadelphia: Temple University Press.

————. 1988a. *Schooling and the Struggle for Public Life*. Minneapolis: University of Minnesota Press.

————. 1988b. *Teachers as Intellectuals: Toward a Critical Pedagogy of Learning*. Granby, MA: Bergin and Garvey.

————. 1993. *Living Dangerously: Multiculturalism and the Politics of Difference*. New York: Peter Lang.

Sandstrom, Kent, Daniel Martin, and Gary Alan Fine. 2003. *Symbols, Selves, and Social Reality*. Los Angeles: Roxbury Press.

Willis, Paul. 1977. *Learning to Labor*. Aldershot, UK: Gower.

13

The Meaning of Class Differences in the Academic World

Bonnie Berry

During my master's program I crossed paths with another student as she was going in to see a professor with whom I had just finished an appointment. My friend and fellow student later told me that after I left the professor's office, the professor commented to my friend, referring to me, "What a sweet, gentle Appalachian woman." I suppose that was an accurate assessment at the time, and I carry some remnants of those traits to this day. Those traits have not served me well, nor have they plagued me.

This chapter will address some of the complications of being less than middle class in a world presumably peopled by the middle and upper-middle classes, my own unremarkable experiences as a lower-status member of academic society, and a theoretical exploration of the meaning of class in academics.

THE TROUBLE WITH BEING LESS THAN MIDDLE CLASS

First of all, there are social expectations and assumptions that are commonly accepted and common knowledge to the middle and upper classes that are not common to the working and lower classes. It is assumed, or at least it used to be assumed, that academics are from at least, if not above, the middle class. Along with those assumptions about class comes an entire set of related assumptions: that we academics know how to handle dinnerware, that we know what wine to order, that we know what to say in social settings without embarrassing ourselves or others, that we have the correct manners at meetings, that we know how to dress appropriately for the occasion (and that we have the money to dress appropriately), and so on. It is expected that we all have similar social experiences, say, in terms of cultural awareness. For example, we should know about fine art and Broadway musicals and we should be well traveled.

The disadvantages of not being economically secure are pragmatic as well as social. The physical scarcity of resources associated with being economically disadvantaged is frightening, unpleasant, and arduous. Never knowing if you can afford to pay tuition, buy books, or buy the necessities of living is, shall we say, anxiety-provoking. In my case, I received my college education in the early 1970s through the early 1980s, at a time when the government would help poor people get through college. My family had such a low income that we qualified for free aid, plus I qualified for smart-kid grants and scholarships. While the government aid covered most of my costs and was absolutely crucial, it was never enough to live well and, importantly, to live like the other college students whose parents had plenty of money for their education as well as anything else they needed or wanted (trips to Europe, clothes, cars, apartments, dinners out, etc.). The pragmatic side of being financially without is nothing compared to the social side. The sense of self-entitlement that middle- and upper-class students feel was something that evaded me and will (thankfully) evade me forevermore. The combined effects of practical and social deficits make one feel not equally worthy and as though one never will be. Worse, one doesn't know how to think of oneself as an equal, socially speaking, and this does not necessarily begin with the academic years. It often starts earlier and may extend beyond that time.

IT'S ALL RELATIVE

My family was and is working class, on a good day. In other words, the more fortunate people in my family are working class and the remainder are poor.

I was born in a cabin. No, really, I was. It was a one-room cabin deep in a woods, with no indoor plumbing and with a fireplace as the heat source. I did not feel underprivileged, because plenty of people in the surrounding rural Ohio environs were poor and working class and, for example, commonly used outhouses, as did we. Our fundamentalist church did not have an indoor toilet. The people in town had toilets but we rarely mixed with them. By the time I was in first grade, we had an indoor toilet. But one of the girls with whom I went to school didn't even have a real floor in her house, just a dirt floor. So, no, I didn't not fit.

When I was about twelve years old, I was sent to a church camp. This was a bit intimidating because many of the other children came from big cities like Toledo. Not to be outdone and certainly not wanting to be exposed as the child of Appalachian parents, I decided to spend my week in disguise. I faked an accent and everything. It worked. I was voted the most popular girl in my bunkhouse and was awarded a prize. Then, at the end of the week, when our parents came to pick us up, there was my mom, with her non-genteel southern accent, locating the parked car as being "over yonder." I burst into tears and buried my burning face in the camp counselor's shoulder. I have since dropped all disguises but instead do not volunteer to talk about my background.

I had assumed that I would drop out of high school at the legal age, sixteen, and work at working-class jobs. Then came a broken vein, and this broken vein was the breaking point. As a teenager, I had worked at a job that was too strenuous for someone of my size and youth. The purple spot on my leg was a nonnegotiable reminder that this was the beginning of other health problems and other indices of powerlessness, as best evidenced by my coworkers. Some of my female coworkers, all of whom were working class or poor, showed up for work with missing teeth, black eyes, and worse. They had unpaid bills, too many children, no money, and no influence.

The sense of powerlessness is impressive among the lower classes, especially for women of the lower socioeconomic stratum. We had even less influence than the men had with social control agencies and thus no protection. More globally, we had little to offer the labor market that a million other untrained and unquestioning people couldn't offer. Mostly, poor people represent a sense of hopelessness, a desert of denied dreams, the reality of having no options. Thinking back on my coworkers, fondly and sadly, they never stated any aspirations. In my case, at the time, brief moments of aspiration arrived with a great deal of marijuana smoking, aspirations that dissipated as quickly as the smoke. To aspire was pointless. Nay, it was painful. It was humiliating. It was dangerous.

With more a sense of resignation than expectation-propelled aspiration, and having literally nothing to lose, I finished school. It seemed an odd decision, given the circumstances.

In college, class relativity became obvious on a daily basis. My undergraduate years were spent at Miami University of Ohio, a university peopled by middle- and upper-middle-class students. Naturally, I didn't ask them their SES, but from their material possessions, manner of speaking, and attitude, I figured them for middle- and upper-middle-class kids. For the first time, really, I was surrounded by people who had never known powerlessness. They seemed to have been protected, and I envied them for that. They had a sense of entitlement that befuddled me. It had never occurred to them that life can be otherwise for other people, and when class issues were discussed in our coursework, these otherwise very smart and nonjudgmental students would say the darnedest things, like, "Well, what else do welfare recipients have to do all day but stand in line waiting for a check?"

It was here, in undergraduate school, that I encountered a common middle-class American feeling: that all of us have choices, that we *choose* our lives. These young people believed that, no matter how humble one's be-ginnings (and theirs weren't), one could achieve anything one set one's mind to. Certainly we all make choices everyday, but the *array* of choices is limited for working-class and poorer people. And the *chances of success* are limited as well, even when an aspiring choice is made. For one thing, and as mentioned, there are the material deficits, such as not having books in the home. For another, there is an absence of experience to draw upon: our par-ents cannot guide us on which colleges would be best to attend or which ca-reer choices to pursue, they cannot relay their own economically and edu-cationally successful experiences.

As an undergrad, I was well liked but, needless to say, I didn't ask anyone to come home with me. I suppose they would have found my family and sur-roundings quaint, but, while they might have found my family and life to be an anthropological curiosity, I would have been, wrongfully, ashamed.

My graduate years took place at a much more class-diverse institution, Ohio State University. A large number of my fellow graduate students were working class and, mostly, there was no need to feel out of place. There were a few occasions, though, when distinctions between the working-class students and middle-and upper-class students bore witness to the class "dif-ference." Our professors, as near as I could tell, were all of middle-class and upper-class extraction and seemed unaware of class distinction among the students. As such, there was an occasion in which a professor remarked about a line from a well-known musical. The professor assumed that we all knew about the musical with the possible exception of the one non-U.S.-born student in the class. The professor explained to this student the mean-ing of the line, although the student seemed to understand already. I didn't know the meaning, but I was probably not alone.

So I became a Ph.D. and a professor, reaching the pinnacle of what one would think is middle-class status. My first post-Ph.D. job was at the Univer-sity of Miami (Florida) where a large portion of the students were (and prob-ably are) privileged. Mistakenly, I had expected respect from these students; after all, I'm a Ph.D. and an assistant professor. As one of my colleagues amusingly pointed out to me, "Of course they have no respect for the faculty. Their maids make more money than we do." Well, there was nothing to do about that disparity or the students' attitude about the disparity. What I needed to work on was forcing a sense of equality between myself and *all* others, and that would come only with practice. To make matters more dif-ficult, my reticence to view myself as equal to all grew from my gender as well as my former SES. Being the first woman hired tenure-track in the de-partment caused no end of confusion for some of the male coworkers, who were prone to sexual harassment and who honestly believed that women were unequal. The young reader might bear in mind that, in the 1970s and 1980s, women were not treated as they are now. Sexism persists, abundantly so, but back then women were harassed with impunity, assumed to be not as smart as men, and generally thought of as second-class citizens. It required a lot of patience to bring my colleagues and, less so, my students, into the light. To possess such a gender-based and class-based sense of self solidified the feeling of inequality. I had been trained to feel "less than," and this feeling manifested itself, for example, in my reluctance to ask for things that others asked for. Others could ask for favors, resources, and consideration as a matter of course, as though they automatically had every right to ask for these things. It has taken a long time to arrive at the novel idea that I am equal . . . about twenty years, to be exact.

In sum, in my academic career, most people do not know my background. Ordinarily, people do not ask, I suppose, because they have no reason to. For instance, there are now no outward signs of my previous status. On the few occasions when people do ask, I have answered this question minimally and noncommittally. When a few people have discovered my background, they often say, "I bet you really appreciate what you have now." I think this means that I should be grateful, or that I am expected to be more appreciative than those not from a poor background, for the "luck" I have had in removing myself from a less-than-advantaged situation. I do not feel grateful or appreciative for achieving my new status. It was merely persistence that got me here.

GETTING THEORETICAL ABOUT IT

My preferred theoretical interpretation for the class-academic interface would assume a critical (variously known as conflict or Marxist) approach. Those who possess social power, in the form of property, income, status, and even education, hope to maintain this power. They have the power to maintain the social structure as is. In the case of the issue at hand and in the context of these current times, an elitist U.S. presidential administration has made it far more difficult for those without means to gain an education. In these troubled times, even the middle class has trouble paying for college, thanks to the Bush administration's ruination of the economy and the administration's cutting back on social programs. Thus, universities have raised their fees to the point that even those who could formerly attend may not be able to. We are presently left with a situation that resembles that of a century ago when only the wealthy could attend college. This, I needn't tell the reader, is totally against equal opportunity. This type of social structure perpetuates class distinctions and prohibits class mobility and lends itself to alienation and anomie on a cultural scale. Moreover, it is destructive for the society as a whole—because it is not just the rich who have something intellectual to offer.

The less educated the public, the more controllable they are. This is true for at least two reasons. First, education is strongly correlated with better jobs and higher incomes. Second, and more important, education is strongly correlated with social awareness. The more educated the individual, the more likely she or he is to be feminist, environmentally concerned, politically progressive, not racist, and a proponent of all manner of egalitarian social agendas. This is one way to examine the meaning of keeping the working and lower classes in their place, uneducated, and powerless.

Now let's take a look at one of my least-favorite sociological theories, one that nevertheless has a lot to say about SES and society: structural-functionalism. Structural-functionalism, as the name implies, is an examination of social forces and social conditions in terms of the function they serve for society as a whole. As the reader is well aware, all societies are stratified; for instance, along socioeconomic levels. In the United States, there are rich people, upper-middle-class people, the middle class, the working class, and the poor (with any number of nuances to describe the various strata). The members of the middle class, often hoping and striving to be upper class, serve the functions of the upper class via their roles as teachers and other professionals. The working class serves the upper class via roles in labor (as cooks, factory workers, etc.).

The structural-functionalist argument has been made that it is a good thing, socially, to have such stratification; indeed, the bulk of the work on this topic has presented the curious notion that poverty is functional. Structural-functionalism can be viewed as a justification for social stratification, with members of the lower SES bearing the brunt of the functionality. Building on earlier work by Davis and Moore (1945), Herbert Gans (1972; 1971) argues that poverty is functional for society as a whole for many reasons, of which I will present only a few. The poor provide a pool of applicants for the lowest-paid and menial jobs, such as washing dishes, thus ensuring that society's "dirty work" gets done. Second, given their low economic position, the poor provide a ready market for substandard products, like stale food, slum housing, and used cars. Third, the existence of the lower stratum improves the chances of economic success for all other socioeconomic groups by reducing competition for the better-paying occupations. Fourth, the poor help the rich get richer; for example, because of a social structure allowing very poor incomes, the rich are provided with more money to invest in corporate and other endeavors.

Essentially, the structural-functionalist argument is, who else would buy day-old bread, join the army, or clean toilets if not the poor? The upper and middle classes benefit from having a lower class (and, I would argue to some extent, a working class) to purchase bad merchandise, to serve as cannon fodder, to do the dirty work, to (in short) be exploited. The last thing those benefiting from such a stratification system would want would be equal opportunity to obtain an education.

Consider the functions of socioeconomic stratification and denial of educational opportunity in light of other social ills. One might say that sexism is functional since it serves to keep men fully and well employed and women underemployed and unemployed; thus, sexism is a good thing. Child labor would be a good thing from the point of view of elite corporate owners, since children are typically paid less for their labor than adults. Oppression of nonhuman animals is functional for society, assuming that humans want to eat, be entertained by, ill-use as labor, and otherwise exploit nonhuman animals. Crime is a positive social force because, using the structural-functionalist argument, convicted prisoners fill prisons and take troublesome young black men off the street, prisons provide employment opportunities for correctional workers, crime creates a need for more prisons (thus creating construction jobs), and prisoners are a source of very cheap (often corporate) labor.

Let us leave structural-functionalism, strictly speaking, and progress to anomie theory. Here we will be revisiting the earlier discussion of life *choices* in the forms of educational and employment opportunities. Robert Merton (1938) picked up where Emile Durkheim (1897) left off in describing situations where social norms are weak, conflicting, or absent. Anomie, best understood as normlessness, is a condition of normative confusion in which existing rules and values have little impact. Merton specifically wondered about social values possessed by societal members regarding work and education, the impact of those values on social mobility, and whether these societal members were willing to abide by social norms (rules) to gain a better foothold in life. To make the social situation trickier, social structural conditions vary depending on economics and other broad social forces to which people must adapt in order to achieve their goals. From this, we approach one of Merton's greatest contributions to the study of achievement (for instance, educational achievement, social mobility, etc.) and denial of aspirations. In essence, alienation can result from denial of the "American dream."

In the United States, we are told that all of us can achieve this dream—the great job, the material possessions, a home, and so on—if we only work hard enough. If you can't make it here, in the land of opportunity, there is something wrong with you as an individual, not with the social structure, which provides equal access. This, of course, is untrue for many of us, but the result of nonachievement is a profound sense of failure. Merton finds that we deal with this gap between aspirations and achievements by several modes of adaptation: conformity, innovation, ritualism, retreatism, and rebellion. Conformists adopt the socially accepted goals (such as upward mobility) and the institutionalized means (such as hard work and education). Most people conform, but working- and lower-class academics do it in spades, with tenacity, and against greater-than-average odds. Working- and lower-class scholars accept the goals as culturally specified (to be a respected scholar and member of the middle class), and they accept the institutionalized means to achieve those goals (years of education, sacrifice, and hard work).

Anomie theory, while not assuming equal freedom of choice for the economically disadvantaged, does most poignantly describe the uncomfortable sense of alienation emanating from the *desire* to achieve not being matched with the *means* to achieve. Lower-status options are not, in fact, what the top-down social structural message (supported by those who have achieved, i.e., the middle and upper classes) makes them out to be. That is, poor and working-class people would like to have but do not, in reality, have equal options. And that is one of the main points, brought home to us clearly and entertainingly by Barbara Ehrenreich's (2001) book about working in lousy jobs. Ehrenreich, in real life a successful journalist, took it upon herself to wait tables, serve as a housecleaner in hotel rooms and homes, work in a nursing home, and labor as a "sales associate" for Wal-Mart. She not only gives a superb description of how difficult it is financially to make ends meet but also conveys a good sense of the hopelessness (in terms of never having a sense of future) of doing such work on a daily basis. She recognizes that she, at any moment, could give up her various menial jobs and get back to her more comfortable life. Herein is the point: Knowing that you have options makes all the difference in the world. And that is not necessarily knowable to those from a long-entrenched background of lower- and working-class lifestyles. Even if we do become aware of our possibilities for achievement, some of us are not so fortunate in achieving mobility. This latter theme is promoted in Iain Levison's (2002) book recounting the immense difficulties of living a working-class life with a very real and dreadful lack of options. Although he is educated, he is stuck in an endless trail of horrible jobs (deckhand on an Alaskan crab boat, etc.) that do not pay what the labor is actually worth but which the laborers cannot speak against without losing their jobs. The sense of hopelessness is palpable.

CONCLUSION

My full name is an Appalachian name. Until adulthood, I hated it and wanted to have it changed legally but didn't have the money. Now, I don't care. It is a part of my identity but is buried under a me-sized mountain of other identifiers. I am a social science researcher, I am successful, I have enough money. My friends and coworkers either don't know or don't care where I come from. Other academics accept me as a good, trustworthy sociologist without knowing or caring what my presenting class was, earlier in life. The lower-status part of me is in the next-to-the-bottom layer of me. I know now what I should have known all along, that I am as worthy as the next sociologist and the next human.

REFERENCES

Davis, Kingsley, and Wilbert E. Moore. 1945. Some Principles of Stratification. *American Sociological Review* 10: 242–49.

Durkheim, Emile. 1897. *Suicide: A Study in Sociology.* New York: Free Press, 1951.

Ehrenreich, Barbara. 2001. *Nickel and Dimed: On (Not) Getting By in America.* New York: Henry Holt.

Gans, Herbert J. 1971. The Uses of Poverty: The Poor Pay All. *Social Policy* 2: 21–24.

———. 1972. The Positive Functions of Poverty. *American Journal of Sociology* 78: 275–89.

Levison, Iain. 2002. *A Working Stiff's Manifesto.* New York: Soho.

Merton, Robert K. 1938. "Social Structure and Anomie." *American Sociological Review* 3: 672–82.

14

Trajectory and Transformation of a Working-Class Girl into an Upper-Middle-Class Associate Dean

Phyllis L. Baker

There is scant social science literature on working-class academics (Granfield 1991; Cox, Matthews, and Associates 2001; Ryan and Sackrey 1984; Tokarczyk and Fay 1993) and little work on the process of the social transformation of class position (Kaufman 2003). In this retrospective narrative I point out that my current life situation as an associate dean at a major regional and comprehensive public institution is a result of a mixture of transformative interpersonal and structural variables. In an analysis of this narrative it becomes clear that transformative interpersonal variables were the most influential factors in the trajectory of my life from a working-class identity to an upper-middle-class and academic identity. Just as surely, though, some transformative structural factors were also present. Although this chapter focuses on the transformation of my class position, it is written with an understanding that I will always be working class.

Focusing on practices of everyday life to decipher larger structures and seeing the social world as a constructed human product has a long and rich tradition in the social sciences. Authors in this framework argue that a social analysis is best done when situated within real activity (Berger and Luckmann 1967; Willis 1977; Bourdieu 1984; MacLeod 1987; Baker and Carson 1999). When standard, traditional, and macrolevel social science theories and frameworks are analyzed within microlevel social contexts, social scientists are able to offer further clarification and critique of those understandings. In line with this interpretive perspective, my narrative illustrates the complexity of socioeconomic class, focusing on its transformation.

The presentation of data in this essay is chronological. Starting with a description of my family of origin, I move on to stories of my undergraduate and graduate school experiences and, finally, end by documenting my experiences

197

as assistant professor and associate dean. I am telling this story as a polemical nexus to the perspective that members of the working class change their class status through hard work and late nights. However, rather than meritocratic variables, class in my narrative is primary in my transformation, as illustrated by the transformative interpersonal and structural variables. This is a personal testimony of my transformation from a working-class girl into an upper-middle-class associate dean (who will always be working class).

EARLY YEARS (1956–1973)

My family of origin is in all ways a traditional working-class family. My father was a cement finisher; in my eyes he was a highly skilled laborer. In the beginning of his career, after World War II, he held three union cards as a brick-layer, plasterer, and cement finisher. For most of his life he did concrete work. He tried to run his own company but was unsuccessful. Excluding a few opportunities every year, concrete work in rural western New York is usually only available eight or nine months out of the year because of the weather. For most of my growing up, during Dad's off months he collected unemployment while he trapped and hunted for money and some food. I felt proud of what he did. My father was a highly sought-after, skilled worker, a handsome, good man.

My mother was raised by her biological mother and stepfather. She never knew her biological father. My mom gave up two sons. She birthed her first son in high school, and he was raised by my grandparents. Additionally, my mother got pregnant before she and my father were married and had to give that son up for adoption. Then, after marrying my father, she had my two siblings and me. My mom is a strong woman who speaks her mind and likes all kinds of people. Her analysis of the social world was quite critical to my understanding of the world; she explained that those who received rewards were those who had the "right last name." I believe this analysis of class laid the groundwork for what would become my critical analysis of society.

Both my siblings stayed in the area in which we were born. My brother followed in my father's footsteps and became a cement finisher. However, by the time he was an adult, there was not much work in western New York State. His career as a cement finisher was not as glorious as my father's. My sister got pregnant and married just out of high school. She went to work in a furniture factory and has held other similar jobs. She recently went to the local business school and graduated with an associate of arts degree, at the top of her class. She is unemployed and depressed. Both of my siblings are bright, capable, and good people but are victims of the class structure and the continued economic downturn of western New York State.

While growing up I never considered attending college. No one in my extended family ever went to college. In my junior year my boyfriend, who was a senior and graduating a year ahead of me, was going to college. So I decided to graduate a year early and go to college. I had nothing else to do, and I knew that I did not want to stay around where I grew up. I loved my family but really needed to get out and start my own life. Following my boyfriend out of high school and to college seemed to be a good idea. As I applied for college, I realized that I could actually go through a combination of grants and loans. I went to a junior college the first semester and then on to what was at the time called the State University of New York at Fredonia.

UNDERGRADUATE SCHOOL (1973–1979)

I started undergraduate school as a working-class woman from rural western New York State following her boyfriend. After one year at State University of New York at Fredonia, I left my boyfriend and followed a couple of my friends to California. We left in my Chevy Vega with a parakeet, some clothes, a little money, and my stereo. After arriving in California, I continued to go to college because it paid my bills and it seemed more fun than what appeared to be my only other alternative, being a waitress. I was not aware of or interested in economically "making my life better"; I was only concerned with getting by and hanging out with my friends.

After I obtained my A.A. from Grossmont College in California and started going to San Diego State University (SDSU), for the first time I saw myself as a good student and someone interested in making change in the world. I moved into a commune with twelve people, seven of whom were Marxist lesbian feminists. I watched from the outside, intrigued and impressed. My rural upbringing had not prepared me for this, but my mother's perspective on the world did. She liked all kinds of people but resented those with the "right name." Her analysis of how the world was run—by those with the right name—prepared me for my interest in women's studies and sociology. She stood up for herself and was strong. She had suffered a great deal of pain in her youth, and she gave me strength and a level head. My interpersonal relationships at this point in my life were critical to the development of my feminist and critical perspective. I became a feminist activist. I started the Women's Resource Center at SDSU, and the sociology faculty really liked me. I participated in marches and sleep-ins. I was comfortable on campus. For the most part, I hung out with other activists and appropriated much cultural capital from them as well as from my middle- and upper-class roommates. Had I not been hanging out with a bunch of upper-middle-class students and activists, I would not have gone on to the university and graduate school.

All together it took six institutions and six years to get my applied bachelor's (A.B.) degree in sociology with a minor in women's studies from SDSU. I finally buckled down and made it through because I fell in love with women's studies and sociology and gained mentors. It was at this time that I first considered the possibility that my life could be something quite different from that of my family of origin. Maybe I could be a professional, maybe even a professor like the ones who had taught me so much about the world.

In addition to the transformative interpersonal relationships and interactions described above, there were also macrostructural variables that affected my class trajectory and transformation. I don't think I could have gone to undergraduate school had it not been the 1970s, when Basic Educational Opportunity Grants were available. These were free moneys for school expenses for those who could not otherwise afford to go to college. There were other options for financial aid in California of which I took advantage, including a well-funded work-study program. Moreover, once I established residency, tuition was really inexpensive.

It was during my senior year at SDSU that I applied to the Ph.D. program in sociology at the University of California at San Diego (UCSD). My mentors at SDSU told me that the only way I could be a professor was to get my Ph.D., and UCSD was the only program in the area. Leaving the area was not something I even thought about doing at the time. I applied for admission into the Ph.D. program during spring semester 1979, right when I was finishing my A.B. I received a rejection letter in the mail. According to the student grapevine at SDSU, there was an understanding that UCSD would not accept SDSU students. I guess I was lucky when I went up to UCSD and the chair of the admission committee at that time, Jack Douglas, said he would give me admission with no support if I could get the others on the committee to also accept my application. I walked around the department and received signatures from other committee members, who included Jackie Wiseman and Fred Davis. I distinctly remember wearing white polyester pants, Birkenstock sandals, and a green T-shirt with a picture of Karl Marx on the front. I was embarrassed by the clothes but had nothing else. I lived in San Diego and chose UCSD not because there were faculty with whom I wanted to work but because it was in San Diego and offered a Ph.D. I wanted to be a professor and change the world!

It was through these interpersonal experiences within such a particular structural context that I found a voice and a place in the world—as a feminist political activist. I decided I wanted to be a professor, and my life was transformed forever. My mother's critique of the world and my choices to leave home, go to California, and stay in college were important variables. However, my best guess is that had the structural context been different at the time, if it had been similar to what it is today, then such opportunities would not have been available, regardless of my interpersonal relationships and interactions.

GRADUATE SCHOOL (1979–1988)

I started graduate school at UCSD in fall 1979 and graduated in spring 1988. It took nine years to complete my Ph.D. My experience at UCSD was much different from my experience at SDSU. The department at that time was considered one of the top qualitative-methods departments in the country, emphasizing symbolic interactionism and ethnomethodology. I did not really know what those things were because I had taken only one methodology class that was quantitative, and we did computer programming. UCSD faculty members at the time included Bennett Berger, Rae Blumberg, Aaron Cicourel, Fred Davis, Joseph Gusfield, Chandra Mukerji, Hugh Mehan, David Phillips, and Bennetta Jules-Rosette. A bit later Kristin Luker came and eventually became the chair of my dissertation committee.

The first day of my graduate experience is still vivid to me. Our seminar met on the sixth floor of the humanities and social sciences building. The seminar room had large windows with a view of the Pacific Ocean. Though I would now appreciate that view much more than I did then, it was still impressive. I was so excited, and I could sense that this was very different from the context of my undergraduate experience. It took a long time to understand how and why it was different; at first I was in awe at all the really bright people around the table. As time went on, my analysis altered to be a bit more critical, as I realized that sometimes what I saw as bright behaviors were really behaviors that were marginalizing me. After being in the program for a while, I realized that I was in way over my head and began to see myself as somehow less than my colleagues. Most of my cohort had master's degrees. I received a C in my preclassical theory course from Caesar Grana. One of my colleagues had to tell me that getting a C in a graduate school course was essentially flunking the course. Luckily, I also took a field methods course from Jackie Wiseman that semester and received an A minus. I eventually had the C changed to a B after doing more work, but I had been labeled as one of several who would never make it through the program, and there was nothing I could do about that. The label stuck with me throughout my career at UCSD.

One of the most fundamental and negative consequences of this label and my participation in this elite institution was that my self-esteem tanked. At the same time, I decided that what I could do best and have control over was partying, so I focused on that. In the early years I became embroiled in a network of cocaine and methamphetamine users. I could do more cocaine than most and had more access to it than most. This initially made me a hit with many of my colleagues but not with my professors. As time went on, I quit associating with most colleagues and was very close to getting kicked out of the program. During my heavy drug use, including a six-month stint as a speed junkie, I very tightly hung on to my dream of becoming a professor. I had no other income options, so I worked as hard as I could to stay in the program. In part, my rescue came in the form of a professor, Bennetta Jules-Rosette, who liked my work and supported me. She told me to get out of the library and "get my feet wet"—to get out into the field. It was not long after that that I was clean and passed my oral comprehensive exams. It took six years to pass those exams. Dr. Jules-Rosette and her students were instrumental to my successful completion of the Ph.D. program.

Though I had certainly been aware of class, race, and gender issues before going to UCSD, it was in graduate school that I really began to adopt a view of myself as different from most of my colleagues. This recognition, the concomitant alienation and marginalization, along with some bad choices on my part, started a downward spiral. At the same time, concealment of my working-class identity, associational embracement of middle-class and upper-middle-class lifestyles, and the love for my activist, critical, and feminist work allowed me to reap rewards. I hung my hat on my political orientation as a critical feminist. This was something else over which I had control. I could do something about my political orientation; I could do less about my class and cultural capital. In addition to having a label as one who would not finish, I had the label as a feminist activist. Because of my need for income and my passion for feminist and critical politics, I managed to stay enrolled, which continued the transformation of my class.

In addition to the above interpersonal variables, there were also structural variables that influenced the transformation of my class. I do not think that today I would be accepted at UCSD. Departmental politics and interests were quite different then, the admissions committee was interested in accepting students from a broad range of backgrounds, and financial aid was much more available. My transformative interpersonal relationships and the structural context motivated and maintained my career at UCSD; however, it was at quite a personal cost.

ASSISTANT PROFESSOR AND ASSOCIATE DEAN
(1990–PRESENT)

I was hired at the University of Northern Iowa (UNI) as an assistant professor in the fall of 1990. When I was hired on a tenure-track line, I more fully took on the role of middle-class professional and hid the other parts of myself. I had been away from drugs for a number of years; I was married and had one child. I accomplished associational distancing from my class by buying a big, four-bedroom house in a new subdivision, where I was surrounded by engineers and stay-at-home moms. We had sod laid for our yard and took out a home equity loan. We had two new cars. Our children went to Montessori school. I constantly bought new clothes for all. However, my husband hated his engineering job and we felt uncomfortable in the neighborhood; I called it our "milquetoast" neighborhood. I enjoyed interacting with most of our neighbors—they were nice—but it just did not feel like home. We seemed different from them. My husband and I could afford our milquetoast neighborhood because we managed to buy a house in California in the late 1980s right before the housing prices soared, and we sold right before they dipped.

On the other hand, I was comfortable with my colleagues from work. I commuted seventy miles one way but really liked my job. I felt accepted by my peers. The couple of years before tenure and promotion were a bit problematic and stressful. I had my tenure clock stopped for a year. The provost's office allowed for this in cases where there were "family emergencies." Having a child was put in that category, for which I will always be grateful, because I was short on the requisite amount of publications and needed another year. At that time, the faculty in our department did not often socialize together, which created an atmosphere where it was not much noticed that I did not hang out. I would teach my courses and then commute back home to write and to live my private life in my milquetoast neighborhood.

I was promoted to associate professor and given tenure at UNI in 1997, and it was a dream come true. I had a good steady paycheck and relatively high status and enjoyed most of what I had to do. I could be myself much more at UNI than at UCSD. Being myself was and continues to be a multidimensional phenomenon. I was working class, but I was also a new Ph.D. from the University of California at San Diego who had worked with many excellent scholars over the nine years and developed excellent research and writing skills. The working-class background continued to fade into the past, and more and more of middle- and upper-middle-class cultural practices and perceptions took over.

We moved from our milquetoast neighborhood seventy miles away to a much more working-class area, one that is much closer to UNI. Our neighborhood is mixed by socioeconomic class; some houses are really big and expensive; others are small and much less expensive. I don't think there is an engineer within two blocks! My husband quit his engineering job, received a doctorate in industrial technology, and is now an assistant professor at UNI. My children attend parochial school, and I recognize the hierarchies established in the elementary and high schools they attend. There appears to be favoritism based on parents' status; however, the important parts of status are not so much class as parental involvement with the schools, whether it is financial contributions or volunteer time. There is considerable privilege for those students whose parents are alums or those who hang out often and participate in school events. Given that neither I nor my husband has many ties to these schools and that we both work full time, we do not have much status other than that afforded to us by our positions as professors. This status is, of course, much more than my parents ever had. Experiencing stratification related to our children's schools furthered and complicated my understanding of class and status.

In a manuscript I recently submitted for publication that is reminiscent of work earlier in my career, I argue that the socioeconomic structures that Mexican women leave and migrate into determine their gendered behavior. Immigrant women's behavior reflects the broader socioeconomic context. Mexicanas from rural Mexico migrate to Iowa because the socioeconomic context of Mexico demands it. As a result, their gendered *behavior* changes because they are forced to leave their families and work outside the home. However, they resist changing their gendered *ideology*, and it remains traditional. Similarly, in my case, the broader socioeconomic context, as well as my interpersonal relationships, was definitive of my transformation. I went to college because my boyfriend did, and I continued going to college because I needed to support myself and I could do that by going to college. As a result, my interests, behaviors, and skills changed. Nevertheless, parts of my working-class self remain working class, like the Mexicanas' traditional gendered ideology. As I become more comfortable in my upper-middle-class job, it seems appropriate that my academic work now mirrors the trajectory of my class awareness.

Though I do not want to admit it, the transformation of my class position continues, and although I do much less associational distancing from my working-class identity, I continue with associational embracing (Kaufman 2003) of my upper-middle-class identity. There are not many things I like better than wine and classical music, though vodka and rock and roll are close seconds. This kind of transformative microidentity management work (Granfield 1991) is necessary to successfully continue in my upper-middle-class job. So, although interpersonal relationships helped me to become a professor and continue to transform my class status, so did the structure of UNI's policies on tenure and promotion and the housing market in California.

I became an associate dean in the fall semester of 1999, creating the need for more and deeper levels of social transformation. I initially felt uncomfortable with job requirements and did not think I did a very good job. Interestingly, as time goes on, my transformation becomes more complete, but I also am less guarded about my working-class culture. I have become proud of my background, of my parents, and of their struggles. After four years as associate dean, I now find it easier to be myself, probably because I am relatively safe in my job and much surer of myself. Structural and interpersonal variables play important roles in the continued transformation of my socioeconomic class.

CONCLUSION

When the social transformation of class position has been an area of focus, many authors argue that those from the working class who are middle-class or upper-middle-class professionals have jumped up the class ladder as a result of working hard, giving support to the notion that our society is meritocratic. For example, Rubin (1976), in speaking about the circumstances of working-class families and working-class college students, argues that "only the hardiest, the most ambitious, the most motivated toward some specific occupational goal will ever get through college" (208). However, an analysis of my narrative does not support this notion.

Though I worked hard at least part of the time, other variables were much more integral to my class transformation. In my situation, luck, happenstance, mentors, friends, and the broader socioeconomic context played the most important roles. As a result, the transformation of my working-class identity to an upper-middle-class identity was primarily a result of associational and interpersonal factors coupled with some macrolevel phenomena. The socioeconomic context included cheap tuition in California, grants for lower classes to attend higher education, and an academic environment that partially legitimated minority and critical ideologies. Rather than supporting a meritocratic system in which I, as an individual, worked really hard to climb the class ladder, my narrative supports a materialist, interpretive, and critical framework in which some of my relationships, some luck, and some structural factors were responsible for my class transformation. As a good social scientist I cannot argue that my case alone allows for rejection of the notion that our society is meritocratic; however, it does present a challenge to it. An analysis of my everyday life experiences within academia and the structured social context grounds and illustrates the complexity of social class. Though social class is reproduced by hegemonic, patriarchal, and capitalist macro-level systems, it also gets played out in everyday life. Thus, within the context of our society, my class transformation stands out as an oddity while helping us to further understand that in the United States, meritocracy is a myth, not a reality.

REFERENCES

Baker, Phyllis L., and Amy Carson. 1999. "I Take Care of My Kids: Mothering Practices of Substance-Abusing Women." *Gender & Society* 13: 347–63.

Berger, Peter L., and Thomas Luckmann. 1967. *The Social Construction of Reality: A Treatise in the Sociology of Knowledge.* New York: Doubleday.

Bourdieu, P. 1984. *Distinction: A Social Critique of the Judgement of Taste.* Trans. Richard Nice. Cambridge, MA: Harvard University Press.

Cox, Matthews, and Associates. 2001. "Working-Class Academics Share Woes, Pointers via the Internet." *Community College Week* 13 (13): 14.

Granfield, Robert. 1991. "Making It by Faking It: Working-Class Students in an Elite Academic Environment." *Journal of Contemporary Ethnography* 20: 331–51.

Kaufman, Peter. 2003. "Learning to Not Labor: How Working-Class Individuals Construct Middle-Class Identities." *Sociological Quarterly* 44: 481–504.

MacLeod, Jay. 1987. *Ain't no Makin' It: Aspirations and Attainment in a Low-Income Neighborhood*. Boulder, CO: Westview Press.

Rubin, Lillian Breslow. 1976. *Worlds of Pain: Life in the Working-Class Family*. New York: Basic Books.

Ryan, Jake, and Charles Sackrey. 1984. *Strangers in Paradise: Academics from the Working Class*. Boston: South End Press.

Tokarczyk, Michelle M., and Elizabeth A. Fay. 1993. *Working-Class Women in the Academy: Laborers in the Knowledge Factory*. Amherst: University of Massachusetts Press.

Willis, Paul E. 1977. *Learning to Labor: How Working Class Kids Get Working Class Jobs*. New York: Columbia University Press.

15

Making the Grade: Impostors in the Ivory Tower

Lyn Huxford

Until I attended a panel on the lives of working-class academics at a sociological conference, I had not given much consideration to how my working-class background had affected my life as a college teacher. Strange that it is sometimes difficult to apply what I teach to my own life. As I sat in that audience listening to the stories of the people on the panel, I felt a strong sense of identification with their experiences and began to reexamine my own. This reflection on the effect my social class background has had on my life as a college professor allowed me to do what I encourage my students to do—exercise my "sociological imagination." Long ago, C. Wright Mills[1] encouraged us to consider the intersection of history, social structure, and biography to better understand how our private troubles may be experiences we share with many other people and thus, in reality, be public issues. Looking at it now, using my sociological imagination, I better understand the insecurities and uncertainties that plagued me so much of my early years, first as a college student and later as a college teacher, and I realize that I am not alone.

In telling my story, I explore how gender, social class, and historical period all coalesced to make me feel as though I was an impostor who had somehow faked her way into the hallowed halls of academe. I now realize that I developed coping strategies in order to survive in that most upper-middle class of social institutions, college. For me, these coping strategies involved the phenomenon of what I call "doing social class" or, more particularly, "doing upper-middle class" as an impostor in the academy. Such coping strategies were necessary because of the internalized classism that created in me a culturally imposed sense of inferiority and shame that many working-class children acquire early in life. Although it has been almost forty years since I began college, in many ways colleges and universities are no more working-class friendly for students or faculty today. By sharing my story I hope to prevent a few younger working-class faculty or students from experiencing the feelings of inadequacy that I experienced, and sometimes still do.

Institutions of higher learning profess many ideals of tolerance and appreciation for diversity, but they are elitist institutions intent on protecting the privileges that come with admission to the ivory tower, and they are not very friendly places for those who do not conform to the dominant norms and values. New faculty are socialized to a set of norms and values that reinforce upper-middle-class normative standards. The expectations to conform are powerful. There exists a prototype of the ideal college professor. It is assumed *he* is well educated and intelligent, and it is preferable that the education be at a prestigious university or liberal arts college on either the East or West coast. Better yet if this education consists of an elite undergraduate institution on one coast and an elite graduate school on another. In some cases, a prestigious liberal arts college in the Midwest or South will do for undergraduate education. These, of course, are not the schools the majority of working-class academics attend, unless they are fortunate enough to receive a scholarship. In addition, the prototype requires years of acquiring the patina of self-assuredness and the arrogance that comes with the knowledge of one's guaranteed place among the elite—along with the cultural capital of knowing good wines from bad wines, an appreciation of fine art and classical music, and the knowledge of how to comport oneself in any social situation.

As I describe my life as an academic, you will quickly see that I was a long way from fitting the prototype; however, I felt a tremendous pressure to conform, even though no matter how hard I tried, I could never measure up to such standards. In many ways I learned to "pass" without ever entirely losing the sense of being an impostor—someone who has, in Goffman's words, a "discreditable identity," that is, someone who has a secret that if revealed will result in his or her being stigmatized and treated as a deviant.[2]

So here I am revealing my secret. Even after teaching for twenty-five years, I feel some hesitation at doing so. After all, I have, at least in my own eyes, become good at my performance as an impostor in the academy. However, as Muzzatti and Samarco have noted in an earlier chapter in this collection, "you can take the boy out of the class, but not the class out of the boy" . . . that goes for the girl, as well.

As I mentioned, I have been teaching college for twenty-five years; all of my full-time teaching has been at the same liberal arts college in the Midwest. I started college in 1964 and did not graduate until 1972. I received my master's degree in 1975 and, finally, my doctorate in 1981. Throughout most of my undergraduate education and all of graduate school, I was a wife, mother, full-time employee, and part-time student. However, to foster understanding of my experiences as a working-class person in the academy, I need to begin with my earliest experiences as a student in the classroom. The working-class insecurities I brought to my life as a professor were baggage acquired early on in the educational system.

LEARNING SOCIAL CLASS: THE EARLY YEARS

I grew up in south St. Louis, Missouri. My parents met during World War II and married as the war ended, and I was born in 1947. My father trained as an electrician in the navy during the war and became a union electrician afterwards. He had a high school education and was an intelligent man who probably would have thrived in college had he ever had the opportunity. He was a conservative southerner who enjoyed arguing issues over the dinner table. My mother did not complete high school and only held jobs for a brief time during my childhood. My father's traditional southern background combined with the gender stereotyping of the era had convinced him that he was supposed to be the only breadwinner in the family. This, of course, greatly affected our income. As I look back on it, I remember what seems like many discussions about money, or the lack of it, between my parents, especially during my elementary school years. We always seemed to have enough food, a roof over our heads, and a car, but I also remember having to wear a lot of boys' clothes that my uncle who worked in the men's department at Sears gave me. Despite this, my parents sent me to the local parochial school, which had to be quite a sacrifice. However, Catholic kids went to Catholic schools even if there was a public school down the street. It seemed that if you were not Catholic, or were a Catholic who did not go to Catholic schools, you did not have much chance for salvation. So I began my education at St. Margaret's, the local parochial school. My early years were relatively uneventful. I lived in a neighborhood that consisted of four family apartment buildings and attended a school where everyone seemed to be somewhat similar in terms of where they lived, what kinds of cars their parents drove, and the clothes they wore. I am certain that I would have become aware of social class differences had I stayed at St. Margaret's, but at the time I was blissfully unaware of such distinctions. I did what city kids did: played with my friends and went to school. A major change occurred, however, as I was getting ready to enter fifth grade.

I lost my innocence at Holy Innocents. My parents moved to a two-family house owned by my aunt and uncle, and I transferred to a different Catholic school, Holy Innocents, where I quickly started to learn the lessons of social-class diversity in the population of the school; I was just too young to realize it.

At Holy Innocents the lessons of social class were subtly taught side by side with math and reading. The students came from a relatively diverse community in terms of social class. Although we all wore uniforms, we were not all equal in each other's eyes or in the eyes of the nuns who taught us. From this point on, I began to learn that some kids were better, brighter, and destined to be more popular and more successful, and that those kids were the ones whose parents were more successful and thus smarter. The more tragic lesson was the flip side—some kids are not as good, smart, or as likely to succeed. This lesson continued to be reinforced throughout my education by many teachers, peers, and the culture as a whole.

Suddenly the world could be divided between renters and owners, a fact that I had been oblivious to before attending Holy Innocents. I learned that the value of the house a person lived in could tell you the value of the person. Looking back, I remember being embarrassed that we were renters. Throughout my childhood until I left home we lived in that two-family flat in south St. Louis owned by my aunt and uncle. My parents paid them a modest sum monthly; the sum was modest because my mother was there in part to help my aunt, who walked on crutches and was sick a lot. But it was clear, in the status-conscious world of my aunt and uncle, who were the haves and who were the have-nots.

Perhaps it is because home ownership is so linked to the American dream that it is this more than anything else that stands out in my mind as what separated the working-class kids from everyone else. I was uncomfortable around the kids who lived in the nice houses. I believed they and their parents were better than my family and me. I wanted to be one of the kids who lived in a nice, single-family home with lots of rooms. In retrospect, I am sad to recognize how I badgered my parents to buy me things that represented the trappings of a middle-class lifestyle, such as clothes like those the popular girls wore. Catholic schoolgirl uniforms did little to obscure the trappings of social class. I particularly remember thinking that if I had a pair of penny loafers with a shiny penny in them I would magically become popular.

Then I knew nothing about the subculture of shame so compellingly described by Loewen[3] as one of the hidden injuries of social class. All I knew then was that I wanted to be one of the popular girls and that popularity seemed linked to possessions and how much money your parents had. I did not recognize the injustice of a system that made me feel embarrassed and ashamed because my parents did not own their own home and did not have enough money to buy me certain luxuries.

Before I started learning the lessons of social class, I had already started learning the lessons of gender according to a very traditional working-class script. In my neighborhood not much was expected of girls other than cooking, sewing, looking good, and being nice. Some of the adult women in my neighborhood worked at menial, low-paying jobs, but the clear message I received was that being a housewife who had a husband with a good job was the goal. This was, after all, the period that inspired television shows such as *Father Knows Best* and *Leave It to Beaver.* Teachers in high school encouraged both the middle-class and working-class girls to take home economics and typing, thus reinforcing this message—no class bias here. Home economics was to teach us to fulfill our expected role as homemakers; typing was so we had something to fall back on in case our husbands failed to live up to the breadwinner expectations placed on them. The gender and social class expectations of the 1950s and early 1960s conspired to place me on the path to becoming the wife of a blue-collar, union workingman. This would have been my destiny had it not been for the intervention of a teacher.

During my sophomore year in high school, a remarkable social science teacher took an interest in me. When he asked to come to my house to talk to my parents, my first thought was that I had done something wrong. Up to that point my grades had been either really good or really bad, depending upon my interest in the subject, and I had become a minor class clown. It turned out that I was not in trouble at all. In fact, his message was that I was bright and that my parents ought to encourage me to attend college. I owe a tremendous debt to this wonderful teacher. Years later, when I fully realized what an exceptional teacher he was and what a difference he made in my life, I tried to find him to thank him but could not track him down. Without his intervention I do not think I would have ever been able to see myself as someone who could go to college. I needed someone I respected to tell me it was possible. I was able to see myself through his eyes as someone who was intelligent and college material. Other than my teachers, I did not know anyone who was a college graduate, and none of my neighborhood friends were talking about attending college. His words had a tremendous impact.

As a result of this teacher's encouragement and with the support of my parents, I began to study hard in order to get into college. How to do it was the problem. The goal was clear; the means were elusive. We did not have any extra money to pay for college tuition, and colleges seemed alien places that we knew nothing about. Looking back, I do not even know if financial aid was available at the time. I learned about scholarships because my uncle (the same one who owned the house we lived in) was a volunteer with Junior Achievement and knew they had a scholarship program. Even though my grades were excellent, I never considered applying for colleges outside of my hometown. That would have been too lofty an ambition. Everyone was telling me I needed to get a full-tuition scholarship or I would not be able to attend college. So my uncle encouraged me to apply for the only one of the Junior Achievement scholarships that paid full tuition, and I ended up getting it—a full-tuition scholarship to Maryville College, a local all-women's college. Ultimately I felt as though my uncle's influence was responsible for my receiving the scholarship. So the very beginning of my college career was undermined by doubts as to whether I really belonged.

THE COLLEGE DAYS:THE STUDENT

In high school I often felt as though I did not fit in, but I never doubted it was where I belonged. Everyone I knew went to high school; the same was not true of college. Somehow I had faked my way into the ivory tower, but it took decades before it became a place I felt comfortable. I lasted two years at Maryville College. The education was excellent, but the environment was totally alien. Most of the young women who attended the college were from very privileged families. As one of my fellow students told me, she might as well major in basket weaving because she was really in college to meet the brothers of her classmates in order to find a prospective husband and to acquire the requisite pedigree to be the wife of a highly successful business leader or medical doctor. When I enrolled in this school, they had only recently stopped having teas on Sunday at which students were expected to wear dresses and white gloves. It was a step beyond a finishing school, but there was still a lot of finishing going on.

Fortunately, I found some challenging teachers and a group of scholarship misfits to hang out with. Our merry band of intelligent misfits consisted of four scholarship students, all from working-class families. We carpooled forty minutes each way from the city to the college, which was located in a very affluent section of St. Louis County. In St. Louis, as in many cities, the city-county divide was a social class divide as well. Despite growing up in St. Louis, I had never been in the area where the college was located.

At the time, it appeared as though all the other students either lived on campus and were from exotic places like New York or Costa Rica or lived in palatial homes and had attended the same elite Catholic girls' high school operated by the order of nuns who had founded the college. These Sacred Heart nuns seemed to specialize in girls' schools for the very privileged. The result was an environment that was not very welcoming to girls from working-class families. Most of the girls were members of an elite club, and membership was restricted.

As I write this I am not sure whether I am being fair to my classmates. I brought to college the internalized classism that I had acquired early in my educational experience; I felt like an outsider before anyone at the college ever uttered a word to me. This environment only served to intensify the feelings of inferiority I had already developed. Before, I had compared my working-class family life to middle-class family life; now I was confronted with people who went skiing on winter break and belonged to country clubs. I never saw any injustice in the differences between my classmates and myself. I wanted to be like them, and I continued to think that their privileges somehow marked them as better than the rest of us.

The experience was not all negative. By observation I acquired some cultural capital that would later be useful when I became a college professor. In many ways I attribute much of my success as an impostor to the observations of upper-middle-class and upper-class life that I made here. But the more important outcome was my introduction to sociology.

When I began college, I had the lofty ambition of being a psychiatrist. As a high school student, I lied about my age to become a volunteer at the local state mental hospital. I was fascinated with the world of mental illness and looked up to the men wandering around the halls in white lab coats. I wanted to be one of them. For my first semester, I eagerly signed up for an introductory psychology class and quickly learned what I had not known—that psychiatrists are medical doctors. I had never seen nor heard of a woman M.D. I quickly gave up that ambition and decided to settle for being a psychologist. That goal lasted another week, until I learned that psychologists need something called a Ph.D. I had never even heard of such a degree; I considered myself fortunate to be getting a bachelor's degree. Left without a goal, I fortunately stumbled into a sociology class. Sociology became my passion. By then I knew better than to ask any questions about what degrees you needed. I often tell this story to my students to illustrate how gender and class can intersect to limit our aspirations. I also use it to illustrate how oblivious we can be to the social forces influencing our lives. Once again I did not question the fairness or justice of such a social arrangement.

After two years in college I dropped out. Several forces came together that contributed to that decision or act—I am not really sure which it was at the time. Throughout the two years in college I continued to feel like a misfit, and by 1968 the social climate had changed dramatically. The counterculture called and I answered. The "drop out, turn on, and tune in" youth culture of the late 1960s offered an enticing alternative to the staid respectability of an all-women's college where I felt I did not belong. Add to this the fact that I met a man who represented to me all the allure of a bohemian lifestyle. I dropped out of school and ran away to New Orleans to "live in sin" with a wonderful man, Jim, who would later become my husband. One of the very first things I did upon moving to New Orleans was to enroll in what is now the University of New Orleans. In fact, the only reason we eventually married was so that I could qualify for in-state tuition in Louisiana. I do not fully understand why I never lost sight of my intense determination to get a college degree. It was very important to Jim, as well. He was my strongest supporter during my pursuit of a college degree. He had already completed his college degree, and it was important to him that I not lose the opportunity to do so just because I had joined him in New Orleans.

For a while I tried to balance the hippie lifestyle we were living in the French Quarter with the demands of school. Even as a part-time student it was not easy to balance such widely divergent demands. Most of my friends were going to bed as I was supposed to be going to class. All too often I followed their example. As a result this was not the most successful period in my academic career.

During this period, we took whatever jobs were available. In our social milieu there was a conscious rejection of the materialism of the establishment. You worked to get by. Within a year we discovered that I was pregnant and we decided to follow a group of friends to Lafayette, Louisiana, in the heart of Cajun country. Once again, one of the first things I did was to enroll in the state university there. Pregnant and poor, I was still determined to continue my education. Although we were living the hippie life, neither my husband nor I was totally committed to the counterculture.

The aspirations instilled in me by my high school teacher remained firm. I was determined to get a college degree; I was determined not to slip back into the accepted script for a working-class girl. The counterculture had provided an ideology rejecting the upper-middle-class world, but at heart I wanted to be a part of it. I wanted the feeling of self-worth and social worth that I thought came with success.

We eventually returned to St. Louis in 1969. My husband got a job in a tuxedo rental store, and I became a catalog assistant at St. Louis University's library. My entire education from that point on was part time. The job in the college library did not pay much, but it did provide the valuable benefit of free tuition for two courses a semester under the tuition remission program.

Sociology in the last half of the 1960s resonated with my working-class roots. I sat in classrooms where power and dominance were examined and the -isms were challenged. It felt far more comfortable than the elitism of the privileged women's college and more compatible with my values and ambitions than the hippie ideology. By then most of the students on campus looked working class—blue jeans were the uniform. The student movement had made allies of a sort between students and workers. In many ways, however, the similarities were superficial. Everyone may have been wearing blue jeans, but underneath those working-class clothes were some mostly upper-middle-class bodies, bodies that were predominantly male.

Finally, in 1972 I completed my bachelor's degree. I was not certain of what to do next, so I just continued to take sociology classes. It never occurred to me to apply for fellowships to other graduate schools, both because of family ties to the area and because of lack of knowledge of how to go about it.

No one explained to me the intricacies of how academic life worked. All of my professors were men. No one took the role of mentor for me, and I had no idea what exactly I was going to do with my sociology degree. I loved being a student but never really felt a part of the sociology student culture. So I stayed where I was because I needed the job. My parents were glad to help with childcare. No one ever suggested that later on academic deans and faculty colleagues might judge me as somewhat deficient because all my degrees were from the same school in the Midwest.

Mentors are so important for working-class students in college and graduate school. The college I attended was a private, Jesuit institution that had very little social class diversity. A mentor in high school had helped me realize that I could go to college, but in college no one served that role—I received excellent grades, but no one helped socialize me to the expectations of academic life. It was assumed that we all understood how it worked.

Did gender and social class shape the expectations the sociology faculty had of me as much as it shaped the expectations I had of myself? I certainly asked no such question at the time. I attributed any deficiencies I felt I had or any sense of not measuring up to the academic standards to my own limitations and weaknesses. Even though I had good grades, it was hard not to feel that I was fooling all my teachers and fellow students into thinking I was smart and capable. The other students seemed so much more polished, articulate, and knowledgeable. I just wanted to sit in class, learn the material, and be invisible. I felt that nothing I had to say could possibly be as impressive as what my fellow students were saying. Silence became my coping strategy. Internalized classism had convinced me that I was lucky to be where I was and I had better not let them discover that I really did not belong. I was still a working-class girl from south St. Louis who had somehow snuck into the halls of the ivory tower. We may have been criticizing the privilege and dominance of the upper classes, but as I looked around me everyone seemed privileged and superior, and I wanted to be like them.

In view of our many critiques of capitalism and discussions of the inequities of the social class system, it astonishes me how unconscious I was of the effect of my working-class background on my experiences. A sociology major ought to have been able to apply the insights of the discipline to her own life. In fact, I still gravitate toward blaming myself rather than the system. Of course, if any of the faculty were themselves from working-class backgrounds they were not talking about it. All of them appeared sophisticated and erudite about all sorts of things that counted—no one was mentioning cultural capital during this period.

As difficult as it was for working-class men, it was worse for working-class women. During this time, not only did we not have working-class models, we generally did not have women as role models. We were truly intruders. The women's movement was gaining strength, but in my classrooms male voices still dominated. Throughout my entire graduate school education, I had only one course taught by a professor who was a woman, and she was a sophisticated European with whom I felt nothing in common, other than gender and sociology. The teachers were male and the method was primarily lecture or Socratic. The majority of students in the sociology graduate program were men as well, and they were the ones who dominated classroom discussion. I sometimes felt that women were put through some sort of ordeal by fire to determine if they were fit enough to be Ph.D.s in sociology. I vividly remember a small seminar class in which the professor singled out the quietest woman in the class for particularly ferocious grilling day after day. After one especially nasty episode, she burst into tears and left, never to return. She had failed the test. Although I do not really remember much about her, it would not surprise me to learn that she was from a working-class background. Were middle- and upper-class women treated differently? I am not sure, but I suspect so. It would be interesting to compare the experiences of middle- and upper-class female graduate students during this time to see if social class privilege lent any protection to women who entered programs dominated by men. I suspect it did.

Somehow, without any guidance, I learned about the *Chronicle of Higher Education* and that it was possible to apply for teaching jobs ABD. I gathered up my courage and looked for jobs. Once again I focused on the immediate area.

COLLEGE DAYS: THE TEACHER

I took the first job I was offered; I considered myself lucky to be offered a position as a criminal justice instructor at a small, church-related college close enough to commute from St. Louis. Notice the use of the word "lucky." I was grateful to be allowed to teach college. I had taught some evening courses as a graduate student and really loved doing it, but I never really visualized myself as a college professor. I really did not belong; I felt so different from the people who taught me. I was so grateful that I was thankful to take the meager salary the school offered.

The situation was somewhat unusual. I was a member of a previously all-male criminal justice department composed mainly of individuals with law enforcement experience. This made me an outsider on a whole new level. Because I was the only one in the department with a Ph.D. in the works, I brought some credibility to the program, but I was generally given the impression by the other department members that I could not possibly know what I was talking about because I had no "street experience" as a police officer or other criminal justice professional.

For its part, the faculty in the traditional liberal arts seemed to have little or no respect for the criminal justice faculty or program. It was tolerated because it brought in badly needed money, but it was clearly at the bottom of the hierarchy of disciplines. Beginning in the late 1960s, a number of "professional" degree programs began appearing at some colleges and universities. These programs were career-oriented majors that included criminal justice, nursing, and business. In retrospect, I can see that such programs would appeal primarily to the working-class college students who were suddenly attending college in greater numbers owing to expanded financial aid programs. The gates to the academy had opened, and the newcomers who slipped in brought with them new disciplines and frequently came from working-class backgrounds.

Prior to this, I had not been aware that there was a hierarchy of academic disciplines, but it quickly became apparent. Philosophy, fine arts, history, and so on were more scholarly and intellectual than these newcomers to the academy. So in addition to the insecurities I brought with me to my first teaching position, I now found myself with another reason for feeling inadequate: the discipline I taught was not a *real* academic discipline. Of course at the time I did not make the connection to social class. How much of this reaction to these upstart disciplines was an attempt to maintain upper-middle-class privilege on the part of the dominant group and to keep the newcomers, many from working-class backgrounds, from challenging the status quo?

Different disciplines are accorded different levels of prestige. The traditional liberal arts disciplines are at the top of the hierarchy. Within the liberal arts disciplines, the social sciences, other than economics and history, are less prestigious than the other disciplines. For example, the label "soft sciences" is often used to demean sociology and psychology as less rigorous newcomers to the academy. If, as I suspect, sociology has a significantly higher percentage of people from working-class backgrounds, this reaction makes some sense. Once again, the effect is to keep the intruders marginalized. Perhaps this is related in part to the fact that sociology is the discipline with the greatest potential for critiquing the status quo, both within the academy and in society as a whole. In fact, this may have made sociology a far more comfortable choice of discipline for me than philosophy or the classics. As difficult as it has been to find a comfortable niche as a college professor, I think it would have been far more difficult if I had taught a discipline such as philosophy or classics.

I was caught between two worlds. I was teaching criminal justice, one of the challengers to the status quo, but I was really a sociologist—and sociology is a traditional liberal arts discipline. This fact did not spare me from the sarcastic comments of some my colleagues in the traditional liberal arts who, as I indicated earlier, saw the professional programs as barely tolerable facts of academic life. After a couple of years, the criminal justice department was dramatically reduced in size as the federal funds to educate police officers disappeared. Soon I was the only one left, and, largely at my impetus, criminal justice became a concentration within sociology. One could hardly have a one-person department, but more important, I wanted respectability; I discovered, however, that respectability does not come easily.

Status and respect in the academy come not just from the discipline you teach but also from attitudes, behaviors, and credentials I knew little about before becoming a college teacher. As I mentioned earlier, I learned that the college you attended could earn you status points. The more prestigious the college you attended, the more points you earned. Add points if it was not in the Midwest or South. If you were from the East Coast you earned points, West Coast, too. I was clearly at a disadvantage. I was born in the area, went to college locally, and received all my degrees from the same local university—I lost points.

A strong classical education earned lots of points. Being familiar with the works of Shakespeare, atonal music, obscure contemporary artists, and the genealogy of *Beowulf* was a clear sign you belonged. Had I stayed at the women's college, I might have gotten some points for this. How you spent your free time was also a key indicator of worthiness. Listening to NPR, having a membership in the art museum, and getting season tickets to the symphony were more indicators of the socially constructed prototype of the college professor. Of course, knowledge and behaviors can be acquired, and if you make enough money, the memberships and tickets can bought. The pressure to conform to such normative expectations is powerful. In some ways the social class origin of faculty is less important than their ability to conform to the expectations. If you can play the game, you can stay. I suspect that most working-class academics do exactly what I did—try to learn to play the part.

Before I learned to play the part, my first reaction was to do exactly what I did as a college student—I tried to be invisible. I avoided casual gatherings because I felt intimidated by what I saw as the obvious intellectual superiority of most of my fellow faculty. I kept my mouth shut at faculty meetings because I did not want to say anything that might lead my colleagues to think less of me. Some of them I avoided as much as possible, feeling as though if they got to know me they would question how I ever became a college professor.

The turning point for me was the appearance of another powerful mentor in my life. This person, a political scientist, and I started carpooling to campus. He was one of the most gregarious, outspoken faculty members on our campus. He became a great friend and avid supporter who encouraged me to speak up; he clearly believed that what I had to say was worthwhile. It was a rather gradual process, but owing to his presence early in my career, I was able to see myself as worthy of being a college professor; the process was very reminiscent of the way my high school mentor encouraged me to see myself as a college student.

Today, I see myself as having learned to be a college professor. I can play the part, but I also allow myself the independence to reject some of the trappings of that upper-middle-class world. I still wear blue jeans to class, much to the dismay of several deans over the years. I drive the oldest faculty car, a 1985 Volvo with peeling paint. I decorate my house with thrift-store finds and hand-me downs. My parties are all potluck and BYOB rather than elaborate dinner parties. I like to think that all of this represents a sort of distinctive style that is well suited to a sociologist. I now tend to say what I think without worrying what other people will think. Of course, some of this may be a function of age and tenure.

I find myself drawn to colleagues who are also from working-class backgrounds. Drinking a few beers with colleague friends at one of the local bars is still more enjoyable than attending elaborate dinner parties with some of the faculty from privileged social-class backgrounds.

IN THE CLASSROOM

Most of what I have described has focused on my sense of being an outsider among my colleagues. The one arena that has consistently been a safe haven is the classroom. The college where I teach still draws a significant proportion of its student body from first-generation students, traditional and non-traditional, from working-class families, although that is gradually changing. I particularly like teaching such students, and I frequently tell stories that include references to my own working-class background because I do not want them to experience the alienation and self-doubt that I did, or I at least want them to know why they are experiencing those feelings. It occurs to me that I am more comfortable letting down my front with my students than I am with my colleagues. I want to serve as a mentor of sorts for those of my students who feel as though they too are impostors. I want to give them what I did not get—a faculty role model who will explain the intricacies of higher education, and most important, a sense that this is where they belong. I am fortunate that teaching sociology gives me many "teaching moments" where I can offer my personal experiences and also provide a theoretical framework and vocabulary that can help students understand the impact of social class on their life chances.

SOCIOLOGICAL IMAGINATION REVISITED

A colleague once described teaching at a small liberal arts college as running a marathon, and here I am in the home stretch of my career reflecting on the hurdles that I encountered along the way. My "sociological imagination" has helped me understand that what I thought were my private troubles are, in reality, public issues and that I have not been running alone. My experiences are similar to the experiences of many others. By using my sociological imagination, I raised my consciousness of the impact of social structure—gender and social class—on my career during the particular historical period in which I have lived. All of this played a significant role in creating the hurdles I had to overcome.

Much of the strength I acquired to jump those hurdles came from the people who are an important part of my personal biography: parents, mentors, husband / best friend, and son. Although Mills did not describe it this way, the personal biography component of the "sociological imagination" is a wild card. We cannot control who will become the significant people in our lives. As I wrote this chapter, I came to realize clearly how at important crossroads in my life significant others played a critical role. Without supportive parents, two important mentors, a husband who always believed in me, and an understanding son, I would not have finished college and found a comfortable niche as a college professor.

Current and future college students and teachers will face many of the same hurdles I did because those hurdles are socially structured. During the last half of the twentieth century greater numbers of women, people of color, and working-class individuals broke down the barriers that had previously restricted their access to the academy. But it is not surprising that we are so often encouraged to see ourselves as outsiders. Dominant groups protect their privileges from the demands of challengers. One way to do so is to convince the challengers that they are not worthy. We must continue to help working-class students and teachers understand that their feelings of inferiority are due to classism and an attempt to maintain the status quo, not any personal inadequacy.

The prototype of the college professor must be reconfigured to be more inclusive of women, people of color, working-class people, and teachers of all disciplines.

It needs to be recognized that there is no one path to becoming an academic, but rather there are multiple paths—all of which are legitimate.

NOTES

1. C. Wright Mills, *The Sociological Imagination* (New York: Oxford University Press, 1959).

2. Erving Goffman, *Stigma: Notes on the Management of Spoiled Identity* (Englewood Cliffs, NJ: Prentice Hall, 1963).

3. James Loewen, *Lies My Teacher Told Me* (New York: New Press, 1995).

16

An Unwashed's Knowledge of Archaeology: Class and Merit in Academic Placement

Michael J. Shott

Thorstein Veblen considered college professors working-class functionaries drafted by the leisure class to teach the Unwashed envy of its sensibilities and the futility of sharing them. Apparently, he stole that idea from Marx, who said something about "false consciousness." To Veblen, the professoriate's self-image as a cultivated, independent elite was mere delusion. Few professors are apt to view themselves or their social position as did the famously acerbic Veblen; college professors were *middle-* or *upper*-class, not working-class, functionaries. Whatever delusions it harbored about its status and role did not prevent the professoriate from reproducing itself and its values, thereby preserving its own privileges against the lower working classes.

Today, Democrats play tennis and some academics come from the working class. Yet higher education remains stratified internally and externally. Externally, both students and faculty are drawn chiefly from upper classes. Internally, institutions and the position they offer are arranged in a graded hierarchy. What is more, position owes to social capital and pedigree as much as to scholarship, a condition that perhaps surprises only academics from the working class. It surprised this one.

My subject is not the improbability of attaining an academic career starting from working-class origins. That is an empirical matter. Nor is it the persistence of class advantage in recruitment to that career, also an empirical matter but one that is amply documented. Instead, my subject is the influence of class on standing or affiliation in the academy. My thesis is that class imposes its own glass ceiling over the career prospects of working-class academics. Class cannot bar the determined from scholarly careers, but it certainly throws down obstacles in the path of their advancement.

WHAT CLASS IS AND CLASSES ARE

Anyone who thinks that he (used generically) can define class rigorously is missing the point. Class is "a fluency which evades analysis" (Thompson 1963, 9), something that happens as much as something that is. As a result, defining and analyzing class is like nailing water to the wall: easy to talk about but very hard to do. For analytical purposes, class must be measured, but it is experienced in daily life as an ineffable sensibility. One definition is as good as another, and mine follows that of Benjamin DeMott (1990, 10): class is "the inherited accumulation of property, competencies, beliefs, tastes, and manners that determines, for most of us, our socioeconomic lot and our share of civic power."

So much for defining class. The next task is to define or recognize class*es*. As a subject, the working class is a matter of history and self-identity but contains a crucial productive element. Workers are neither self-employed nor supervisory (Wright 1985, 45), that is, they do not control the conditions of their economic function or existence, whether money, physical capital, or their own labor. In this view, classes are defined or at least recognized simultaneously; the existence of a working class requires a professional class above it, itself divided into a lower stratum of managers and an upper one of true capitalists. The act or process of defining a class at once implicates others and the system to which all belong. All of this is a turgid way to define "working class." Its members might describe it differently: they work with their hands, not their heads, and, except at church, they don't wear white shirts and nice shoes. If you have dress shoes for Sundays and holidays, you are in the working class.

These definitions of class and classes seem to leave out academics. On the one hand, we only partly control the conditions of our economic function. On the other hand, all of us are supervisory in some degree and, until the 1970s anyway, we wore nice clothes to work. Wright's (1985, 47) view of academic exceptionalism finessed the question; to him, academics controlled their own labor but not the broader context in which they labored. This seems a rather, well, labored definition that inspires wonder about Wright's own class consciousness. Historical trends in academia—alienation of administration from scholarship, fragmentation of authority and expertise— mirror, not contradict, broader trends in the social conditions of labor (Bowles and Gintis 1976, 204–6). Illustrating Marx's thesis, academics may be reluctant to recognize their own working-class status.

A WORKING-CLASS TESTIMONIAL

So much for class and classes in the abstract. I am an archaeologist, practically an impossible career for a child of the working class before the 1970s and still a rather unusual one. Archaeologists acquire prestige and affiliation from combinations of inherited sensibilities, academic origins, research interests, and locales. My career choices and path offer one case study in class status and professional standing. In archaeology, if you want to work at Harvard or UCLA your intrinsic scholarly merit is irrelevant, but you had better not care too much who wins football games, affiliate with state schools whose names contain geographic modifiers, or conduct fieldwork in unglamorous parts of North America. These are academic versions of the unwritten codes of class identity and conduct that pervade society.

I have conventional working-class credentials. Chief among these is my former ignorance of that status. I didn't know that I was in the working class and grew up believing instead that mine was a middle-class family. After all, in America wasn't everyone's? During my childhood, my father drove a truck and my mother kept house. We had a large, close, extended family, most of whom lived nearby and the rest in the world's far corners in military service. I was well fed, well cared for, and well loved.

I grew up in Massachusetts, attending public schools and then a public university because private ones cost too much and because I did not know how to game the SAT racket and was innocent of grantsmanship and self-presentation. I was the first in my family to earn a bachelor's degree. (Of course, the degree was from a no-account university of the sort that class mavens like Fussell [1983] would scorn.) Until the age of twenty-one, I had not flown or traveled west of Ohio or south of Washington, D.C. My international experience consisted of one rain-soaked afternoon in Niagara Falls, Ontario.

Undergraduate Education

Awareness of my class status developed slowly. New England is unusual in the United States for its abundance of private colleges and universities and its comparatively brief history of public higher education. Most residents are Catholics who uncritically esteem Catholic universities and harbor dark suspicions about public ones. (In the 1950s, the Speaker of the Massachusetts House referred to the University of Massachusetts as a "Masonic lodge," to Catholics roughly equivalent to the current president declaring that West Point is on his Axis of Evil.) As a result, private always has been favored there over public. So far as I know, Massachusetts was the only state to found a private university—MIT—with public land-grant funds provided by the Morrill Act. As a formality, it also founded a public agriculture college that eventually became the University of Massachusetts, my alma mater.

After the Civil War, white working-class Americans north and south were lured from their natural identity with working-class blacks by appeals to race. My own Irish ancestors, for example, became white as a matter of social construction, not biology, and for base emotional reasons that contradicted their natural identification with working-class blacks (Ignatiev 1995). In the same way, more faithful to home than class, working-class New Englanders tend to identify with the region's private universities, class bastions if ever they existed. For most, this identification is grounded in nothing more than an accident of geography, because few children of the working class attend those schools. They retain fond feelings for Harvard even though it has never reciprocated. It may as well be on the dark side of the moon for all that Harvard ever did for them.

From an early age, New Englanders of all social classes acquire an exquisitely fine sense of discrimination regarding universities. At the pinnacle, of course, is Harvard; at the base, public universities of all varieties. Between them are private schools finely graded by a mysterious combination of geography, admission rate, mean SAT scores, and their football teams' records. Public schools are all the wrong things: big (by national standards New England ones actually are small, but they are perceived there as too big), nonselective, rowdy, not in Boston. My university lacked even the sense to have a good football team, the only grounds for distinction that regional public opinion would grant such institutions.

Working-class New Englanders perceive this institutional hierarchy, but they are hopelessly deluded about its basis. They may understand that wealth and pedigree bear on placement in the higher-education hierarchy, but they mistakenly identify merit, however that is measured, as the deciding factor. If one is very bright, Harvard beckons, no matter one's class. If Harvard doesn't beckon, then one mustn't be very bright. If one lands in a *state* school, then undeniably one isn't bright and gets what one deserves.

This mentality is as pervasive as it is corrosive to working-class esteem and prospects. My experience in higher education from undergraduate, to graduate student, to researcher, to teacher convinces me that the quality of one's education owes much more to how one goes to school than to where one goes, and that merit has practically nothing to do with placement in the higher-education firmament, either as student or professional. Claims to the contrary for their "stuffy and uncompromising distinction" (Fussell 1983, 160), my experience with products of the self-styled elite universities convinces me of the fallacy of assuming their distinction (these people are no less talented or educated than others, just no more so), if not always their stuffiness. But this realization is shared by few; people routinely ask where, never how, you went to school. My understanding of this was years in the making, not the result of an epiphany the day I walked into my first undergraduate class.

Indeed, I assimilated the common view to my own case. I settled out at Massachusetts because I wasn't smart enough for better schools. At first I was disappointed, even ashamed, to be there. In time, I grew to cherish the education I received there. The change of heart was no accommodation to unavoidable circumstances; rather, I realized that, contrary to everything casually assumed about it, the university was quite good. After I earned the B.A., the logical next step was graduate education to prepare for a scholarly career as an archaeologist. I was too dumb to know that I wasn't supposed to try.

Graduate School and Beyond

I truly became aware of my working-class origin only by attending graduate school at a very private midwestern public university. The realization grew not just because Princetons, Oberlins, Harvards, and Dukes surrounded me—as I said, a very private public university—not just because their passports (they had passports!) bore exit stamps from Switzerland and Chile, not just because their parents were ambassadors, executives, and academics, not just because they had grants—free money—and I did not, and not just because some drove late-model cars and I drove, well, nothing because I couldn't afford a car. All of those things contributed. Nor, with several memorable exceptions, did the realization come from overt class prejudice. Some graduate school peers are among the nicest people I know; anyway, those who were not so nice had more subtle ways of expressing our status differences than making open reference to class, the verbal equivalent of a blunt instrument and therefore déclassé. Like *Look Back in Anger*'s Alison Porter, they wounded with silence or a few well-placed words more than with frontal assaults.

Our respective financial conditions nicely reflected our different class backgrounds. To finance my first year of graduate school, I mortgaged future earnings with loans and a work-study job (in graduate school, for heaven's sake). So far as I know, every one of my cohort peers funded his or her graduate education partly or entirely with fellowships, most drawn from public funds. As I said, most of my peers were bright people, but none brighter than I, who lacked such funds but whose family, at least to an infinitesimal degree, subsidized with its tax dollars the graduate education of my more privileged peers. Talk about underwriting the affluent. Ever since, graduate school fellowships have seemed to me more an upper-class entitlement than a public good.

Anecdotes do not make complete arguments, but they make good points. One evening early in my graduate career I was drinking beers with colleagues, as graduate students do. Somehow, the talk drifted to the occupations of students' parents and, like many conversations, worked its way around the table. When it reached me, I said that during my childhood my father drove a truck and my mother kept house. First came the chuckles that follow a small joke, then silence while everyone waited for me to tell them what my parents really did. Produce documentaries for PBS? Teach at

Wellesley? Manage trust funds? I have neither the right nor the desire to feel ashamed of my parents, so it didn't trouble me to say, "No, really, that's what they did." The next silence was awkward, but soon the conversation righted itself and moved on. A small moment, insignificant by itself, but one that revealed my fellow students' expectations and the distance and experience that separated us.

None of this was debilitating, however frustrating it may have been. Perhaps my greatest surprise in graduate school was the dawning realization that my peers, despite their backgrounds and the unexamined advantages they conveyed, were no more talented than I. Yet their placement in the undergraduate cosmos unquestionably was higher. If placement was a question purely of merit, how could this be? In retrospect the answer is obvious. Living the experience, however, took some time to disabuse me of the misconceptions under which my working-class mind labored.

Their native ability did not distinguish my graduate-school peers from me. Instead, mostly it was their confidence and sense of security that set them apart. Neurosis is a middle-class indulgence. Fear is a working-class condition. My peers were at a graduate school considered prestigious because they deserved to be. For the most part, in fact, they did; they were a fairly bright group. I was there by virtue of some oversight and lived in fear of its discovery. At the start it was clear that most cohort peers knew less about archaeology than I did—by pure dumb luck I was an undergraduate at a time and place that served a serious archaeology student quite well—but knowing the subject was not a condition of admission nor a guarantee of status once admitted. My peers knew something infinitely more important: What you knew mattered less than what you were and how you acted. In graduate school, you got along by getting with the program, socially as much as intellectually. My peers had the social capital to thrive that I lacked.

And thrive I did not. My colleagues were shrewder and much more surefooted in negotiating the thickets of academia. My first two years of graduate school involved unlearning what I knew more than learning anything in particular. My performance in classes was unexceptional. I soldiered on but nearly washed out, finally muddling through (or what I expect from my professors' perspective amounted to as much). At length faculty came to regard me as unpromising, perhaps not a good fit for the program. Most of them were decent people, but they had common human failings, one of which was the tenacity of first impressions. As far as I know, most who trouble themselves to think about it still regard me as a remedial case who settled out where he deserves to be.

My original goal was to study Andean archaeology. I spent several field seasons in the Andes, but practical concerns eventually motivated me to work in my graduate school's own backyard, the Midwest. Now, my graduate department cultivated a the-world-is-our-plum mentality manifested in the geographic patterns of research among its faculty and students; the number and variety of entry stamps in one's passport was a practical measure of status there. One faculty position is reserved for local prehistory but has not been held for thirty-five years by any archaeologist with prior local experience or any interest in the region. The few of us so unwise or blinkered as to choose to work in the Midwest were regarded with the combination of surprise, pity, and disguised scorn customarily reserved for circus freaks. At the time, I was aware of but indifferent to this attitude, not realizing how it would bear on my career prospects.

Especially in a self-consciously nouveau country like the United States, archaeology is an esoteric discipline. What little most people know of it they casually confuse with digging for dinosaurs. Archaeology, therefore, is regarded as an elite pastime; either it is a hobby or, if a profession, only one for those who don't need one. Because the discipline lacks the high public profile of other fields and the perception of relevance to modern life, the academy's archaeological prestige is earned by some combination of pedigree, the view that discovery conveys authority by right ("I found this site or tool so am an authority on all scholarly matters that relate to its study," a view as legitimate as supposing that anyone who drives a car is a competent mechanical engineer), locus of research (*not* employment; where you do your fieldwork, not where your university is located), and genuine merit. Leave aside the first, which is indefensible, and the last, which is unobjectionable. For present purposes, leave aside as well the right of discovery. The salient point is the prestige attached to research in the area of my choice, the American Midwest.

A glance at how archaeology is practiced in the American academy reveals many paradoxes for a field that claims universal intellectual, not just geographic, scope. To some significant degree, an archaeologist's standing among his peers owes to where he works, not how, how much, or how well he works. In the academic ranks, the study of North American prehistory is underrepresented by comparison to other continents, especially to apparently glamorous areas like Latin America (Shott 2000). From the point of view of the United States, Latin America is a combination of all the right stuff: "accessible, cheap, and appropriately exotic" (Pi-Sunyer 1998). It is the land of lime margaritas. By comparison, the land of lime Jell-O seems painfully unglamorous. As a result, midwestern practitioners are rare in what most archaeologists and others regard as the first rank of American research universities. To judge from the scant regard paid it in American academic departments, the Midwest is the least of the least, its study unfashionable for intertwined cultural and aesthetic reasons. Indiana Jones may be a romantic character in American popular culture, but not because of any connection with his namesake state. His archaeology was a great game set, from American perspective, in distant and exotic locales. Indiana Jones is a Hollywood invention but one distressingly near the truth of popular misconception. In the academic organization of practice, Hollywood is mirror, not fantasy.

What explains the neglect of the Midwest and the corollary esteem of distant places? First-world archaeologists routinely work in places attractive as much for their natural beauty, culture, and remoteness as for their research character. There is nothing intrinsically wrong with such preferences except that the prehistory of equally valid but less glamorous areas is neglected in the process and the careers of those who work there circumscribed. Patterns of archaeological fieldwork coincide remarkably well with the distribution of resorts, tourist hotels, national parks, vineyards, and medieval pilgrimage routes. Purely on archaeological grounds, there seems no good reason why Andalucía, say, should be better studied than Iowa, but it is obvious why it receives both more tourists and more archaeologists. Commerce may follow the flag; archaeology follows the travel brochure. (A perhaps more cynical view is a disciplinary equivalent of world-systems theory. The wealthy global North [North America, western Europe] imports from the South [everywhere else, particularly Latin America and Africa] raw materials in the form of archaeological evidence, then exports back its refined manufactured goods as theories, published literature, and acquired prestige.) Whatever the reasons, so far as midwestern archaeology is concerned, if you dig there, they won't come, "they" being tourists, readers, funding sources, prestigious universities. More to the point: you won't go, anywhere, that is, but the Midwest.

At length my working-class fear was manifested in several ways, perhaps chief among them the fear of unemployment without benefit of the Ivy League social-welfare system. ("Can't find a faculty slot? We'll make you Assistant Deputy Dean of Left-Handed Women from States Whose Names End in the Letter A, or Executive Officer to the Master of Fumfroo House." Or, "My cousin is on the Prudential board. She'll find you something there." Or, "My college roommate is a congenital idiot. He runs Covert Ops at Langley and, if he knew what it was, could be persuaded that he needs a Farsi speaker with extensive Middle Eastern travel experience.") Most graduate school peers wouldn't dream of applying to, let alone accepting employment from, places like the Carnegie "comprehensive" university that employs me. The Harvards et al. wouldn't, in their view, stoop to that level, because they knew that they didn't have to, that no matter their records— and many of them are perfectly good scholars—they would receive offers from the Berkeleys or Boston Universities or Chicagos of the world. Failing that, they always could become Assistant Deputy Dean of Something or work for Citibank, Booz Allen, the Metropolitan Museum, or whomever their social apparatus provided outside the academy.

So here I am, and there they are, by and large.

HIGHER EDUCATION IN CLASS SOCIETY

"University education is the power which is destined to overthrow every species of hierarchy . . . remove all artificial inequality and leave the natural inequalities to find their true level."

Lester Ward (1872, cited in Bowles and Gintis 1976, 27)

If irony is the simultaneous contemplation of opposites, American society is deeply ironic. Simultaneously it holds dear two contradictory beliefs: that it is classless and that it offers upward mobility. If there were no class differences, there would be nothing or nowhere to move upward to. Mobility presumes the path and destination that the myth of classlessness denies. Society does not reconcile these contradictions so much as it cherishes both while blithely ignoring the contradiction between them.

From the Jeffersonian ideal of an aristocracy of virtue, the democratizing influence of education has been an important element of the American mythos. Education opens doors for the deserving, no matter how humble their origins. Higher education particularly serves the democratizing purpose, and its advocates like Ward long have traded on this belief to win it support. In effect, it is regarded as the instrument that corrects the injustices that the prevailing mythos assumes do not exist. Higher education is celebrated as the solution to a problem whose existence is denied.

But if to some education is the path to success, to others it conditions the young to fill fixed roles in class society. Certainly, some regard as a myth education's democratizing function (e.g., Bowles and Gintis 1976, 209–10; Kahlenberg 1996, 96–101). They note that, generation to generation, SAT scores and access to privileged higher education consistently correlate with wealth and other status measures. Old Europe used titles and accidents of birth to make its invidious distinctions. As unfair as its society was (and is), at least it had the virtue of basing distinction on something transparently arbitrary. Europe is slowly working its way through a centuries-long process of dispensing with such silliness. America takes a different route, using a perceived higher-education hierarchy to make its class distinctions. This path is more pernicious, because American society is experiencing no comparable process of change. As a result, "having a degree from Amherst or Williams or Harvard or Yale should never be confused with having one from Eastern Kentucky University or Hawaii Pacific College or Arkansas State or Bob Jones" (Fussell 1983, 152). In this view, education forges and reproduces, not breaks, the shackles of class (Bowles and Gintis 1976), a statement as legitimate as it sounds melodramatic.

Internal Ranking in Higher Education

Our habit of thought is to sharply distinguish secondary from higher education, high schools from universities. Both are in the business of educating the young, but they are separated by a qualitative difference in state. Language serves the distinction; high school faculty are teachers, university faculty professors. We may teach, as my university misses no opportunity to stress, but we are not mere teachers. (Actually, we are to our students, who are blissfully unaware of the distinctions that faculty are so jealous to preserve; routinely they refer to us as teachers. The worst thing that a student can call some of my colleagues is "Ms." or "Mr." In college, it is "Professor" or "Doctor" or just plain "Sue" or "Jim." High school teachers are addressed by the generic honorific, faculty by different, elevated ones or the perversely familiar given name.)

But if "school teachers . . . are the economic proletariat of the professions" (Mills 1951, 129), universities and their faculties are no monolithic stratum that stands unambiguously in elevated rank above them. Harvard and Ball State are not equal in the sight of God or, what really matters, the *U.S. News and World Report* annual university edition. People may argue the comparative merits of Michigan and Chicago, but few would hesitate to rank both above, say, Oregon, and no one would waste time wondering if Tulsa or Northern Iowa deserved mention in the same conversation. As the existence of an upper class requires lower ones, the existence of a Harvard requires truckloads of Emporia States and the graded set of Northern Colorados and Cincinnatis between them. These perceptions of rank have precious little to do with the native ability of faculty at the respective institutions; many at low-ranked schools are very good scholars indeed, and you, dear reader, are invited to draw the obvious corollary. Yet the most brilliant economist at Auburn or political scientist at South Dakota State need waste no time waiting for that plum appointment to the Council of Economic Advisers or the State Department. Those positions are reserved for Harvards and Stanfords, no matter how exceptional the faculty elsewhere or how ordinary the faculty at those exalted places. Rank has its literal privileges.

From a faculty perspective, the Carnegie Foundation's (1994) classification forms a rough-and-ready hierarchy: Research 1 universities are above Research 2 universities are above Doctoral Universities are above Comprehensive Universities like mine. Liberal arts colleges comprise a sort of side category equal, in some respects, to Research 1 institutions. We in the vastness of the middle ranks can measure our remove from either extreme in a variety of ways that include salary, location, and subjective prestige. If some of us have risen above the level of high school faculty, we are daily reminded of the many ways in which we have not risen nearly far enough. From high school to Harvard, therefore, educational institutions are arrayed in a hierarchy of near-medieval complexity and refinement, an educational Great Chain of Being.

Class Effects among Students and Faculty

I take for granted, so will not trouble to document, the fact that student access to higher education is externally stratified. That is, college students of all varieties are unrepresentative of their age cohorts because they are drawn from higher socioeconomic ranks. More arguably perhaps, I take for granted the further point that student access to higher education is internally stratified. College students of higher socioeconomic rank are drawn to particular institutions, the result being that the student population at elite colleges and universities is highly unrepresentative even of the larger college population. The Harvards of the world certainly take this condition for granted and trade on it routinely; there is no good educational reason but very good social ones why Mount Holyoke, for instance, has its own campus stables. The result is a hierarchy within a hierarchy, college students over others and students from la-de-da schools over the rest of the college population.

In the same way, university faculty are unrepresentative of society by their inherited socioeconomic rank. This is the professional version of external stratification, strictly equivalent to the student one. Synthesizing earlier research, Oldfield and Conant (2001, 172) concluded that middle- and upper-class dominance of the academic ranks is a stable condition that can be traced back at least to the 1950s. There seems little reason to doubt that it originated much earlier. Their survey of University of Illinois faculty showed, not surprisingly, that it was not representative of American society but significantly skewed toward the middle and upper classes (2001, 179).

A mid-1990s survey of archaeologists reported some data on socioeconomic status, a suitable proxy for class (Zeder 1997). Its respondents were mostly but not entirely academics. I treat the data as representative of the professoriate, even though archaeologists in nonacademic positions (chiefly in government agencies and private consulting firms) are likelier to be of working-class origin than those in academic positions. My treatment therefore is conservative, tending if anything to exaggerate the numbers and proportions of working-class versus higher-class respondents. Yet most respondents self-identify as middle class or higher, only 22 percent as working or "lower-class" (table 16.1). (Indeed, treatment *is* conservative. In unpublished data broken down by occupation, only 21 percent of academics self-identify as lower class, 24 percent as upper class [M. Zeder, personal communication, 2003]). The distribution of proportions differs slightly by sex, with somewhat more women than men self-identifying as upper class. This difference is mostly at the expense of the lower class, because middle-class

Table 16.1. Proportions of Archaeologists by Socioeconomic Class

	20–39 %	40–59 %	60+ %	Total %
Women				
Upper	27	26	25	27
Middle	56	53	60	54
Lower	17	21	15	19
(n)	(62)	(344)	(40)	(614)
Men				
Upper	18	18	28	19
Middle	59	57	50	57
Lower	23	25	22	24
(n)	(253)	(639)	(118)	(1010)

Source: Zeder (1997: Table 2.1).

proportions are similar between women and men. Longitudinal trends are equivocal in these figures, but lower-class proportions are not higher in younger age cohorts. Indeed, proportions by class are remarkably stable among women of different ages. Among men, lower-class proportion varies little, and a slight decline in upper-class proportion from older to younger cohorts is almost entirely balanced by a corresponding increase in middle-class ones. The pattern is clear: younger archaeologists continue to be recruited mostly from middle-class or higher ranks, not from the working class.

Perhaps most arguable of all in the popular mind if undeniable on empirical grounds, faculty are further ranked by socioeconomic status within the academy, in a way largely commensurate with the perceived ranking of institutions. A 1960s study found that inherited social class determined position by affiliation in the higher-education status hierarchy independently of scholarship or even scholarly pedigree as measured by prestige of one's Ph.D.-granting institution (Crane 1969). A decade later, the fact of internal stratification persisted. To summarize a mid-1970s survey, "Class background bears not only on who becomes a professor, but even more closely on where he or she teaches. . . . The more prestigious, research-oriented institutions have drawn their professors disproportionately from the higher social strata. . . . Conversely, academics from working-class and farm backgrounds turn up most heavily in the lower-status colleges" (Lipset and Ladd 1979, 323). The conclusion is undeniable that "the rewards of prestigious academic positions are much better correlated with measures of pedigree than of productivity" (McGinness and Long 1997, 362). This is internal stratification. For both students and faculty, then, a great chasm divides the Boise States and Harvards of the world.

Class Effects in the Archaeology Professoriate

Zeder's data showed clearly that archaeology in the academy is externally stratified. Is it also stratified internally? Sporadically over several years, I studied the relationship between scholarship and position among American archaeologists in academia. Even now the study remains incomplete. Here, I summarize results that suggest class effects in patterns of hiring and employment of academic archaeologists. The necessary data include institutional affiliation of archaeologists and measures of affiliated institutions' rank or status, of scholarly productivity, and of each archaeologist's class status. I briefly discuss these measures below and justify them and their various permutations at greater length elsewhere (Shott 2004).

I collected data on institutional affiliation as of the 1996–1997 academic year, drawing a random sample of the more than seven hundred archaeologists listed in the American Anthropological Association's (1996) guide to departments for that academic year. (In the United States, archaeology is taught and practiced mostly within larger anthropology departments.) There is no comprehensive national ranking of anthropology departments or the archaeology programs they contain. National rankings of research universities exclude comprehensive universities and liberal arts colleges, where many archaeologists are employed. They cannot be used to rank institutions because too many would be omitted. Several sources rank American universities on numerical scales; I used Gourman (1996), whose rank scores ranged from about 2 to 5 on the ratio scale. Gourman ostensibly ranked only undergraduate education, but undergraduate and graduate faculty are not separated in American practice, so I treat the scores as valid measures of perceived rank and call them "affiliation."

"Scholarship" was measured (tediously) as number of books and articles, using MELVYL, a bibliographic database housed at the University of California that indexes scholarly literature held at the UC campus, nearby research libraries, and Harvard University's Tozzer Library. I discuss the ranking of presses and journals and the parsing of multiple authorship elsewhere (Shott 2004). As mentioned above, archaeologists' class status was solicited and compiled in an earlier study of the archaeology profession, but those data were not available for study. Lacking systematic information on class, I adopted the poor expedient of undergraduate institution as a proxy for class. Here again I used Gourman (1996) to measure rank. Other studies, noted above, showed that class and undergraduate affiliation are correlated, if not perfectly. Further lacking systematic information on undergraduate affiliation, I consulted online university bulletins, catalogs, alumni directories, and biographical profiles published in conjunction with scholarly articles, and I also queried some archaeologists by e-mail. Thus was undergraduate institution determined for 123 of the 186 in the random sample (66 percent). Unfortunately, inability to determine undergraduate institution is not distributed randomly. Major private universities' bulletins proved much less likely to list faculty undergraduate institutions than did public ones or liberal arts colleges, a bias only partly counterbalanced by use of other sources. I must assume, but cannot demonstrate, that the sub-sample of the random sample whose undergraduate affiliation I learned remains a valid random sample. I call the Gourman measure of undergraduate affiliation "pedigree."

Data of this nature are inherently problematic. Top-ranked college football teams often lose to unranked opponents, and a national ranking of orchestras vouchsafes little about the quality of a musical experience. Rankings violate the inherent complexity of social phenomena by reducing multivalent properties to single values, much as would reducing Renaissance masters to a common numerical scale miss the point of their meaning and impact. ("If Michelangelo is a 6.9, then Raphael must be at least a 6.6.") But numbers can be useful depending on how they are used, and they permit forms of analysis that can reveal patterns worth knowing.

I undertake more thorough analysis of these data elsewhere. Selected findings suffice here. Pedigree and affiliation correlate ($r = .28$, $p<.01$); partial correlation to control for the independent effects of scholarship little alters results ($r = 26$, $p<.01$). (I report r, but nonparametric r_s yields nearly identical values and attained significance in all analyses.) Partial correlation of affiliation and scholarship to control for pedigree is somewhat lower ($r = .19$, $p = .04$). Both influence career prospects and affiliation, but pedigree matters more than scholarship.

Correlations are low if significant and scatter plots diffuse, both from imperfections in measures and because factors besides merit and pedigree influence affiliation. But the correlation between pedigree and affiliation patterns differently between archaeologists whose professional affiliations are with public versus private universities. It is weak for public institutions ($r = .16$, $p = .15$) but highly significant for private ones ($r = .48$, $p<.01$). Among public institutions, high professional affiliation is not confined to those of high pedigree. Among private ones, lower pedigree confines the (admittedly small) sample to lower affiliation, but archaeologists of higher pedigree are distributed across a wide range of affiliated ranks. Where pedigree is modest, affiliation is low; where pedigree is high, affiliation is low, high, or in between. Still, only the highly pedigreed enjoy high professional affiliation. Private schools particularly esteem pedigree in the archaeologists they employ.

Stepwise multiple linear regression (MLR) is a more powerful but less robust way to examine patterning in evidence. For all sampled archaeologists, MLR admits rank of the institution that awarded the Ph.D. degree, pedigree, and scholarship in descending order (multiple $r = .43$, $p<.01$). Measured by additional variation explained by its entry, scholarship accounts for about 3 percent of variation, although pedigree accounts for only about 5 percent it-self. For archaeologists employed by private universities, MLR to identify de-terminants of affiliation enters only rank of the Ph.D. institution and pedigree (multiple r = .47, p<.01); scholarship is not a significant contributor to affili-ation. Pedigree, a measure of inherited class status, influences affiliation, a measure of achieved professional status, more than does scholarship.

Obviously, measures are crude, the merit of archaeologists resides in more than just scholarship, and there is great variation among individuals. This is both undeniable and unsurprising, because many good archaeologists have good positions with high-ranking affiliations. There is no perversely inverse meritocracy in archaeology, no upside-down pyramid where the least are highest and the best least. But unless intrinsic merit and native ability some-how are related to class status, it is inescapable that access to position in the academy protects and reproduces class privilege. This is a turgid way of say-ing that class matters more than merit in determining career prospects.

It is an exaggeration to say that the archaeological profession is in deep denial about this truth. Instead, archaeology is blithely indifferent to it. The profession rightly is concerned about opportunity by race and gender. As in society at large (Kahlenberg 1996), class is ignored or minimized by com-parison. What class consciousness that archaeology possesses is confined to its subject, not its practice. Compared to the archaeology of women, of slavery, of homosexuals, class is a minor entry among the proprietary in-terests of recent archaeological research. Even as a subject, it is promoted only rarely in the United States, for instance by a self-acknowledged mem-ber of the professional class who regards the promotion as a way to indulge the personal interests of the working class (Duke and Saitta 1998). What-ever the sincere good intentions behind the effort, they bring class to our attention for our benefit. Good intentions do not entirely offset the patron-ization implied, the presumption that the working class's imagination can-not transcend its own history and conditions. However well intentioned, this attitude is of a piece with the implicit presumption that only black stu-dents should be drawn to black studies, only women to women's studies. What about those of us in the working class who, like the middle or pro-fessional class, have interests beyond our class status and history? If there should be no Mayan epigraphy or Egyptian dynastic history for the work-ing class as opposed to everyone else (and there shouldn't), there should be no proprietary archaeology of the working class for working-class archaeologists.

Leave aside the particulars of my own case and comparative merit. Briefly, my scholarly record is the equal of those of most archaeologists who hold higher positions in higher education's great chain of being. The disparity be-tween my record and status is due partly to chance, the opportunity distor-tions of market restriction in higher education, and, as discussed above, my choice of research area. Mostly, though, I believe that is owing to pedigree. To some significant degree, I am where I am because I'm from the wrong side of the academic tracks. This status and origin has limited my opportunity and prospects. But my conclusion has an obvious corollary: some disciplinary colleagues have records at least as good as mine and positions no better, if not worse. Some have no position at all. Indeed, the unexceptional nature of my position is the point; there is no grand conspiracy to deny any one person his rightful position, whatever that may be. There is instead casual indifference to merit in my discipline and equally casual indifference to the pervasive, enduring advantages of class.

In the path of advancement lies the further problem of guilt by association. No matter his ability or record, an archaeologist placed at a lower-status university has this affiliation itself as a barrier to overcome in the path of advancement. To some degree, academic departments stake their reputations and self-images on the hiring process and tend to gauge their standing in proportion to the prior institutional affiliation of those they hire. They may pay lip service to individual merit as a criterion ("We hire the best person available, no matter his or her affiliation"), but they often seem to choose less on the relative merit of individuals than the perceived stature of where they come from. Only the most self-assured departments can boast internally (to deans, say, who control their budgets) or externally (to disciplinary colleagues elsewhere who judge their standing and their grant proposals) that they recently hired the best available and that he or she just happens to come to them after fifteen years at Bugtussle State Teachers College. "Bugtussle State?" their audiences might gasp. A dean might say, "If that's the best they could do, they must not be a good department. I'll show them. I'll cut their budget." Or a colleague might decide, "Henceforth, I'll collaborate with Sue or Jim at Exalted University, not this pathetic loser who just hired someone from—what's it called?— Bugbump A&M?"

Complaints about access to status sound like dissing one's own university. To refute this criticism may seem defensive, but isn't. No one need apologize for ambition, nor is it proof of disloyalty. I am grateful that my university hired me and supports my scholarship to some degree. Ambition for higher status implies no disrespect for my employer's standing or ingratitude for its support. My university knows perfectly well where it stands in the higher-education cosmos and trades on that knowledge both with its governing body and its own students. It is a respectable school that meets a legitimate social and educational need (although it tends sometimes to indulge its constituencies' misconceptions). Our best students are the equal of those anywhere. No one "stoops" to work here, no matter how much the Harvards might think so. Like most of my colleagues, I take seriously my responsibilities to it. Yes, I would be happier at a research university, a judgment less on my institution than on its fit with my predilections and career goals, as well as the range of prospects elsewhere.

To some, ambition also implies presumption if not pathos. Who am I, they might say, to think that I deserve to be at a research university? Higher education is a meritocracy, and the fact of my status is proof of my, let's say, modest merit. As in student admissions, if one is deserving then Harvard beckons; if Harvard doesn't beckon, then one isn't deserving. The flaws in this logic are both empirical and principled. Empirically, witness the evidence of class bias in university faculty noted above and at length elsewhere in these pages. The notion that higher education is a meritocracy may comfort the comfortable; it would be funny if its implications for the uncomfortable's career prospects were not so grave. In principle, the logic is no different from supposing that the displaced or ill deserve their plight because they experience it.

CLASS REMEDIES?

If class effects are demonstrated and widespread, then they demand correction. Oldfield and Conant (2001; see also Kahlenberg 1996, 101) considered at length the merits and rationale of such corrective measures. Class-based affirmative action, or whatever we choose to call it, broadens opportunity, corrects past injustices, and does not partly disadvantage poor whites ("white" as constructed social identity, not biological trait) while redressing inequities that others suffered.

The appeal for class-based hiring is principled. But, perhaps true to my class's cynicism, I am deeply skeptical of its prospects. The current sociopolitical climate militates against expansion of protected status, which is opposed even by many who would benefit from its effects. Anyway, race- and gender-based protection was driven by powerful ruling-class self-interests. It is no original observation that the first generation's beneficiaries of gendered affirmative action were conspicuously privileged to start with. Crudely, such policies benefited the spouses, sisters, and daughters of the (primarily) men who advocated and implemented them. Their appeals and justifications played out in mass media, not the pages of obscure scholarly books like this one. Almost by definition, class-based policies benefit few of the people or their families who are in a position to act on the justice of the appeal.

Still, there are good reasons to contemplate the prospect and justice of class-based remedies. The world is unfair, and each day's newspaper describes hardships and suffering against which the status of working-class academics shrinks nearly to insignificance. So much is undeniable, but also irrelevant. Correcting inequities neither worsens nor prevents the correction of greater social ills. In contrast, ignoring inequities or tolerating them because, after all, some people have it much worse, is a counsel of despair. By that reasoning, nothing ever will change because there is always something or someone more deserving elsewhere. Sometimes the world is improved in small steps.

If not unseemly, at least it may appear churlish to complain about one's academic standing when so many who do not hold them seek academic positions. To the extent that access for the meritorious is foreclosed, the complaint in fact is churlish by degree. But the same class-based inequity that bars access to some bars status to others. In that respect, at least, our dilemmas are similar.

CONCLUSION

Sporting metaphors are unfashionable in academia, but I don't apologize. Access to status in archaeology is like a professional baseball team whose major-league rosters were populated as much by AA and AAA players as by legitimate major-leaguers. Minor-league rosters would contain legitimate major-leaguers in equal measure.

Sammy Sosa played for the Cubs. Baseball would not abide his languishing with the Elmira Blue Sox. Baseball teaches useful lessons: that unionism has benefits, if sometimes equivocal, that merit is rewarded, but also that life is unfair and capital trumps all, as recent baseball history amply demonstrates. As does life, baseball offers eternal mysteries—why the Cubs can't ever win—and lessons about merit that academia might heed.

Like some colleagues, I am not in the major leagues. Yet I can hit the academic equivalent of major-league curveballs, if not as well as Sammy, and would be much happier in a world where merit mattered as much as does pedigree. Until then, I soldier on like my working-class colleagues everywhere. For now, the next game with the Mahoning Valley Scrappers beckons.

REFERENCES

American Anthropological Association. 1996. *American Anthropological Association 1996–97 Guide to Departments*. Washington, DC: American Anthropological Association.

Bowles, Samuel, and Herbert Gintis. 1976. *Schooling in Capitalist America: Educational Reform and the Contradictions of Economic Life*. New York: Basic Books.

Carnegie Foundation. 1994. *A Classification of Institutions of Higher Education*. Princeton, NJ: Carnegie Foundation for the Advancement of Teaching.

Crane, Diana. 1969. "Social Class Origin and Academic Success: The Influence of Two Stratification Systems on Academic Careers." *Sociology of Education* 42: 1–17.

DeMott, Benjamin. 1990. *The Imperial Middle: Why Americans Can't Think Straight about Class*. New York: Morrow.

Duke, P., and D. J. Saitta. 1998. An Emancipatory Archaeology for the Working Class. *Assemblage* 4. www.shef.ac.uk/~assem/4/4duk_sai.html.

Fussell, Paul. 1983. *Class*. New York: Ballantine.

Gourman, Jack. 1996. *The Gourman Report: A Rating of Undergraduate Programs in American and International Universities,* 9th ed. Los Angeles: National Educational Standards.

Ignatiev, Noel. 1995. *How the Irish Became White*. New York: Routledge.

Kahlenberg, Richard D. 1996. *The Remedy: Class, Race, and Affirmative Action*. New York: Basic Books.

Lipset, Seymour M., and Everett C. Ladd. 1979. "The Changing Social Origins of American Academics." In *Qualitative and Quantitative Social Research: Papers in Honor of Paul F. Lazarsfeld,* ed. R. Merton, J. Coleman, and P. Rossi, 319–38. New York: Free Press.

McGinness, Robert, and J. Scott Long. 1997. "Entry into Academia: Effects of Stratification, Geography and Ecology." In *The Academic Profession: The Professoriate in Crisis,* ed. P. Altbach and M. Finkelstein, 342–65. New York: Garland.

Mills, C. Wright. 1951. *White Collar: The American Middle Classes*. New York: Oxford University Press.

Oldfield, Kenneth, and Richard F. Conant. 2001. "Exploring the Use of Socioeconomic Status as Part of an Affirmative Action Plan to Recruit and Hire University Professors: A Pilot Study." *Journal of Public Affairs Education* 7: 171–85.

Pi-Sunyer, Oriol. 1998. "Ethical Issues for North American Anthropologists Conducting Research in Mexico: The National Dimension." *Human Organization* 57: 326–27.

Shott, Michael J. 2000. "Geographic Emphases in American Archaeological Practice." *Society for American Archaeology Bulletin* 18 (2): 22–27.

———. 2004. "Guilt by Affiliation: Merit and Standing in Academic Archaeology." *The SAA Archaeological Record* 4 (2).

Thompson, E. P. 1963. *The Making of the English Working Class*. New York: Vintage.

Wright, Erik Olin. 1985. *Classes*. London: Verso.

Zeder, Melinda. 1997. *The American Archaeologist: A Profile*. Walnut Creek, CA: AltaMira.

17

Class Enriching the Classroom: The "Radical" as Rooted Pedagogic Strengths

Livy A. Visano

TEACHING AS LEARNING

Class-informed teaching is inherently constituted in teacher and student relations that are committed to "being" and "becoming" conscious. By moving well beyond the mindless modernist business of "doing," teaching about class engages the converging processes of *"reaching in"* and *"reaching out."* First, reaching in, the intrapsychic dimension of the knowledge–identity nexus, focuses on self-consciousness as an active meaning-creation activity that connects the past selves in the present to transcendent possibilities. This self-awareness moves beyond the prevailing Western rational, scientific, and linear models to more intuitive acts of knowing grounded in the "power of self-definition" (Giroux 1995, 133). As Nietzsche (1887) observed, of all the knowledge that we seek, self-knowledge is the most difficult to achieve, primarily because one's own set of ontological assumptions, intellectual traditions, and knowledge escape scrutiny. Since an understanding of the world is filtered through one's understanding of self, introspection or inner conversation enables the self to think through relations, actions, symbols, meanings, and other sociocultural components (Brunner 1999). Effective class-informed teaching is contingent upon self-awareness, an inner search for freedom, equality, and dignity. As hooks (1990, 157) states, "one of the deepest expressions of our internalization of the colonizers' mentality has been self censorship." By recognizing the protective benefits of privilege and the limitations of material existence, teachers become better suited to identify their communities, their ways of life, their labor, and, more important, their ways of thinking. Fear, however, vitiates the actions of the privileged and arrests the development of "social" empathy that is so necessary

241

in coming to terms with one's own position vis-à-vis the experiences of the marginalized.

Second, reaching out, intersubjective pedagogic self-other interactions are a recognition of the ongoing and transbehavioral constructions that occur between the inner and outer perspectives. The ability of teachers to know themselves *and* to understand others through sympathetic introspection requires collaborative exchanges based on mutual recognition that exists in all forms of social and cultural interactions. An emphasis on inclusion, readmittance, and reinterpretation communicates connectiveness. In Giroux's words, knowledge "never speaks for itself, but rather is constantly mediated through the ideological and cultural experiences" (1988, 100). Learning through reciprocal involvement reflects a pedagogy that is "engaged" (hooks 1994), "transformative" or "critical" (Wink 2000, 123), and "community-based" (Mooney and Edwards 2001). As bell hooks (1990, 8) elaborates: "Critical pedagogy (expressed in writing, teaching, and habits of being) is fundamentally linked to a concern with creating strategies that will enable colonized folks to decolonize their minds and actions, thereby promoting the insurrection of subjugated knowledge."

Critical pedagogy challenges normative patterns of teaching and urges "a social praxis" that helps "to free human beings from the oppression that strangles them in their objective reality" (Freire 1985, 125). Teaching, therefore, is a social enterprise that tells us just as much about the "teaching" individual or organization as about the phenomenon being taught. To ignore the lived realities of teachers and learners alike is a perniciously anti-intellectual act that refuses to understand the significance of *context* and *content* as constituting an analytic framework for articulating identity, subjectivity, and social interactions. Context, the set of structural and experiential forms, conditions the content of teaching and learning. Both social contexts (affiliations, resources, and skills) and personal contexts (ideology, motivations, and self-concept) mediate the message—the subject matter of learning. The coterminous forces of context and content are not only integral to teaching but also anchor the often ignored engagements with life experiences. As will be later documented, the self is always located in particular relations between discourses of power, deeply ingrained living experiences. Accordingly, working-class experiences, as ontological categories, ground the basis of experience and therefore knowledge.

The everyday life as class practices cannot be concealed nor dismissed as merely the background of social activity; rather, it is necessary to reveal how class foregrounds everyday life experiences (de Certeau 1988), habits, constraints, and inventive strategies. For Lefebvre (1992), the daily life, especially the daily recurrences from leisure to labor, is the site in which one measures the progress of human becoming. It is the everyday life experiences that account for social ontologies, for expressions of knowledge, and for how we are mired in the mystifications of materialistic projects. Admittedly, any study of everyday life would be a completely absurd exercise, unable even to grasp anything of its object, were it not done expressly for the purpose of transforming it (Debord 1967).

In addition, it is argued that class, a fundamental element of the living and lived experiences, contributes to contemporary analyses of identity and difference. Class is a complex and multidimensional concept that has been too frequently abused to reify workers as a static, pathologized, and marginalized economic category. Further, within the politics of recognition, class has been too readily dismissed as a banal and essentialist ideology embedded in prevailing institutions or too quickly lost in its intersections with ethnicity, race, or gender. Working-class identity and experience consist of dynamic counterhegemonic struggles and resistance that have historically and cross-culturally facilitated emancipatory pedagogies.

To professors of critical criminology in a neoliberal environment of learning, it remains a formidable challenge to teach effectively and inclusively about the power and politics of difference. We often hesitate to put theory into practice because of the associated cultural and political risks. Specifically, as teachers, we risk looking incompetent to our colleagues and students if we experiment unsuccessfully with new ways of teaching (Brookfield 1995, 232); and we risk being marginalized by a hostile culture that views the critically responsive academic as "subversive" (Kerlin 1995). Though much research exists on women and minority group members in academe, there continues to be a dearth of studies focusing on the impact of social class background on academic careers. Typically, working-class identities and class consciousness belong nostalgically to some contrived bucolic past, either to be forgotten or alternatively reified. Class today among the contemporary intelligentsia is irrelevant (Munt 2000, 1) and only incorporated as a fleeting research interest, especially in mainstream criminology. But all academics have a duty to account for the type of framework they employ in resolving thorny contradictions regarding their own curricular and personal commitments to race, gender, class, and sexual orientation, in addressing their own privileges, and in implicating themselves in knowledge production.

The aim of this chapter, therefore, is to analyze the differential impact of working-class experiences on teaching and learning. Specifically, how is the working class the fabric that weaves the fibers of belief, value, and lived experience for academics? What is the degree of penetration of the ideological on the institutional? How do working-class ideologies "fit" in framing basic institutionalized practices? Similarly, this chapter draws attention to the crucial role dominant institutions play in influencing working-class cultures. How do ideological and institutional governmentalities mediate the experienced and articulated social relations concomitant with the hegemonic narratives in everyday lives?

CRITICAL AUTOETHNOGRAPHY

The autobiography is used as a self-referential tool to interpret previous experiences in order to understand class positioning. This dialogic autobiography, a critically responsive pedagogy, provides practical knowledge for living life dynamically and creatively. Moreover, this critical awareness grounds teaching and learning; this rooted consciousness emancipates the teacher from further reproducing inequities and social injustices. By drawing on autobiographical accounts of academics from the working class, we have established some fundamental elements of the difficult transition from a working-class environment to the privileged life of academics (Lacey 2000, 41). *The self in context* is a method for achieving necessary tactics of life that emerges through time. Taking experience seriously, this methodological practice seeks to discover the implications of class, categories that reference classist identities, and the politico/socio/cultural structures that marginalize working-class and ethnic communities. The ensuing narrative profiles the extent to which we as teachers "realize" ourselves in the subterranean world of anecdotal evidence and personal testimony—fragments that constitute critical sources of information (Heyes 1999).

A critical autoethnography, or self-study, displays multiple layers of consciousness, connecting the personal to the political. Consistent with Smith's (1987) methodology of uncovering organized ways of knowing, configurating class and self-identity "in terms of connectedness/embeddedness," this exercise asks us to make public our stories in an attempt to remind us of the impact of "being and belonging" to the working class, which too many people, for far too long, have tried to erase. The autobiographical approach is important because it not only authenticates and locates the "organic" position (Gramsci 1971) but clearly defines the organic intellectual as someone who is positioned to have experienced and is experiencing the particular consequences of living from certain social juxtapositions. As a result of the articulation of a set of problems associated with one's life and the lives of other working-class people, one develops an increasing familiarity with opportunities to think through issues in order to effect change in the oppressive structures of dominance. For example, it is critical to locate myself in this project, and within particular experiences and social histories, to make salient for the reader the experiences and ways of understanding that inform my theoretical framework, most notably, in the absence of mainstream academic literature, especially in criminology. In representing myself and relating to others in similar circumstances, these interweaving fragments of biography facilitate an interrogation of dominant interpellations that have been integrated with and implicated in our daily lives. I am convinced that this self-reflective method of knowledge making and understanding of the everyday world is more compelling and valid than the prevailing positivistic modes of inquiry. The latter falters miserably in providing pedagogic thoughtfulness (Taylor and Settelmaier 2003) that demonstrates how social and cultural forces shape practices of knowing.

THE RADICAL AS ROOTED: A NARRATIVE OF PROMISE

Of course, the story that follows will itself be deviantized for offending certain "high" moral grounds and for challenging conventional perspectives. To the threatened, the arguments herein will be easily discarded as rancorously polemical and controversially provocative, forever beating on rhetorical drums. Regrettably, the loose ethnographic forays of mainstream criminological cookbooks have failed to stimulate critical curiosities, refused to challenge the congested closures of criminological canons, and denied experiences that defy the defining gaze of authoritative definitions. The narrative of working-class criminologists "is a political observatory" (Foucault 1979, 281) not a misfit zoology absorbed in the exhibitionism of the criminal entertainment industry. Instead, this story succeeds even if only ideas are mobilized and readers eventually politicized to think more subversively in empowering themselves. Since, as Foucault (1979, 304) admonishes, "we are in the society of the teacher-*judge*, the doctor-*judge*, the educator-*judge*, the social-worker-*judge*," it will not be surprising that the reading of fragments of pain and humiliation will occasion some fetishized voyeurism that alienates and reifies the life experiences of "those others." Hopefully, this political project invites the more circumspect reader to self-engage ideologically and historically in the conditions and consequences of classism, racism, misogyny, and heterosexism.

AS THE "FOREIGNER"

My family landed in Quebec City on a cold day in November of 1951. Penniless refugees, we had lived for the previous six years in eight different refugee camps in three different countries.

The ordeal began on the morning of March 13, 1945. My mother answered a knock on the front door of her family home in Zadar on the Dalmatian coast (formerly a part of Italy, now a part of Croatia) to find two commanding police officers and a government intelligence officer. Threateningly, they informed her that she and her family had fifteen days to report to the local dock, where they would be shipped to another city to be detained as refugees. Forced into exile from their country, my parents joined the thousands of other Italian nationals removed from their homes and placed in refugee camps.

Hungry, forced to sleep on cement floors of a large warehouse in Split, and in fear of local authorities, my family was shipped to Bari, Italy, like unwanted cargo. Those who resisted were killed. Six of the group with whom my family traveled were taken aside, still in full view of the rest, and slaughtered by machine gun for having defied the local authorities.

The Italian government refused to recognize us as nationals. Like the thousands of other refugees, we felt betrayed by a government that had relinquished all responsibility and forced us to become wards of the International Refugee Organization (IRO). Six years later, we were ordered to a camp in Germany, where we were told we would be shipped to Canada or the United States or Australia for resettlement. My twin sister and I were born in the camp in Naples and have absolutely no memory of these earlier experiences, but my two older brothers, my older sister, and my parents remember vividly the hardships of dislocation.

Authorities of the IRO and Catholic Immigrant Aid oversaw our resettlement in Fairview, Alberta, a remote, small, rural community hundreds of miles north of Edmonton. No one in the family spoke any English or knew anything about this country called Canada, our new "foster" home. My first recollections are vague memories of a very long, cold, and dark train trip from an unfamiliar port in Quebec City to some unknown destination. Immediately upon arrival in this snow-covered, very cold, distant, and barren region, we were warmly welcomed by the local community—poor farmers, workers, and First Nations residents who clothed, housed, and fed us. The local minister secured a temporary job for my father as a dishwasher in one of the very few restaurants in the town. The cold winter months were unbearable, the culture shock was unimaginable, and the employment prospects dismal.

Tired of the poverty and the extremely long and cold winter, my father and my older sister, barely seventeen years old at the time, left Fairview to go to Sudbury, Ontario. A Croatian family with whom we had shared cramped quarters in the German camps and with whom my mother remained in contact insisted that life in their newly adopted town would be more bearable, given the better employment prospects. My father and older sister left eagerly to explore the possibilities and to pave the way for the rest of us. Several months elapsed before we were reunited, hopeful that we could settle more securely in this small mining community.

Sudbury presented many of the already all-too-familiar challenges we faced as unskilled foreigners unable to speak the language. With two adults and five children in a two-bedroom basement apartment, it was crowded, but we were grateful we were all together. The support of other working-class families helped to sustain us. Others of European background, similarly relocated, became our extended family. As kids, we referred to these family friends as uncles, aunts, and cousins. The loyalty, respect, and generosity that characterized these relationships are among our most cherished memories.

My father worked in construction in the so-called "pick and shovel" crew until he was laid off when the construction contracts deteriorated. My oldest brother, then twenty years old, contributed to the family income by working as a miner, drilling nickel in a mine in the Blind River basin. The small space was manageable; my parents converted the living room into a bedroom and the dining room into a living room. The division of labor was clear and simple: my mother managed the household while my father desperately sought employment. To support the meager family income, we took in boarders, other immigrants from Italy and Libya. My oldest sister soon left to marry an Anglo-Canadian but continued long after to help support the family. Her greatest contribution was in the employment she would secure for my father in Sudbury and later in Toronto.

Although we lacked many amenities, life was peaceful. Friends would visit regularly, generously offering money and food. I recall many fascinating stories. We, as children, listened attentively to the histories recounted by the older working-class folks about how Canadians rode the trains protesting labor abuses; we learned about Nicola Sacco and Bartolomeo Vanzetti—two Italian immigrants executed for crimes they did not commit—the Depression; the wars; and the like. One close family friend, Mat Petranovic, a laborer who visited us daily, educated us in the oral tradition with his experiences and other stories of life in China and Cuba, about Canadian politics, and so on. My mother, Mat, and my godfather—an Italian-trained medic turned sweeper at the Sudbury smelter of INCO, the area's largest mining company—constantly reminded us of the importance of education. One family story that remains vivid in my mind is of my maternal grandfather. Having migrated to the United States in 1910 as a twenty-year-old looking for employment, he joined the widely persecuted International Mine Workers of America union. Undecided and unsettled, he traveled back and forth a few times between Philadelphia and his hometown in Zadar. Though he returned to the United States in 1912 and again in 1918, he could not adjust to the harsh living conditions in Philadelphia at the time and finally settled back in Zadar with his parents and siblings.

As children we played games with homemade paper toys; my siblings and I never had, nor do we recall ever missing, the many toys and the sporting equipment like skis, skates, and toboggans enjoyed by so many of our friends. We did purchase a camera when I was in grade 7. I became the family photographer and excelled in taking family pictures. I recall the hours during my adolescence that we spent as a family listening to the music of Johnny Cash on a white Marconi radio perched above a tall refrigerator.

But much of this newfound peace was shattered on April 8, 1958, when at 9:10 p.m. we answered a quiet knock on the front door. Our priest had come to notify us of the accidental death of my twenty-year-old brother, who had just been killed when the mine in which he was drilling collapsed. The following day, the front page of the local newspaper, the *Sudbury Star,* read:

> One man was killed and two others were seriously injured when they were hit by a 2½ ton fall of rock at the eighth level at Lake Nordic Mine, Tuesday night. Dead is a former Sudbury man. . . . He is believed to have died instantly. . . . Mine authorities said the three-man crew had just started drilling when the accident happened.

This news report did not mention the other twenty-nine miners who had died "accidentally" a year earlier, nor was there ever a report of the eleven miners who died a few months later in the same basin. Miners were easily replaced. There were other immigrants and sojourners from the Atlantic provinces who could easily be hired to take the place of the dead men. One of them was my father. But his employment as a miner was cut short; he was forced to quit when all his ribs were crushed by an underground train.

Food stamps fed the family until my father secured a job with the city as a garbage collector—a position he enjoyed for twelve years. I am still struck by the uncanny deference that my father had toward his boss (perhaps out of fear of losing his job) and by the pride he felt in his work.

My second-oldest brother by five years took a full-time job as soon as he was old enough. He started as a sweeper in the smelter for INCO, following in the footsteps of my godfather. Given my brother's poor performance in high school (due in no small part to the challenges presented by the language and cultural differences), work was the only option for him, as it was for many other members of working-class immigrant families. At work, he excelled as an active union steward, proudly parading his large silver-colored metallic lunchbox adorned with numerous stickers proclaiming his identification with the United Steel Workers.

There are many memories that in hindsight demonstrate an extreme insensitivity, bordering on hostility, toward those students who did not "fit." I remember my twin sister complaining about her vision in grade 1. Instead of recommending an eye examination, the school attributed her problems to her poor English and failed her. I recall in grade school the colossal ignorance of teachers who would repeatedly reprimand immigrant working-class kids for not having had their parents assist them with their homework. Leaving aside the simple fact that our parents were exhausted by the end of the day and could not speak English fluently, by the time we were in advanced primary grades, many of us were more schooled than our parents. The extracurricular activities such as going on school trips, playing on organized hockey teams, playing in school bands, and attending summer camp required money, which few of the working-class kids had. Left behind, we created our own entertainment, but not without experiencing the inevitable tensions of kids who wanted to belong and to participate.

Education for those of us who did not "measure up" was difficult. I came close to failing grades 3, 5, and 7 but finally excelled in grade 8, receiving the highest grade in the class. Despite this achievement, the school authorities continued to try to stream my friends, my brother, and me into vocational programs. In grade 9, the school counselor recommended that I attend a technical training school despite my sustained A-grade performance. We were all continually made to feel stupid as foreigners and as working-class kids singled out and humiliated for our cultural differences and accents. At times, the most belligerent teachers physically beat us.

In the face of all the institutional pressures to quit and forgo education, it was family support and encouragement that sustained me. Throughout these years our mother relentlessly extolled the virtues of education despite the challenges that schooling presented for all of us. I suspect the tragedy of my oldest brother's death—knowing that mining as a career was otherwise what we could expect—further inspired our academic pursuits. The value placed on education was high, and it was considered a collective accomplishment. When I had a test, I remember my family as being very supportive, making many sacrifices. My brother would stay away from the small room we shared so that I could study undisturbed. By this time my twin sister and I were excelling in high school, both attaining incredible grades and later gaining admission to university. Decades later, while working full time and with a young family to support, my brother completed high school and earned his bachelor's degree in education. When he returned full time to university to complete his master's in education, we rallied to his assistance. We were and still are extremely proud of his achievements, and his wife's support of his education was essential.

Throughout our adolescence and youth, the family represented a safe refuge. Dinner conversations were lively and bonds among us deeply cemented. To the outsider, Sudbury is a hell hole, a barren wasteland—the result of decades of environmental degradation. But to us it represented honest working-class values and a genuine sense of community. This sense of community extended to our friends. During leisure pursuits, time away from study and household tasks, I enjoyed the company of my peers who, having succumbed to the pressures of authority, were not in school. Those in our gang who worked financially supported the leisure activities of those of us in high school. These school dropouts were very proud to have friends who were in school, and on occasion they expected us to teach them. This respect and loyalty existed in many cohesive working-class youth cultures in all activities, from shooting pool to just hanging out on street corners.

Billiards represented much to us as a source of income as well as entertainment. I recall one incident at a billiards hall when a group of us working-class

high school students were busily engaged in a game. A group of more economically privileged boys from the same high school class entered and bullied
us—taunting us with such slurs as "wops," "dagos," "mafia," and "spaghetti
benders." Within seconds, the dropouts rather forcefully removed the intruders. The bullies never bothered us after that.

Hanging out with my dropout friends was not a response to the rejection
I felt but rather was due to the attraction of a more comforting world of
working-class peers who shared my values of loyalty and respect. Interestingly, we seldom noticed the same levels of loyalty among the predominantly Anglo-Canadian middle-class youths. We did notice how bored they
seemed—bored in school, bored with their cottages, bored with their families and friends, bored with all their materialism.

Our mother devoted her life to her children, ensuring that we had three
hot meals a day and that we were healthy and happy. Equally important for
her was a general education that taught us the skills to proudly define ourselves spiritually, to know how to judge the value and worth of a person by
the quality of the relationship and not the size of the wallet, and to know that
family working-class values were positive.

Since my parents could not speak English, as children we assumed considerable responsibilities—dealing with medical and financial matters, citizenship issues, finding employment for my father. We had no time to waste
fighting each other; we were too busy looking after each other and assisting
with the family chores. Another precious value that we learned was the refusal to submit unquestioningly to outside authorities. Even though I went to
church every Sunday, as an altar boy I watched the abuse of authority and
saw how the priest would defer to the more well-to-do of the parish. Unlike
middle-class kids, working-class youths were taught wary obedience to "deserving" authorities, to question and to be curious, to respect the concept of
respect, and to be critical of shallow, sycophantic displays of deference. For
this reason, my working-class peers found schooling, based on dominant
values of materialism, competition, and acquisitiveness, difficult. Relative
deprivation, poverty, unemployment, minority status, limited opportunities,
inequality, school conflicts, and limited access to opportunity structures
were significant in shaping our worldview. To many outsiders, the working
class, especially as represented by the unskilled laborer, was a common or
popular identity that admittedly did not measure up to "normalized" middle-
class standards or to the authoritarian disciplines.

School, the church, and places of employment were steeped in an Anglo-
centric white culture, history, and way of understanding the world. Anything
Italian or working class was dismissed as foreign and ridiculed as vulgar. My
birth name is Livio, but my early teachers immediately changed my name to
Livy, a more palatable and less foreign moniker. This practice of imposing
values and thereby colonizing identity persisted throughout high school and

university. When I was in grade 12 several Catholic teachers/priests constantly made derogatory remarks about Italians, who they assumed were either bricklayers or in the mafia. A quiet, and sometimes not so quiet, resistance to authority was the result of this nefarious negation.

AS THE "OUTSIDER"

In my experience, early socialization shaped ideology and common sense (Giroux 1983). When I first arrived in Toronto (a large metropolitan city) as a first-year undergraduate student, I was struck by the anonymity of unskilled workers and the shameless disregard with which others treated them. I was surprised to notice the absence of metal lunchboxes, such a permanent fixture in the Sudbury household.

At university the workload was heavy. Social and Political Thought was a challenging program of study from which I profited immensely. During this stage the process of living in residence for three years with limited financial resources was not uncomfortable. My previous background helped in this regard. I was familiar with and practiced at doing more with much less. I was grateful to my mother, who would send "care packages" of food, and grateful for the small allowance provided by my twin sister (who was working part time as a bank teller), which augmented my meager summer savings.

During my first summer at university I helped my father with his janitorial duties, an unpaid task that once again was rewarding for the lessons it offered. I observed closely how others disparagingly treated us, identifying us as lesser people because of the job we were doing. Some would go out of their way to remind us of our status; the majority, however, just ignored us as if we were invisible. I experienced the vulnerability that comes from the real risk of layoff that comes with this type of work. While the privileged university students would lounge around the swimming pool, my father and I were busily cleaning it and the building, waxing the floors and burning garbage in the basements.

During the following summer months and throughout my university education, I worked in factories, warehouses, construction, fast food establishments, and restaurants, loading trucks, painting houses, running deliveries, and waiting tables, all to pay my tuition. But the value of giving back was firmly entrenched. I volunteered at the Scott Mission (a social service agency aiding the poor and hungry) and contributed to the work of a variety of community-based organizations including the Metropolitan Toronto Social Planning Council, Race Relations and Policing Councils, several antiracist agencies and organizations, labor organizations, Students for a Democratic Society, and the Canadian Party of Labour. I attended many anti–Vietnam War demonstrations and the Cesar Chavez grape-boycott protests in the early

1970s. I was encouraged by my older brother to get involved; he was my mentor in praxis throughout university, just as he was my protector during high school and just as he was my teacher of "street smarts" in elementary school. His commitment, passion, and knowledge of labor issues were impressive. I have always hoped to measure up to his high standards of activism.

At the encouragement of the late professor Robert Harney, I applied to and was accepted into law school following graduation. But the experience was incredibly disturbing and my time in this program short. Both the content and the delivery of material were extremely class biased, devoid of any considerations of social justice. It was in law school that I also felt a profound sense of discrimination based on class and ethnicity. Routinely, two of the professors would single out the very few "Italians" for ridicule. Because of the fixed seating arrangement, they knew immediately on the basis of surname who "did not belong" and reminded us in a variety of ways of this "fact." I voiced my concerns to the dean at the time, the late Ron Ianni, himself an Italian from northern Ontario. He investigated my complaints and recognized the obstacles the bigotry presented. We both agreed that I would enjoy studying criminology instead, which would offer me the opportunity to critique the law rather than to practice it.

After my criminology master's degree I worked full time in an after-care agency. I resigned in protest with a handful of others because of what we perceived to be unfair labor practices that resulted in the firing of a black case worker. Shortly after this experience, I was hired to work for the federal government's parole service, where I became the vice president of the local Public Service Alliance, a large national union. Still in contact with my professors at the University of Toronto a few years later, I was encouraged by Professor Austin (Ted) Turk to pursue a Ph.D.

We observed a curious phenomenon while at university. While there were only a few of us from working-class backgrounds and preciously fewer faculty members rooted in the working class, there were many more students from privileged backgrounds opting to live a marginal existence. Just as the working class was striving to become a part of the nouveau riche class, these students of privileged background were presenting themselves as the nouveau pauvre. These "fashionably poor" students tentatively immersed themselves situationally. Though they had the economic make-up of the working class, they most certainly did not have the cultural, and their talk of social justice seemed incongruent with the salaries, properties, travel opportunities, and lifestyle from which they came and to which they would return.

While completing my M.A. and Ph.D. I was teaching at three different universities as a part-time instructor. With the Ph.D. in hand and the assistance of my supervisor, Professor Dennis Magill, I was fortunate to secure a tenure-stream appointment to one of Canada's most progressive universities. At

York University, I participated in antiracist struggles (as a member of a number of race relations committees) and continued with union work (serving on the executive committee of the faculty association). After several requests and some administrative delays, I was granted a transfer to the Atkinson faculty, whose primary mandate at the time was in serving working-class adults, minorities, and part-time students. Likewise, my research interests have always focused on the impact of culture on inequality, from my master's thesis on organized crime with an emphasis on the deviantization of Italian Canadians, my doctoral dissertation on deviant behavior with a focus on gay and straight kids who hustle, to policing of race, to media depictions of youth.

My involvements with various community-based organizations continued. In the late 1980s several of the critical criminology professors formed a collective to publish the *Journal of Human Justice,* of which I was a patron. As a faculty member, I helped found the Access Action Council and volunteered with the African Canadian Legal Clinic, Youth Empowerment Committee, Police Race Relations Committees at 14th Division, and chaired the Community Advisory Committee of Corrections Canada. Later, I moved toward something with which I had never before been officially involved: the Italian community in Toronto, in particular, the Italian Congress, the Columbus Centre, the Italian Centre for Diabetes, and VitaSana; for a brief time, I was the Elia Chair of Italian Canadian Studies at York University.

After a long labor-management dispute at York University and countless hours on the picket line, I was encouraged by my many colleagues to run for dean. As dean of the second-largest faculty, I was nevertheless aware of my class and ethnic background. I was routinely reminded of it, directly and indirectly, in the relationships and practices with which I was professionally engaged. My learned colleagues were not immune to the pressures of stereotyping and occasionally would characterize my critical decisions or actions as those of the "mafia" or a "thug."

Having moved from the foreigner to the outsider, certain nonnegotiable values remain. Class loyalty, honesty, family rootedness with one's children, siblings, and elderly parents, and an incredible appreciation for finding a like-minded life partner are the values I hold most dear.

ON REFLECTION

Many decades later, the country in which I live still remains as foreign to me as the country of my birth. The experiences of my family's collective lifetime are indelibly etched on my consciousness.

Even with a strong academic performance by working-class students, in primary and high school we were treated differently. Although facilities and resources were available, they were not accessible to us. Marginality mediated both the situational context of relations and the wider structural contingencies. What was lacking in material amenities was more than compensated for by deep and rich connections, and it was there that we found strength. In hindsight, I would say three related factors were fundamental in building and maintaining the world of the working-class youth, as I experienced it: constituting skills of actors (survival mechanisms), reactions of valued others, and self-identity (self-confidence).

As a university student and as an adult worker, I, like many from working-class backgrounds, encountered the combined forces of isolation and alienation with an alarming frequency. My previous life experiences had not prepared me well for the more heightened deceptions and disguised displays of bigotry that silences on the basis of class, gender, race/ethnicity, and sexual orientation. Much learning took place during the transition from student to full-time worker, where institutional and ideological expectations often conflicted and helped frame a different kind of thinking or knowing at different stages of getting connected, staying connected, disconnecting, and reconnecting.

During my undergraduate and graduate studies it was clear that working-class students existed in several worlds while never feeling fully adjusted to or part of middle-class realms. Most students of working-class background do assimilate, especially in communication style; they have to in order to survive. Appearance and language (verbal and body) communicate values. Language accommodation is more easily managed than cultural integration. Language has voice. But giving voice, often absent in many of my undergraduate university lecture halls and graduate seminars, silences the right to speak (Troyna 1994, 8), with or without an English accent.

As a full-time, tenured academic, it is clear that class background plays a major role in the "academic hierarchy." In different environments the working-class subjects are forced to hide their identities and conceal certain dispositions (Bourdieu 1989). Many of us must contend with these dual realities, often internalized as what Christine Overall (1998) calls "role muddles" generated by the conflicting expectations that arise from roles that are socially dissonant. The university culture provides a coherent narrative of identities, social recognitions and a sense of "we-ness" that stresses the similarities or shared attributes around which group members coalesce. The professional frames of reference normalize institutional practices and protect privilege. But a critical approach regards identity as an integral dimension of teaching in disseminating knowledge. Privileged class interests manipulate by "de-politicizing" and "cooling-out" critical or oppositional research. Privilege as a sophisticated means of domination seeks to transform the individual into an assembly-line conception of self, thereby furthering vulnerability and credulity. Financial compensation is not only an integral index signifying the prominence of certain actors, institutes, or centers but also is a normative guide of professional standing in the "teaching" culture. Status articulates an investment in a culture that misappropriates a moral language and celebrates possessive individualism, leaving behind only mirrors and windows through which knowledge is framed. Seldom is there a call for a moratorium on competitiveness, let alone on state- and industry-sponsored research centers and studies. Within this orientation, the culture of collegial complicity has diverted attention away from authentic voices and action. The pedagogies consistent with protected professionalism, lucrative consultation, and research institutes with special funding arrangements have ushered in a new "banking system" that commodifies teaching (Farr 2000). As Dei (1996, 21) suggests, "schools are not only agencies for cultural, political, and economic reproduction, but are also sites of contestation between groups differentially situated in terms of power relations."

CLASS LESSONS

Working-class experiences facilitate the development of an interrogative stance that is informed by history and political economy when looking at the familiar. Class enables a *sociological imagination* (Mills 1959) that links personal troubles with public/social issues; it allows people to connect patterns in their lives with the events of society; to appreciate the intersection of biography and history when approaching phenomena deemed to be "controversial"; to delve into the social sources, meanings, and implications from various vantage points, using different analytic lenses; and to become more demystified and tentative in their traditional appraisals of controversial or social issues. In other words, class invites all faculty and students alike to partake more fully in their own learning, to formulate fundamental questions about the nature of our own learning. Typically we as working-class academics are invited to become strangers and are asked to be courageous in deconstructing traditional texts by concentrating on the contradictions and closures inherent in conventional commentaries; to respond to the critical faculties that we have developed; to document our experiences, consciousness, and intentions and their relational contexts, especially when examining the teaching and learning processes as political projects; and to position ourselves ideologically and historically. This anticlassist perspective challenges the privileged normative characterization of teaching as a given and static process of meaning construction in relation to our social realities. Finally, at the personal and interpersonal levels, critical education provides an understanding of the human condition. This emphasis on the experiential confers an *authenticity*. To be truly authentic and work for change means undertaking assessment and reassessment of the self within changing contexts. Based on experience, this process requires negotiation, tolerance, and change as one acts in the present and at the same time reflects on one's status. This dual process of action and reflection offers a source of insight and further change. Experience is important only if it is authentic. Regardless of whether the experience is researched or lived, teaching is respected by students if the presentation of socially sensitive material is based on a variety of flexible approaches.

Authenticity is a commitment to resistance. As Trotman (1993) clarifies, authenticity moves beyond western thinking to begin the work of constructing alternate social realities. Authenticity encourages an awareness of the other and envisions the self as a knowing being, a powerful person who possesses a clear understanding of his/her place in the world (Trotman 1993). In journeying toward pedagogical authenticity, we strive to creatively dispute, via a socially responsive teaching and learning process, normative conceptualizations of "difference." This involves linking education and action in order to generate strategies for an equitable, sensitive, and coherent set of immediate and long-term responses that enhance social justice. Lamentably, traditional criminological canons reflect the primacy of deference, of genuflecting before the altars of self-proclaimed experts, rather than differential defiance based on the politics of self. Traditional models of teaching and learning criminology continue to judge differences, colonize compliance, and shackle imagination. What is required is a more emancipatory and transformative pedagogy, grounded in various struggles (gender, race, class, and sexual orientation). Equally significant is the realization of the limitations of traditional approaches to crime, narratives that support particularistic truth claims rather than more socially just methods. My own response has been to continue to explore the subjective dimension of my working-class past in order to rethink the origins, meaning, and consequences of teaching "class" in criminology-related courses. These approaches are designed to question, rather than reinforce, the moral, political, social, economic, and intellectual organization (or regulation) of society (Jakubowski and Visano 2002). Thus for instructors striving to put critical pedagogical strategies into action, the task of providing students with more inclusive curricula in an open and critically responsive pedagogical environment becomes quite overwhelming. Through a more critical education, we will uncover our assumptions, learn more about our own learning, self-consciously challenge the dominant ethos, and develop oppositional currents. Praxis, as an ideologically informed action-based orientation to knowledge or truth claims, essentially meets the methodological demands of progressive teaching by encouraging the teacher to grasp a critical knowledge about the nature of criminalization. A close proximity to, or familiarity with, alternate social realities enables the teacher to capture more fully the experience of criminology; the nature of the teacher's experience communicates and thereby breathes meaning into criminological debates. Thus, the idea of experiential and intellectual integration refers to the relational, positional, and provisional functions of interpretation. Thus, we can speak of standpoint epistemologies—attitudinal knowledges and their corresponding ideologies—myths, symbols, metaphors (Arrigo 1998).

Class-committed teaching and research invite the process of experiencing the connections between oneself and the "other," about expressions of power and cultural controls. For many criminologists, class-committed pedagogies run the risk of being set apart and relegated to the margins; quite frankly not much of a risk for those who have experienced it in daily realities. Regulation, through its reproduction of particular (proper, permitted, encouraged) forms of expressions, fixes (or tries to fix) particular signs, genres, repertoires, codes, as normal representations of "standard" experiences, which represent human beings as far more standardly "equal" than they can be in fact (Corrigan 1990, 111). The act of identifying oneself as "from the other side of the tracks" "as those others" places an individual historically in specific narratives, images, and values, identity to the history of the people. But, if we understand hegemony, as articulated by Antonio Gramsci (1971), "domination is exercised as much through popular 'consensus' achieved in civil society as through physical coercion (or threat of it) by the state apparatus, especially in advanced capitalist societies where education, the media, law, mass culture etc., take on a new role," we must then ask ourselves, how do ruling ideas come to "rule" and how can we break through these ideas or challenge them? For Gramsci, hegemony suggests that social processes, through which meanings are produced, constructed, and signified, are characterized by struggle and contestation, and the meanings that come to be privileged have been fought for, consented to, and legitimated. Stuart Hall (1992, 281) argued that this work has to be addressed on two fronts. On the one hand, we have to be at the very forefront of an intellectual theoretical work, because it is the job of the organic intellectual to know, not just pretend to know. But the second aspect is just as critical: organic intellectuals cannot absolve themselves from the responsibility of transmitting ideas, through the intellectual function, to those who do not belong, professionally, to the intellectual class.

CONCLUSION: THE STRUGGLES CONTINUE

Power, privilege, and profits prevail in a culture that defies difference. Class identity, experience, and class politics are reworked and recreated throughout life courses. According to Habermas (1974), the knowledge that humans produce is strongly determined in part by the interests that motivate them, namely, technical, practical, and emancipatory (Heyes 1999). Critical theory emphasizes emancipation through enlightenment, an enlightenment produced through self-reflection. Self-reflection ideally reveals distorted self-knowledge and institutional domination that prevent undistorted knowledge and the achievement of true interest. The real task of transformation is to discover for ourselves who we are; but part of this discovery entails a dialogue with our history and with the developmental influences that have affected us as whole persons, politically, culturally, and spiritually (Heyes 1999). For Foucault, this is "a history of the present" (1979, 31), and not a history of the past in terms of the present. Our academic contributions are more likely to come out of a personal, creative, politically engaged self, one that has a social and not simply academic purpose (Olsen and Shopes 1991, 200). Otherwise the phenomenology of privilege continues to formulate and format exclusionary practices that marginalize and negate the identity of "others." Like Bryan (2000), whose call to action fittingly defers to hooks, we are reminded of the importance of education for critical consciousness:

> Politicisation of the self can have its starting point in an exploration of the personal wherein what is first revolutionised is the way we think about the self. To begin revisioning, we must acknowledge the need to examine the self from a new, critical standpoint. Such a perspective, while it would assist on the self as a site for politicisation, would equally insist that simply describing one's experience of exploitation or oppression is not to become politicised. It is not sufficient to know the personal but to know—to speak it in a different way. Knowing the personal might mean naming spaces of ignorance, gaps in knowledge, ones that render us unable to link the personal with the political. . . . It is understanding the latter that enables us to imagine new possibilities, strategies for change and transformation. (hooks 1989, 107)

NOTE

A special note of gratitude is extended to Stephen Muzzatti and Vince Samarco for their intellectual courage and encouragement of working-class commitments. The author wishes to acknowledge with great gratitude the details provided by Maria and Gino Visano, who spent dozens of hours taping their stories and reviewing patiently the details of their lives. No small accomplishment for anyone, especially for those in their late eighties and early nineties! My siblings Gianni, Franca, and Fulvia were equally supportive; I am also grateful for the love and support from Brenda, Anthony, and Tammi.

REFERENCES

Arrigo, Bruce. 1998. "Marxist Criminology and Lacanian Psychoanalysis: Outline for a General Constitutive Theory of Crime." In *Cutting the Edge: Current Perspectives in Radical Criminology and Criminal Justice*, ed. J. Ross, 40–62. New York: Praeger.

Bourdieu, Pierre. 1989. *Distinctions: A Social Critique of the Judgement of Taste*. London: Routledge.

Brookfield, Stephen D. 1995. *Becoming a Critically Reflective Teacher*. San Francisco: Jossey-Bass.

Brunner, D. 1999. "Performance, Reflexivity, and Critical Teaching." *Journal of Critical Pedagogy* 3, no. 1 (November).

Bryan, Agnes. 2000. "Exploring the Experiences of Black Professionals in Welfare Agencies and Black Students in Social Work Education." Ph.D. diss., University of Bath.

Corrigan, Philip. 1990. "Social Forms: Human Capacities." *Essays in Authority and Difference*. London: Routledge.

de Certeau, Michel. 1988. *The Practice of Everyday Life*. Berkeley and Los Angeles: University of California Press.

Debord, Guy. 1967. *The Society of the Spectacle*. New York: Zone.

Dei, George. 1996. *Anti-racism Education: Theory and Practice*. Halifax: Fernwood.

Farr, M. 2000. Brave New BA. *CAUT Bulletin*. University Affairs (March).

Foucault, Michel. 1979. *Discipline and Power*. New York: Pantheon.

Freire, Paolo. 1985. *The Politics of Education: Culture, Power, and Liberation*. Granby, MA: Bergin and Garvey.

Giroux, Henry. 1983. *Theory and Resistance in Education: A Pedagogy for the Opposition*. Granby, MA: Bergin and Garvey.

——. 1988. *Schooling and the Struggle for Public Life: Critical Pedagogy in the Modern Age*. Minneapolis: University of Minnesota Press.

——. 1995. Teaching in the Age of Political Correctness. *Educational Forum* 59 (Winter): 130–39.

Gramsci, Antonio. 1971. *Selections from the Prison Note Books*. New York: International.

Habermas, Jürgen. 1974. *Theory and Practice*. Boston: Beacon.

Hall, Stuart. 1992. Cultural Studies and Its Theoretical Legacies. In *Cultural Studies*, ed. Lawrence Grossberg, Cary Nelson, and Paula Treichler. New York: Routledge.

Heyes, Cressida J. *APA Newsletters* 99, no. 1 (Fall).

hooks, bell. 1989. *Talking Back: Thinking Feminist, Thinking Black*. Boston: South End Press.

——. 1990. *Yearning: Race, Gender, and Cultural Politics*. Boston: South End Press.

——. 1994. *Teaching to Transgress: Education as the Practice of Freedom*. New York: Routledge.

Jakubowski, Lisa, and Livy Visano. 2002. *Teaching Controversy*. Halifax: Fernwood.

Kerlin, Scott. 1995. Pursuit of the Ph.D.: "Survival of the Fittest, or Is It Time for a New Approach?" *Education Policy Analysis Archives* 3 no. 16 (November 8).

Lacey, Joanne. 2000. "Discursive Mothers and Academic Fandom: Class, Generation, and the Production of Theory." In Munt, *Cultural Studies and the Working Class*.

Lefebvre, Henri. 1992. *The Critique of Everyday Life*, vol. 1. London: Verso.

Mills, C. Wright. 1959. *The Sociological Imagination*. New York: Oxford University Press, 1978.

Mooney, Linda, and Bob Edwards. 2001. Experiential Learning in Sociology: Service Learning and Other Community-Based Learning Initiatives. *Teaching Sociology* 29 no. 2: 181–94.

Munt, Sally. 2000. *Cultural Studies and the Working Class: Subject to Change.* London: Cassell.

Nietzsche, Friedrich. 1887. *Genealogy of Morals.* New York: Vintage, 1973.

Olsen, Karen, and Linda Shopes. 1991. "Crossing Boundaries, Building Bridges: Doing Oral History with Working-Class Women." In *Women's Words: The Feminist Practice of Oral History*, ed. Sherna Berger Gluck and Daphne Patai, 189–204. New York: Routledge.

Overall, Christine. 1998. *A Feminist I: Reflections from Academia.* Peterborough: Broadview.

Smith, Dorothy. 1987. *The Everyday World as Problematic: A Feminist Sociology.* Toronto: University of Toronto Press.

Taylor, Peter Charles, and Elisabeth Settelmaier. 2003. *Critical Autobiographical Research for Science Educators.* Curtin University of Technology, Australia.pctaylor.com/news.html (accessed July 5).

Trotman, Althea. 1993. African-Caribbean Perspectives of Worldview: C. L. R. James Explores the Authentic Voice. Ph.D. diss., York University.

Troyna, Barry. 1994. Blind Faith: Empowerment and Educational Research. *International Studies in Sociology of Education* 4: 3–24.

Wink, Joan J. 2000. *Critical Pedagogy: Notes from the Real World.* New York: Addison-Wesley Longman.

Index

About the Contributors

Phyllis L. Baker is the associate dean of the College of Social and Behavioral Sciences at the University of Northern Iowa. She received her Ph.D. in sociology from the University of California–San Diego. Her published work frames her concerns about inequality, paying particular attention to marginalized groups of women. Her current research is on recent Mexican migrant workers in Iowa.

Jennifer Beech is assistant professor of English and writing center director at the University of Tennessee at Chattanooga. She has published essays in the *Journal of Teaching Academic Survival Skills* and the *International Writing Center Association Update*; she also is the author of several pieces directly related to working-class literacies, to be published in edited collections.

Bonnie Berry earned her Ph.D. in sociology and currently serves as director of the Social Problems Research Group in Washington State. Her research interests include studies of social inequality (such as animal rights), social movements, social aesthetics (for example, the fat acceptance movement), and right-wing ideology and its effects on terrorism. She is author of numerous journal articles and the book *Social Rage: Emotion and Cultural Conflict*.

Julie Ann Harms Cannon earned her Ph.D. in sociology at the University of Nebraska in 1997, specializing in sociological theory, race, class, and gender and feminist theory, methods, and pedagogy. She is currently a member of the sociology faculty at Texas Tech University. Her research

273

interests include the women founders of classical sociological theory, student perceptions of campus racial climate, and amateur stripping.

Lyn Huxford is a professor of sociology at McKendree College in Lebanon, Illinois. She received her Ph.D. in sociology with specializations in criminology and social problems from St. Louis University in 1981. In addition to teaching, she serves as coordinator of the Center for Public Service at McKendree College, and is an active volunteer with HIV service organizations in the St. Louis metropolitan area. Her current research focuses on service learning and critical pedagogy.

David Kauzlarich is an associate professor of sociology at Southern Illinois University–Edwardsville. He has written in the areas of state crime, nuclear weapons, international law, and human rights violations. He is coauthor of two books, *Crimes of the American Nuclear State: At Home and Abroad* (with Ronald C. Kramer) and *Introduction to Criminology, 8th edition*, with Hugh D. Barlow. He is currently working on a criminological theory text.

Donna LeCourt is an associate professor of English at the University of Massachusetts–Amherst, where she teaches graduate and undergraduate courses on the cultural and ideological nature of writing and the teaching of writing. She is also director of the university writing program. Her most recent work on identity politics, class, and the teaching of writing will appear in a forthcoming book titled *Identity Matters: Schooling the Student Body in Academic Discourse*.

William J. Macauley Jr.'s work focuses on the lack of diversity in the discursive privilege of academic culture and the barrier that creates for working-class students and academics. The transience of academic culture, and its concomitant disembodied discourse, is of particular interest. He teaches at Mount Union College in Alliance, Ohio.

Daniel D. Martin has a Ph.D. in sociology from the University of Minnesota. He is the author (with Kent Sandstrom and Gary Alan Fine) of *Symbols, Selves, and Social Reality: A Symbolic Interactionist Approach to Social Psychology* and several journal articles. He teaches courses in urban sociology, inequality, and social movements and organizations. Dan has received numerous teaching awards including the Panhellenic Association Outstanding Professor Award, the Miami University Service Learning Award, and the Honored Professor Award.

Stephen L. Muzzatti was born to working-class immigrant parents in Toronto. He received his Ph.D. in sociology from York University and is an assistant professor of sociology at Ryerson University. He specializes in political economy, cultural criminology, and critical theory, with an emphasis on youth and popular culture. He has written on such diverse topics as criminological theory, Marilyn Manson, pedagogy, state crime, and motorcycle clubs. He is a member of the American Society of Criminology's Division of Critical Criminology and coeditor of the division's newsletter.

Michael Presdee has been a Royal Marine Commando, a homeless expatriate living on the streets in Canada, a tax officer, and a schoolteacher. Mike has taught at Adelaide University, the University of South Australia, Christchurch University College, and the University of Kent and has served on the executive bodies of the Australian and New Zealand Sociology Association and the British Sociology Association. He is the author of *Cultural Criminology and the Carnival of Crime* and has published over forty articles. He is currently Senior Lecturer and Head of Criminology at the University of Kent and external examiner at Open University.

Dawn Rothe is currently a sociology graduate student at Western Michigan University. Her undergraduate work was done at Southern Illinois University–Edwardsville. She has coauthored *Enemies Everywhere: Terrorism, Moral Panic, and U.S. Civil Society* and *The International Criminal Court and the Control of State Crime: Problems and Prospects*. Her research areas include critical criminology, political sociology, and social theory.

C. Vincent Samarco was born to working-class parents in Detroit. He has published numerous essays and short fiction in a variety of magazines and journals. He teaches contemporary American literature and creative writing at Saginaw Valley State University. He also teaches creative writing at the Saginaw Correctional Facility.

Kent Sandstrom is a professor of sociology at the University of Northern Iowa. He is also the executive officer of the Midwest Sociological Society. Kent has won the Outstanding Teaching Award at the University of Northern Iowa, and he has received the Herbert Blumer Award from the Society for the Study of Symbolic Interaction. His most recent publications are *Symbols, Selves, and Social Reality: A Symbolic Interactionist Approach to Social Psychology* (Roxbury Press, 2003) and *The Handbook of Thanatology* (Sage Press, 2003).

Donna Selman-Killingbeck has a Ph.D. in sociology from Western Michigan University. She has an M.A. in criminology and a B.A. from Eastern Michigan University. Her areas of interest include social justice, race and ethnicity, and prison privatization. Her current projects include an examination of the role of corporate America in Michigan's welfare-to-work program and an ethnography of Mid Michigan Couch Surfers. She teaches at Eastern Michigan University.

Michael J. Shott is from a working-class New England family, which means that he has working-class defects like angst and fear of venture. A member of the academic Unwashed, he has attended public schools since 1961. Shott is an archaeologist at the University of Northern Iowa who studies midwestern cultures of thirteen thousand years ago, how latter-day Mexicans make and use pottery, and, more broadly, how the archaeological record formed.

Livy A. Visano earned his Ph.D. in sociology at the University of Toronto and is an associate professor of sociology at York University, specializing in law, culture, and inequality, with a focus on critical criminology, critical legal studies, cultural studies, youth, and ethnographies. He has authored numerous books including *Teaching Controversy* (with Lisa Jakubowski) and *Crime and Culture: Refining the Traditions*. He is currently researching the differential impact of the media on delinquency.

Janelle L. Wilson was born in a small town in mid-Michigan. Following high school, she attended a community college, was turned on to sociology, and received an associate of arts degree. She continued her education at Saginaw Valley State University, receiving a B.A. in sociology, and then at Western Michigan University, where she earned an M.A. and a Ph.D. Her teaching and research interests are in social psychology, socialization, and the sociology of everyday life. She is an associate professor of sociology at the University of Minnesota–Duluth, where she teaches courses in social psychology, deviance, and qualitative methods.